LET THE GAMES
BEGIN

LET THE GAMES BEGIN

MY LIFE WITH OLYMPIANS, HOCKEY HEROES, AND OTHER GOOD SPORTS

RALPH MELLANBY
AND MIKE BROPHY

FOREWORD BY BRIAN WILLIAMS

Fenn Publishing Company Ltd.

BOLTON, ONTARIO

Fenn Publishing Company Ltd.

A Fenn Publishing Book / First Published in 2009

Copyright 2009 © Ralph Mellanby and Mike Brophy

The content, opinion and subject matter contained herein is the written expression of the author and does not reflect the opinion or ideology of the publisher, or that of the publisher's representatives.

Fenn Publishing Company Ltd.
Bolton, Ontario, Canada
www.hbfenn.com

The publisher gratefully acknowledges the support of the Canada Council for the Arts and the Ontario Arts Council for its publishing program. We acknowledge the support of the Government of Ontario through the Ontario Media Development Corporation's Ontario Book Initiative.

We acknowledge the financial support of the Government of Canada through the Book Publishing Industry Development Program (BPIDP) for our publishing activities. Care has been taken to trace ownership of copyright material in this book and to secure permissions. The publishers will gladly receive any information that will enable them to rectify errors or omissions.

Text design: Martin Gould
Printed and bound in Canada

Library and Archives Canada Cataloguing in Publication

Mellanby, Ralph
      Let the games begin : my life with olympians, hockey heroes and other good sports / Ralph Mellanby.

ISBN 978-1-55168-364-5

1. Mellanby, Ralph. 2. Sports–Canada. 3. Athletes–Canada. 4. Television broadcasting of sports. 5. Television producers and directors–Canada–Biography. 6. Sportscasters–Canada–Biography. I. Title.

GV742.42.M44A3 2009   796.092   C2009-902054-8

Printed and bound in Canada
09 10 11 12 13 5 4 3 2 1

TABLE OF CONTENTS

For my grandchildren: Courtney, Carter, and Nick.
—R.M.

To my father, Mike Brophy, who taught me life's most
important lessons: work ethic, humour, and the value of family.
A true leader by example.
—M.B.

FOREWORD

I have known Ralph Mellanby both personally and professionally for forty years.

His expertise and innovative thinking in televising hockey are well known.

In twenty-three years with *Hockey Night in Canada* (twenty as executive producer), he helped the franchise maintain and solidify its role as part of the very fabric of our country.

It was Ralph who was responsible for hiring Howie Meeker and Don Cherry, and then standing firm when the CBC wanted to jettison Cherry after only a month on the job. Ralph once remarked, "Don spoke neither official language, but he knew the game inside out and I could see his remarkable ability to say what so many people were thinking yet were afraid to say." Cherry says, "If it wasn't for Ralph they would have fired me early on. Ralph had the guts to stand by me and support me."

Ralph mentored a generation of young of broadcasters (production and technical) myself included. I will always remember the advice he gave me in the summer of 1974 when I left CFRB radio in Toronto to join CBLT–TV, the city's CBC station. Ralph said simply, "Be yourself. They hired Brian Williams." His contributions though to the development of sports television in North America go far beyond hockey. He produced both the Canadian Open Golf and Tennis tournaments. In all he worked a total of thirteen Olympic

Games for Canadian and American networks and was a key figure in world television coverage for the 1988 Winter Games in Calgary and the 1996 Centennial Games in Atlanta. He also produced the early CBC coverage of the Toronto Blue Jays and the Montreal Expos. It was Mellanby who, along with the then head of CBC Sports John Hudson, had the brilliant idea to hire legendary NBC broadcaster (and former New York Yankee) Tony Kubek to partner with the late Don Chevrier and become the first television play-by-play team for the Jays.

Ralph has been involved in producing the coverage of so many great moments in sport. Now you have a chance to read the stories and meet the people behind these productions. One of my favourites (and it is in the book) involves Mellanby and the late American singer John Denver at the 1984 Winter Games in Sarajevo.

Years ago the CBC's Ontario Region produced a series entitled *Celebrity Tennis*. Ralph was one of the celebrities (and was actually an excellent player). As a young broadcaster, I did the play-by-play along with former Canadian Davis Cup player Peter Burwash. I am often reminded that I once said during a telecast "that Ralph seldom double-faults."

Decades later I can still say there is no double fault here. Ralph has indeed served up an ace. Let the games begin.

Brian Williams
CTV Olympic anchor
August 2009

INTRODUCTION

Ralph Mellanby was born in Hamilton, Ontario, on August 22, 1934, but his father's job as editor of the *Windsor Star* took the family to Essex County, where Ralph attended Essex District High School. Upon graduation, Ralph studied communications at Wayne State University in Detroit, Michigan, and worked part time as a prop boy at CKLW-TV in Windsor. He graduated from Wayne in 1958 with a B.A. in communications, by which time he had worked his way up at CKLW from stagehand to cameraman to floor manager.

In 1959, Ralph accepted a position as cameraman on *The Soupy Sales Show* at WXYZ-TV in Detroit. The following year, he moved to WGN Chicago as a sports production assistant where he got his first opportunity to direct football and baseball. At this time, new television licences were being granted in Canada. Bud Hayward, president of the newly licensed CFCF-TV in Montreal, received a call in late 1960 from an ad-agency friend in Chicago telling him he should consider hiring a talented young Canadian producer who was making a name for himself in the Windy City. When CFCF-TV went on the air in 1961, Ralph Mellanby was on staff, hired to direct not only Canadian Football League games, but anything else that was thrown his way, including *Pulse News, Nightcap, Johnny Jellybean, A Kin to Win, Know Your Sports,* and *Pinbusters.*

In 1963, CTV began broadcasting Wednesday night NHL hockey games and Ralph was assigned to direct both Montreal Canadiens and Toronto Maple Leafs games. This was the beginning of Ralph's long association with NHL hockey.

In 1966, CTV's Montreal production supervisor Pip Wedge asked Ralph to take over direction of *B.A. Musical Showcase*, a musical variety program with a game-show component. While still a sports producer, Ralph found he enjoyed working with musical and performing talent as well as directing scripted productions. And it was this experience of showbiz that made Ralph the logical candidate when *Hockey Night in Canada* executive Frank Selke Jr. was looking for a new executive producer for this important Imperial Oil advertising vehicle.

The combination of Ralph's sports experience and his newly acquired flair for show business enabled him to bring many creative ideas to Canada's television hockey coverage, and fully justified the Canadian Sports Network's confidence in him. In 1968, after two years on CSN's staff, Ralph negotiated a non-exclusive ten-year contract; in addition to his work on hockey for CSN, the deal allowed him to work on other projects.

Ralph remained involved with *Hockey Night in Canada* for twenty-three years. Thirteen of the key on-air and production personnel he hired during that time were subsequently honoured by the Hockey Hall of Fame. The only personality not to have made it (as yet) is Don Cherry, whom Ralph hired in 1980 to appear on hockey telecasts.

Ralph's sports expertise earned him extensive involvement in Olympics Games coverage, beginning with his direction of hockey at every Winter Olympic Games from 1976, in Innsbruck, Austria, to Lillehammer, France, in 1994. In 1985, he was hired by CTV to lay the foundation for CTV's role as host broadcaster at the Winter Games in Calgary in 1988. In 1989, he formed his own company, Ralph Mellanby Associates, to handle several sports productions for CTV. He was senior producer for the Summer Games in Barcelona, Spain, in 1992 and was the director of venue production in Atlanta, Georgia, for the 1996 Summer Olympics there. He also worked for Turner Broadcasting and ABC as co-host broadcaster for the 1991 Pan-American Games in Havana, Cuba, in 1991.

Ralph won five Emmy Awards, all for various Olympic Games productions, including his much-lauded coverage of the "Miracle on Ice," when the United States stunned the hockey world by defeating the Russians and then capturing the gold medal at the Lake Placid Games in 1980. He also won two Kennedy Awards, an Ohio State Award, and a Lifetime Achievement Award from Sports Media Canada.

His other major sports credits include involvement in the production of fifteen Canadian Open Golf Championships and multiple LPGA events; twelve Canadian Open Men's and Women's Tennis Championships; scores of CFL series, playoff and Grey Cup games; and the production of the first Montreal Expos and Toronto Blue Jays major-league baseball games. He was also vice-president of television for the Canadian Football League for two years, 1989 and 1990.

In the entertainment field, Ralph and his friend Brian Robertson formed the Mellanby-Robertson Production Company, which created the *Governor General's Performing Arts Awards*. Ralph and Brian were founding producers of the television version of the *Royal Canadian Air Farce.* They also produced various specials, including the *Andy Williams Christmas Show.*

In 1998, Ralph received an honourary Doctor of Laws degree from the University of Windsor. Ralph's first book, *Walking with Legends*, was a bestseller in 2008.

1

PIGSKIN PARADE

Most people associate me with the sport of hockey, and that is understandable given that my job as executive producer of *Hockey Night in Canada* was a very high-profile one. It was the top-rated television show in the country and I drove that bus for more than two decades.

What a lot of people don't know is that it was football that brought me back to Canada from the United States, where I had been working at WGN-TV in Chicago.

In 1960, CTV, which wasn't yet on the air, got the rights to broadcast Canadian Football League games and was looking for a Canadian with football broadcasting experience. The CFL was to be the cornerstone of the CTV network, in much the same way that ABC and Fox in the States (where the sport is like a religion) built their networks on the back of football.

Truth be told, football was sacred in my family. It was a way of life in Hamilton, where I lived until I was ten years old. A steel town, the folks of Hamilton prided themselves on their toughness, and there is no tougher sport than football. That was especially so in the 1920s, '30s and '40s. Even during World War II, the Tigers kept playing while a new local team, the Wildcats, was born. Everybody assumed Hamilton's passion for football would be enough on its own for two teams to operate successfully, but the reality was it made it nearly impossible for both teams to meet their financial obligations, so in 1950 they merged, becoming the Hamilton Tiger-Cats. Three years later, under the guidance of coach and general manager Carl Voyles, the Tiger-Cats defeated the Winnipeg Blue Bombers to win the Grey Cup.

Before the Tiger-Cats were born, my dad worked at the *Hamilton Spectator*. His boss, Alex Muir, also served as the president of the Hamilton Tigers in the Big Four, one of the pre-CFL leagues. I used to go to many games with my dad—that's when I first fell in love with the sport. Jimmie Simpson was a player, trainer and referee and is in the Canadian Football Hall of Fame as a builder. He also played baseball with my dad. They were great pals; in fact, Simpson was my godfather.

Being around my dad I met a lot of great football people, including Ivor Wynne. The stadium the Tiger-Cats play out of today is named after Wynne, though many Hamiltonians said at the time it should have been called Jimmie Simpson Stadium.

When my dad told me we were moving to Windsor when I was eleven, it broke my heart. Luckily, though, I soon found out Windsor also shared a passion for football, both Canadian and American. I quickly became a Detroit Lions fan, though I never lost my affection for the Canadian game.

I also discovered that Windsor was something of a football factory. Many star players got their start in the sport there. Joe Krol, who passed away in December of 2008, was unquestionably the biggest star to ever come out of Windsor. He played fifteen seasons in the CFL during the 1940s and '50s and won six Grey Cup championships. Another Windsor native, Tommy Grant, enjoyed a fourteen-year CFL career spent mostly with the Hamilton Tiger-Cats. There is a lengthy list of Windsor guys who became Hall of Famers, including the player I consider the greatest receiver of all time, Bobby Simpson.

After we moved, my dad became involved with the Windsor Rockets of the Ontario Rugby Football Union. When I was twelve, my dad got me a job selling programs at the Rockets' games. It didn't seem like work to me because I got to see the Rockets play for free. Boy, was I perplexed about whom to cheer for when the Rockets battled my old team, the Wildcats! One of the players I'll never forget who played for the Rockets was Roy Battagello, who became my high school football coach when I was attending Essex High School. Roy was an early inspiration and mentor.

As I grew older, I used to bump into Detroit Lions players when they came across the border into Canada to hit the bars in Windsor. In those days, the bars used to have live shows on stage, and the lighting guys at the TV station would pick up some extra work at the shows. Back then, Lions players didn't want to be spotted hanging out in bars in Detroit. I recall seeing the great Bobby Layne once at a Windsor nightclub, White's Elbow Room, on the night before the Lions were to play in the 1957 NFL championship game against the Cleveland Browns. I was shocked because it was 2 a.m. Layne was injured and wasn't expected to play the next day, but I was still shocked that he would be in a bar the night before such an important game. (Fact is, I used to see Layne at the bars in Windsor all the time, often with the Lions' place-kicker, Jim Martin. Layne was very affable—if you were white. Being from Texas, he didn't care for the black players. At that time, the Lions only had one black player on their team, John Henry Johnson.)

I needn't have worried about Bobby. With backup quarterback Tobin Rote at the helm, the Lions crushed the Browns 59–14. Guys later told me that if Layne had been more dedicated as an athlete, he could have been one of the greatest players ever. I met the great Jim Brown once and he told me, "If that guy had lived a better lifestyle, he could have been twice the player he was." I am proud today that I got to know Layne, even it was only in the Windsor bars.

Even though I didn't play football beyond high school—I concentrated on baseball—it was in my blood. An executive from our station in Chicago knew about my work and he called his pal Bud Hayward in Montreal. Bud was the president of CFCF-TV and sat on the board of directors of CTV. "I know you are starting up with football," my pal told him. "I don't know who you are going to get to direct the games for you, but we have a young Canadian kid down here that graduated from an American school in Detroit and he's here on a student visa. He works on our sports and I'm sure he would be fabulous for you guys in Canada and for your football."

I went to Montreal for my first interview, then to Toronto for a second. And that is what brought me back to Canada: to direct football, not hockey. It was an easy decision to leave. I was young, around twenty-five years old, and I would have had trouble staying in the States because I was there on a student visa.

Moving to Canada to do football enabled me to meet a number of CFL legends including players, managers, coaches, and broadcasters. Most, such as Annis Stukus, the Hall of Fame player, coach and executive who was CTV's analyst, were wonderful. I must say, though, having worked in Chicago, I was a little spoiled in terms of what to expect from the talent. So it goes without saying I was a little disappointed by Johnny Esaw's production knowledge displayed in our early meetings.

Esaw had called the Grey Cup game in 1951 at Toronto's Varsity Stadium, and in 1960, was named sports director at CTV. Johnny was our boss. He would just sit there during the meetings, bringing little to the table. In those days, the sponsor had somebody from the ad agency right in the truck with you, kind of like Big Brother peeking over your shoulder. Esaw was concerned with keeping the sponsors happy.

I was accustomed to looking ahead at what might unfold in the game and how we were going to shoot the CFL—you know, the technical obstacles we might face. But there was never any talk about that. I would walk out of those meetings shaking my head, thinking to myself, "Who gives a shit about Carling O'Keefe? I care about the telecasts—the product." Over the years, that never changed. I was looking for a teacher to give me a list of dos and don'ts, and I felt that Esaw gave me very little guidance. So I laid out the production plan on my own.

My first game was an exhibition game—the Alouettes against the National Football League's Chicago Bears in Montreal. The game wasn't broadcast in Canada; we used it only as a rehearsal. For some strange reason, I had a feeling everybody was waiting for us to fall on our face. But everything went smoothly. My pals at WGN, who showed the game back in Chicago, were very happy with the job we did, and Red Grange complimented me after the game.

Our first actual broadcast was a game between Montreal and Hamilton, played at Molson Stadium in Montreal. Since Carling O'Keefe was the sponsor, Esaw told our broadcast crew not to mention the stadium by name. (Carling O'Keefe and Molson's were competitors.)

Annis Stukus was the colour commentator. I was sitting in the truck, the ad agency guy was sitting in the back row with me, and the first words out of Stukus's mouth were, "It's a beautiful day here at Molson Stadium." I thought the agency guy was going to bash me over the head. Even Esaw was speechless for one of the few times in his life.

We broke for commercials and the floor manager called down to me in the truck. "Ralph, Annis says he's sorry." I still laugh when I think back to that faux pas.

* * *

Some of my fondest memories of covering football revolve around the people I met, not necessarily the games or my role in the broadcasts.

When I worked in Chicago I got to know the legendary Red Grange, who worked as the colour analyst for the Bears games on TV. I was in my early twenties, and to meet Grange, who was dubbed the "Galloping Ghost" in his playing days, was like meeting Babe Ruth. Grange was a football legend, a member of both the College and Pro Football Halls of Fame.

I'll never forget the first time I met him as long as I live. I was a production assistant and he walked up to me and said, "Hi Ralph. I'm Red Grange." As if I didn't know! Here's one of the most famous football men in history, and he introduces himself like he was some guy who just drove in from New Jersey. He had a ruddy complexion and red hair. It was the late '50s and he was probably in his sixties by that time.

My dad was still alive, and I called him with the news of my memorable meeting. As a newspaper guy, there wasn't much that impressed my dad, but even he was blown away when he heard about my meeting with Red.

"The next time I see him, what should I ask him?" I wondered.

"Ask him how he got his nickname, the Galloping Ghost."

So the next time I saw Red, I asked him the question from my dad.

He looked at me, rather disinterested, and said, "I really don't know. I think some newspaper guy game it to me."

No, it wasn't my dad who gave him the nickname. With a handle like the Galloping Ghost, you would think there'd be a pretty good story to go along with it. It's funny—when you are arguably the greatest football player of the century, little things like the origin of a nickname apparently just roll off your back. They mean more to others than they do to you.

I told him that my dad had wanted to know the story behind his nickname. So Red said, "I can make one up for you if you want."

We both chuckled.

He was a great guy. And keep in mind, this was in the days long before instant replays, where colour analysts can flex their muscles and demonstrate their knowledge of the sport. Red had to find other ways to capture the viewer's fancy. He was a great storyteller, much like Dizzy Dean was in baseball. In those days, you had to fill in with stories about the players and the history of the game. Nowadays, you don't have time for that because of replays and new technologies that suffocate the telecasts.

Without question, one of the biggest stars in the CFL during my days broadcasting games was big, tough defensive tackle Angelo Mosca. The Waltham, Massachusetts, native was drafted by the Philadelphia Eagles in 1959 after playing his college ball at Notre Dame, but he elected to join the CFL's Hamilton Tiger-Cats instead. Years later, he confided in me that the Tiger-Cats actually offered him more money than the Eagles. "Much more money," Angelo insisted.

Mosca won five Grey Cups during his illustrious career, but is best known for an out-of-bounds hit on British Columbia Lions star

Willie Fleming that knocked him out of the fifty-first Grey Cup game. With Fleming out of the game, the Tiger-Cats went on to win.

As mean as he was during games, Mosca was big-hearted with a great sense of humour. At his first practice while he was playing for the Montreal Alouettes, coach Perry Moss yelled for somebody to hold the tackling dummy. Moss yelled, "Mosca, grab a dummy!" Mosca walked over and picked up Moss. The coach was furious. Needless to say, Big Ang didn't last too long in Montreal.

Angie is my neighbour in Niagara now, so I see him every once in a while. I was close enough to him over the years that he came to my going-away party when I was leaving for Calgary. It was held at the Boulevard Club in Toronto. I was known as a hockey guy at that point of my career, and Angelo, of course, was a football guy.

People asked, "What is Mosca doing here?"

"He's one of my great tennis buddies," I'd tell them.

Well, if you saw the size of Angie you knew that wasn't true. He is gigantic! When his football playing days concluded, Mosca became a famous professional wrestler, fighting under the name King Kong Mosca.

I was struggling with a very painful hip that ruined my golf and tennis seasons in the summer of 2008. I wasn't really interested in having hip-replacement surgery, though. Angie, who has had both knees and hips replaced, called me one day.

"It's great, Ralph! You've got to get it done."

I told him I wasn't sure, but Ang was having none of it.

"You get that hip replaced or I'm going to beat the shit out of you!"

I went upstairs and told my present wife, Gillian, "I'm getting my hip replaced." I'd rather have the operation than face Angie!

I am very happy to see him still involved in the CFL as an ambassador and speaker for the Hamilton Tiger-Cats. He is a great Canadian football legend and I am proud to call him my friend.

* * *

I'll never forget Tex Coulter. A centre and offensive tackle, Coulter attended the United States Military Academy and played for Army before joining the New York Giants from 1946 through 1952. He concluded his career in the CFL, playing four seasons with the Alouettes. When he retired, he became a radio broadcaster, working alongside Dick Irvin. He also became a renowned sports artist and was considered one of Canada's top painters.

Once, while we were driving to Ottawa to do a football game, another driver cut Tex off. What was amazing was the fact Tex stood six foot seven, yet he drove a tiny car. The guy who cut Tex off obviously didn't know who he was dealing with. He motioned for Tex to pull over, and of course Tex obliged him. Well, Tex rolled himself out of the car, and I'll never forget the look on the guy's face. He took one look at the size of Tex, raced back to his car and got the hell out of there. Tex looked at me and said, "Think he was scared?"

I have stayed friends with a lot of the people I met during my CFL days, among them the great quarterback Russ Jackson. For years I served on the Fair Play Commission under Prime Minister Brian Mulroney's government with Russ. He is one of my favourites and I love to spend time with him—a real class act.

Hockey players are often said to be the most accommodating professional athletes, and I believe there is some truth to that. But one thing I noticed was how smart most football players are. It makes sense, though—football players are college educated, while many hockey players drop out of high school to pursue their dreams of playing in the National Hockey League.

As a player, Russ was the ultimate quarterback. He was bright and a leader, not to mention a gentleman. A fellow Hamilton, Ontario, native, Russ enjoyed a brilliant twelve-year career in the CFL. Signed originally by the Ottawa Rough Riders as a defensive back, Russ wound up quarterbacking them to three Grey Cup victories. A member of the Order of Canada, the Canadian Football Hall of Fame, and Canada's Sports Hall of Fame, Russ Jackson was named outstanding player in the CFL four times.

Every time I've see him through the years, I've always been impressed. He looks great, and is in such great shape you'd swear he could walk through a wall. What has always stood out about Russ is his ability to teach others. You can't be around him for too long before you learn something. He's smart and opinionated.

He'd say, "Now, *Hockey Night in Canada?* Here's a problem I've got with your show…" And he'd tell you something that bugged him. He was usually right. I guess that's why he was such a great teacher.

Another one of my favourites was Leif Petterson. A sure-handed receiver during his eight-year CFL career, Petterson played in two Grey Cup games and was runner-up for the most outstanding player award in 1979, the same year he led the CFL's Eastern Conference in pass receptions.

By the time I met Leif, I was working exclusively in hockey. He told me he was interested in getting into broadcasting when his playing career ended. Well, Leif certainly had a face made for television with his striking good looks. He also had a great personality.

Leif also desperately wanted to join the Boulevard Club in Toronto and knew I was a member. He phoned me at home.

"I understand you're a big shot there," he said to me.

"No," I said, "but I *am* on the board of directors."

I said I'd see what I could do, and he was accepted. A while later, he told me he really wanted to learn to play tennis, and since I was a decent player, I said I'd teach him.

As he began to learn how to play tennis, I'd get him games with middle-of-the-pack players, not the best players in the club. He wasn't ready for that…yet. But Leif improved so fast, it didn't take long before he moved up the ladder. Within a year of my teaching him how to play, he was competing against the top players in the club and actually won the club championship. The Boulevard Club was known for its tennis, so Leif was beating some terrific and very experienced players.

I'd run into him every now and then and say, "How come you never ask me to play tennis anymore?"

"Ralph, let's be honest, I'm too good for you." And damned if he wasn't! Within a few years he grew to be one of the best tennis players in Ontario.

When the Canadian Football Network was born, I put in a good word for Leif to be part of the broadcast crew. The producer was John Shannon, who later went on to take my old job as executive producer of *Hockey Night in Canada*. Dave Hodge was going to do the play-by-play, and Leif was a terrific colour commentator.

Just as with tennis, Leif took very quickly to the world of television. He had great insight, having been a wonderful CFL receiver for so many years, and quickly rose up the ladder to become one of Canada's most gifted and respected broadcasters. Sadly, Leif died suddenly of a heart attack in 2008 at the age of fifty-seven. He was a great football player and one of Canada's finest television football analysts.

* * *

I had been out of football for quite a while, having switched to Olympic broadcasting, when I got a call from my old friend Doug Mitchell. I had gotten to know Doug while I was living in Calgary, working on the 1988 Winter Games. Doug, who by this time was the commissioner of the Canadian Football League, following the great Jake Gaudaur, wondered if I might be interested in becoming the league's director of communications.

It was 1989 and I told Doug I couldn't do the job on a full-time basis, but I would be happy to lend a hand when I could.

I'd always admired Doug Mitchell, but I didn't realize what a great commissioner he was until I started to meet the owners. Talk about a collection of hardheads. The CFL's head office was in Toronto, where I lived at the time. Doug had brought in Gary Buss, who had been one of the owners of CHCH-TV in Hamilton, as head of sales and Dan Fahey in public relations. We also had a genius as our communications director, John Iaboni. We had a great team in the league office, but I went to the owners' meetings and I couldn't believe it. Few had any background in sports management. This was a pro sport being run by a bunch of amateurs. I mean, they didn't even start some of their games on time. It was bush league!

The worst of the bunch—and trust me, there were some solid candidates—was Harry Ornest, owner of the Toronto Argonauts. This guy would knock me in the media. He'd say things like, "All Mellanby does is sit at home all day. He doesn't do any work; all he does is sit there and look at his awards." We were trying to establish credibility at the league's head office and we had an owner like Ornest running us down. The guy was a menace. From my standpoint, Harry Ornest was the worst thing to ever happen to the CFL. He had no vision whatsoever. We wanted to put microphones on our coaches for the TV broadcasts, but he said no. In fact, it was pretty much no to every idea we came up with. Doug backed me, but it was an uphill battle. Thankfully, I was only doing the job on a part-time basis or I would have gone out of my mind.

I thought the NHL was poorly run until I started working with the CFL. Boy, was I confused. At my first visit to the league's annual meetings I spoke about television. I was asked what my primary objective was, and when I told them I wanted to lift the blackouts, I thought they were going to hang me in the courtyard of the golf club where we held the meetings. At that time, games were not televised locally unless a specified number of tickets had been sold. The owners felt that putting the games on TV would keep people out of the stands, which was just plain dumb. Bill Wirtz, the owner of the Chicago Blackhawks, subscribed to that same theory right up until the day he died and watched as his team became less and less relevant to the public with each passing year. When he died, his son Rocky took over the operation of the franchise, and one of the first things Rocky did was get the home games back on local TV.

I never knew from one day to the next whom I might be dealing with. A community-owned team like the Saskatchewan Roughriders was constantly changing the people on its board. People flowed in and out, so there was no consistency. I was lucky to have Alan Ford there, however, and he shared my vision. I guess it also helped that my late wife, Janet, had been his babysitter when he was a kid in Regina. She always called him "Little Alan Ford."

I was astounded at the attitude of most of the owners. They all looked out for their own interests, not the best interests of the league. Poor Doug Mitchell—the deck was stacked against him. He went grey in that job. He left after just a couple of years, and I left the following year. To my way of thinking, his genius has never been replaced. Doug and I used to dream about expanding the league to Halifax and maybe Saskatoon. In my opinion, the owners drove him out of the job. They wouldn't allow him to do the things he wanted to do, so he finally said, "Enough is enough!"

The CFL brought in people like Bill Davis, the former premier of Ontario, to work in the head office after Doug left. Then Roy McMurtry —another well-known politician. I thought, "This isn't politics, it's football." The fact that they played football at the University of Toronto didn't qualify them to run a professional football league.

Finally, they turned to Donald Crump, who had been Harold Ballard's treasurer at Maple Leaf Gardens. Enough said.

* * *

Today, believe it or not, I am still a big fan of the CFL. And I think today's group of owners are young and fantastic. They understand the importance or working together and marketing their product. They have become so much better at merchandising and they know how to promote their stars. I wish I were involved in the league today. I am certain today's owners would be open to my ideas—they are so much more creative. Plus, there is so much more technology. I think the future of the Canadian Football League is bright.

Today, I remain on the advisory board of the Calgary Stampeders with Doug Mitchell, who is chairman.

I actually helped the Stampeders in 1990. I was working at Turner Broadcasting in Atlanta, which broadcast the Goodwill Games.

I approached the network on behalf of Doug to see if it would be interested in holding the Games in Calgary. I convinced them the people in Calgary would support the Games, and that there was a huge volunteer base there. Plus, the city had had the experience of staging the Olympic Games a few years earlier.

We brought Ted Turner to Alberta, and as he looked around, he was clearly very impressed with what he saw. I knew we were in.

"I've got to buy some of this land," Turner said.

"You can't buy it; it's a national park," I told him. "Besides, you can only own so much land if you are an American."

"What kind of a shitty law is that? This reminds me of Montana, and I own most of that land."

Doug and his committee also had a great fan in Mike Plant, the president of the Goodwill Games, who was my confidant at Turner Broadcasting.

I made sure when they agreed to hold the Games in Canada that there was a cancellation clause in the contract. If, for some reason, they decided to cancel the Games in Calgary, they would have to pay a multimillion-dollar fee. It's a good thing for Doug they agreed to that clause. When Ted Turner sold Turner Broadcasting, the Goodwill Games were cancelled. So there we were with the cancellation fee. What were we going to do with it?

Doug had the brilliant idea to invest the money and use the interest to help Calgary projects. The Stampeders were on their last legs and desperate for financial support, so we gave some of the cash to the football team. I don't think the Stampeders would have survived without that injection of money. Today, part of our Calgary Goodwill Games gang is involved on the Stampeders' board, and Doug is the head. Boy, was I happy with our Grey Cup in 2008.

* * *

One of the greatest men I ever met covering football on television was Frank Rigney, who was named one of the top fifty Canadians of all time. Frank was a fabulous TV analyst for CTV and the CBC—maybe the best ever. Every time I would go to B.C., where he had his houseboat, I'd play a round of golf with him at Capilano Golf and Country Club. Like Tex Coulter, Frank was a big man at six foot six. Talk about hitting a golf ball—this guy could crush it! And he always beat me.

One time, I brought a TV executive along with me and we played a match in Vancouver. We played a game Frank called Bingo Bango Bongo, and to this day I still don't understand the rules. It was Frank and CBC Producer Ron Harrison against me and my buddy. All I know is that, at the end of the match, Frank said, "Your pal owes me $50 and you owe Ron Harrison fifty."

I said fine. But my partner said, "I'm not paying you. I didn't understand the rules." And he didn't pay. So I had to cough up for both of us.

Frank had some medical issues, and the last time I saw him he'd had one of his legs removed. I was thinking to myself, "If I can't beat him now, with just one leg, I'll never beat him." I went into the locker room with my friend, and there was Frank, at his same old locker, taking one leg off and putting another one on.

I said, "What the hell is that?"

"It's my golf leg. The other one is my walking leg."

So we got up to the first tee and I said, "If I can't beat you on your course today, then I'll never beat you."

He just smiled at me and said, "How many strokes do you want?"

I shot 89 and he shot 88. He birdied the last hole to beat me. It was amazing to see him get in and out of the cart with his golf leg on and still hit the ball that well.

When we were done, I said, "If I can't beat a guy with one leg..."

He looked at me and said, "Ralph, I could have had the other leg removed and I still would beat you. In fact, I could throw in one arm." He was right.

For my money, Frank Rigney was the best football analyst in history. It was his humour that set him apart. He worked with the great Don Wittman and really lightened up the broadcast. What hurt Frank was when they brought the third guy into the booth. Frank didn't control the show anymore and he lost some of his lustre—but not on the golf course.

Another fabulous commentator was the late Ron Lancaster. One of the greatest quarterbacks ever to play in the CFL, Ron was worshipped and loved by everyone, especially in Regina.

When he got into broadcasting, I didn't think he'd do well. When he talks he has a southern drawl, so he doesn't come across as being nearly as bright as he actually is. I didn't think he'd get the information out quickly enough.

Well, once again I was wrong. He was great! He had humour and, of course, having been a superstar in the CFL, he had amazing insight. When they brought in the replays, Ron Harrison, his director, told me he got more out of Lancaster than anybody else. He and Wittman fit like a glove. What a team!

Ron was great for me when I joined the CFL. He was coaching in Edmonton at the time, and when I went out there, we went to dinner. When you are in the presence of Ron Lancaster, a glow comes over you like you are sitting in the sunlight. He picks you right up.

I was bitching and moaning about the CFL and he said, "Ralph, don't let the owners get to you. We need someone of your talent at the Canadian Football League. We need you."

That really made me feel good. In fact, it played a big role in me not quitting. Ron passed away in the summer of 2008. Not too long after, Don Wittman left us. Guess our Lord needed a great football announcing team up there. Well, he got the best.

I owe a lot to my days telecasting the CFL. It was my big directorial breakthrough, and I loved it. I am also proud of the legacy that I have left with the CFL in the way of great executives.

Keith Pelley, who was president of the Toronto Argonauts and did such a fantastic job restoring the team's popularity, was one of my guys who I helped start in the business. Scott Mitchell, Doug's son, got his early start on my Calgary Olympic project. Now he's president of the Hamilton Tiger-Cats. My friend Bobby Ackles, one of the bright lights as former president of the B.C. Lions, has a boy, Scott Ackles, who is president of the Calgary Stampeders.

Scott worked on the opening and closing ceremonies in Calgary—and even met his future wife on the project.

I am proud of my legacy in television giving so many producers their starts. Who would have thought that I would have also helped start so many football executives. Now that's something!

2

BUILDING A BRAND ON
HOCKEY NIGHT IN CANADA

The 1966–67 hockey season was a monumental one for the National Hockey League. For starters, it was the final year of the Original Six, the end of a twenty-five-year era during which a major sports league had been run as a cottage industry. One year later, the NHL would double in size to twelve teams, and a niche sport that had generated small pockets of interest was finally well on its way to becoming a truly big league. It was also the year the Toronto Maple Leafs won their last Stanley Cup, beating the Montreal Canadiens in six games. The Maple Leafs were one of the NHL's most successful franchises and had just claimed their fourth championship in six years. Who could have imagined at the time that the most important franchise in the league would then embark on a more-than-forty-year odyssey of incompetence and become a laughingstock?

It was also the season when I accepted the job as executive producer of *Hockey Night in Canada.* You are forgiven for not remembering that.

Hockey Night in Canada was the number one television show in Canada, and I was put in charge of taking it to the next level. I am forever grateful that those in charge didn't buy into the theory that if it ain't broke, don't fix it. Despite its success, *HNIC* did need repairs, especially during the intermissions. Sponsors felt the show lacked pizzazz, and among the things they were particularly unhappy with were pre- and post-game shows that had grown tired and somewhat boring.

33

I was thrilled to be given this opportunity. Having previously worked as a director on *Hockey Night*, I already knew a lot of the people I would be working with. That made my transition to executive producer a lot easier. Not knowing what the future held, I looked at the job as a five-year proposition; I had no idea it would encompass a twenty-year chunk of my life, not to mention the most remarkable and memorable stages of my career.

Having come from entertainment-based television, I was very confident I could make an impact on the show. And I didn't feel as though I was painting myself into a corner career-wise by accepting the position. I knew that if things didn't work out to my expectations, I could always go back to doing what I had done—and thoroughly enjoyed, I might add. I had a lot of options if things didn't work out, especially in the United States.

I was still living in Montreal at the time, and continued to do so until 1971, when I moved to Toronto. My bosses kept me in Montreal at first because they felt *La soirée du hockey*, the French-language broadcast of *Hockey Night*, also needed help. I loved the city, so I enthusiastically agreed.

I really cared about the French show. Although few English-speaking viewers have ever seen the broadcast, it is an important part of the *Hockey Night* franchise. It is a high-impact show, and I knew I had to get somebody to work alongside René Lecavalier. I brought in Gilles Tremblay, who had played nine seasons with the Canadiens, scoring 168 goals and 330 points while helping the Habs win four Stanley Cups, before retiring as a player because he suffered from asthma. He wound up being honoured by the Hockey Hall of Fame for his work as a broadcaster. Amazing!

Even though the sponsors wanted changes, my philosophy was to take things slowly. Granted, the show needed an injection of energy, but I couldn't lose sight of the fact that it was immensely popular. It would be a big mistake to come in and immediately make sweeping changes. I didn't want to knock down the walls; I wanted to crumble them slowly. Most of the changes that first year had to do with technical advances that were available to us—we were just starting to broadcast in colour, and slow-motion replays were on their way. But I also hired two young men, Dick Irvin and Dan Kelly, to work on the Montreal broadcasts, while Keith Dancy was dropped. These were necessary changes because we wanted to bring young, vibrant guys into the show.

Hockey Night in Canada was owned by the MacLaren advertising agency, and at the end of my first season, at a party for the ad executives and sponsors, Bud Turner, who was an executive vice-president at MacLaren, told me his company was pleased with my work. It was comforting to hear that, and I decided then that I could get a little more adventurous in terms of changing the show.

The time was right. With the addition of six new teams, the NHL was like a new league: there were twice as many players, many of whom were known only to the most diehard fans; new managers; new executives; and, from a TV perspective, new opportunities.

We didn't use the word in those days, but what I set out to do was "brand" the show. I wanted the show to stand on its own two feet, so to speak, and move into the future with its own identity. No longer would it be "Imperial Oil, Molson, and Ford present *Hockey Night in Canada*." It would simply be *Hockey Night in Canada*. Up to this point, each period opened up with different theme music—the sponsors' jingles. I felt that the show should have its own signature theme music, as well as a logo that people would instantly recognize and link with *Hockey Night in Canada*. As much as I wanted people to tune in for the hockey, I wanted them to understand it was a TV show called *Hockey Night in Canada*. It was all branding to me.

I'd studied the way the American networks were covering sports, and one thing I noticed right off was that ABC and CBS had all their talent dressed in matching blazers. This technique immediately identified them with their network. But I wanted to take it a step further: I wanted my on-air crew to have a look and sound that identified the *show*, not the network. We aired on CTV on Wednesday nights and Saturdays on CBC. In either case, I wanted viewers to know they were watching *Hockey Night in Canada*. So our hosts, announcers and analysts would wear jackets crested with the *HNIC* logo, regardless of which network they were on.

It was tough to sell my bosses and the sponsors on my plan, but it was something I believed in and something I felt was really needed to boost the show's credibility. I was very fortunate that my president, Ted Hough, bought into my notion. And the success I'd had my first year as executive producer, doing little things like upgrading the intermissions and bringing in some fresh talent, meant I could really count on the sponsors as well as the executives at MacLaren to back me as I pushed forward.

In some ways, it was an adventure, because I had to work through an ad agency. A top designer who had created a lot of sponsor logos for television came up with the *HNIC* crest. He walked into my office one day with what would become our logo—the dark stick and the white puck on the blue background—and I loved it.

"Do you know what it is?" he asked me.

"Sure," I said, "it's the stick and the puck."

"No, no, no," he said. "It's hockey *night*. That's the moon, not a puck—that's why it's white. And that's not a stick, it's the country being divided. And the light-blue background is the twilight."

I thought to myself, "Holy crap! What have I got myself into here?" But the bottom line is, I didn't really care about his interpretation. I just loved the crest.

The designer was the one who recommended to me that we dress our talent in blue jackets so that his logo would stand out.

Our talent wasn't pleased upon hearing that we were moving to a uniform style of dress, although I think their objections were rooted mainly in skepticism. The first guy I approached, out of respect for his status, was legendary broadcaster Foster Hewitt. I figured that if I could sell him on the new blue jackets, the other guys would fall into line.

Well, Foster never took the blue jacket off. Even when he went out onto the ice at Maple Leaf Gardens for the very last time, he was wearing his *Hockey Night in Canada* blazer. And he was damn proud of it! The guys were proud to wear the blue jackets, and suddenly I had producers and directors wondering if they could wear the blue jacket, too. They also wanted to be identified with the show. Okay, good idea.

The jackets came from Mickey Allen Clothes in Montreal, where a lot of the players in the Original Six era bought made-to-measure wardrobes at a decent rate. As far as I was concerned, they had to fit perfectly. Mickey tried to make a deal with me whereby I was provided with free suits, but I wasn't able to give him a promotional credit on the show, because the sponsors wouldn't go for it. He was fine with that; he said his payback would be in knowing that the players would know where the *Hockey Night in Canada* announcers got their great-fitting jackets, and would then shop at his outlet. We wound up having a long-term relationship, because every couple of years the show would have to get new jackets made at a reduced rate. I eventually got my clothes made there, too, but I always paid for them. Our show was so big that I didn't want to owe anybody anything or for there to be any perceived conflicts of interest.

One of my biggest tasks in my first year was to bring the Montreal and Toronto offices together. Prior to my becoming executive producer, the Montreal office thought only in terms of the Canadiens and the Toronto office thought only about the Maple Leafs. (You have to remember, there were only two Canadian teams at that point.) Our office and staff were divided, and I wanted one *Hockey Night in Canada* team—not *Hockey Night in Toronto* and *Hockey Night in Montreal*. My goal was for the staff to identify with the show and the brand, not the team whose games they were covering.

To bring the two groups together, I organized a golf tournament for the people that worked in both cities — French and English. I didn't have one colour of jacket and crest for the English show and another for the French.

There were other subtle changes I insisted on. Jack Dennett, who in my opinion was Toronto's greatest broadcaster, was originally from Calgary. I would tell him to throw that fact into the broadcast every now and then so that people in Calgary would sit up and take notice of one of their own. Dick Irvin was from Regina, Danny Gallivan from the Maritimes, and Brian McFarlane from the Ottawa Valley. Our guys were instructed to mention where the players came from, to give the show more of a national feel. Having grown up in a small town—Essex, Ontario—I knew how exciting it was to have your town's name mentioned on a national broadcast.

Without question, the biggest and longest-lasting impact I made on the show was with the theme song. My idea was to have a song that made people automatically think of *Hockey Night in Canada*, kind of like the theme for Johnny Carson's *Tonight Show*.

I had no idea at the time that our song would become Canada's second national anthem. The song has been recorded numerous times and, with apologies to Stompin' Tom Connors who wrote "The Hockey Song," is regarded as the best hockey song ever.

The people at MacLaren insisted that I contact Betty Hastings, whom they had always used for their commercial jingles and show themes. Because of my involvement in the entertainment world, I felt I had enough connections with the top people in the industry to make it work on my own. Among others, I knew Guido Basso, who was born in Montreal and became a first-call studio musician, arranger, composer, conductor and bandleader in Toronto; the brilliant musician Hagood Hardy, as well as Jerry Toth, another multi-talented musician and, in my opinion, the best arranger in Canada.

I contacted five top composers, among them Tommy Ambrose and Hagood Hardy, and gave them a small amount of money to submit original piano recordings. They were all good. But Betty Hastings told me about a woman she had worked with before, and said she'd like to ask her to submit an entry, too. That woman, Dolores Claman, had written a theme for a film that had been shown by the province of Ontario during Expo 67. Fine, I said, now we'll have six entries.

I agreed to meet with Dolores, whose writing partner was her husband, and she seemed a little different to me. She was a little standoffish and not overly enthusiastic about the project. Quite frankly, I was a little put off by her attitude. If somebody had asked me to write a theme song for the biggest TV show in Canada, I might be a little more excited. Dolores was very businesslike, and it struck me she wasn't open to any suggestions. I got the feeling it was going to be her way or the highway.

The demo recordings came in, and it just shows how far we've advanced since then. Today, composers can use synthesizers to recreate the sounds of the different instruments, and with the aid of a personal computer they can record all the elements and hand in something that sounds very close to the final arrangement. In those days, it was bare bones: the tunes were played only on a piano. Listening to them, you had to imagine how they'd sound being played by a full orchestra. With Dolores's entry, I could do that. I loved her song, and I fought for it. I played the tapes for the big shots at Imperial Oil, Molson, Ford, and MacLaren, including George Sinclair, the president of MacLaren, who was Gordon Sinclair's brother. I told them Dolores's entry was the one I liked best. It was the one I believed would be the best for the show—I had no idea it would become one of the most popular songs in the history of Canadian music.

When it came time to record the theme, I lobbied for the top musicians in Toronto, people I had come to know over the years—we ended up with a twenty-six-piece orchestra. And I called for several different variations to be recorded, to be used at different points in the broadcast.

In the end, it became part of the fabric of hockey and of Canada. In fact, one year, after the Canadian media laid a beating on the U.S. media after the NHL's annual mid-season All-Star Game, the Canadian players started humming the song on the bus on their way back to their hotel. Within a few seconds the bus was filled with the strains of the *Hockey Night in Canada* theme song.

Gordon Sinclair, one of Canada's leading journalists in his day, did a piece on the radio and called the song Canada's second national anthem.

Looking back, there is a part of me that regrets fighting for the song because of the way the contract was structured. I wanted to buy out the song outright—simply pay Dolores a one-time fee for her work and be done with the matter. But the people at MacLaren were coming from an advertising perspective, so they treated it as a piece of music for a commercial — as a result, Dolores would be paid residuals. I felt it was a one-sided deal, in her favour, but I was outvoted.

I ended up in the president's suite at MacLaren, along with my boss, Ted Hough, and I'll never forget the conversation. The vice-president of MacLaren, Bud Turner, who was in charge of *Hockey Night in Canada*, said, "Ralph, let's just keep peace in the family. She has handled all of our music and anything we do with our sponsors, so let's just do it her way."

As we were walking out, Bud said to me, "I think that worked out rather well."

"I think it's the wrong way to do it," I insisted.

He tried to reassure me, saying, "Ralph, the theme will only be on for a few years."

In those days, that was pretty much the case. A song would last for three or four years before it got tired and would be replaced. Little did we know it would be around for forty-two years.

In the summer of 2008, Dolores demanded even more money out of the CBC in order for them to continue using the song. I understand that the network offered her a million dollars for all rights to the song in perpetuity, but Copyright Music, which represented Claman, was asking for between $2.5 million and $3 million. As a result, the CBC decided it had paid her enough money over the years and dropped the song. CTV quickly stepped in and acquired the rights, and now uses it for its hockey broadcasts on TSN and the French-language Réseau des Sports.

On one hand, I can understand CTV's desire to own the song, but every time I hear it, I think of *Hockey Night in Canada*, although I suspect that over time a younger audience will identify it with TSN and RDS's broadcasts.

I think that Dolores made a boatload of money off that song over the years, and I think she was fairly treated by the CBC. Every executive producer that followed me—Ron Harrison, John Shannon, Don Wallace—would call me and wonder why there were restrictions on when they could and couldn't use "the song." It was a shame. I also felt badly for director of sports Scott Moore and the CBC; I felt that loyalty on Dolores's part should have been a factor—not so!

The funny thing is, the song wasn't an immediate hit. Over the years, I think *Hockey Night in Canada* made the song. If it had been on any other show, it wouldn't have enjoyed nearly the impact or longevity. In other words, the show made the song; the song didn't make the show.

As for Dolores, she moved to England and has lived there for years. I always had the impression she didn't like *Hockey Night in Canada*. I don't think she cared much about hockey or the show or its people. Just my opinion.

All in all, I look back on my years at *Hockey Night in Canada* with great fondness. I was never satisfied with what we did, and that kept me motivated to always keep trying to make it better.

I was always on the lookout for something new and different to spruce up the show. We played *The King of Hockey*—the worst hockey movie ever made—in segments over four games, just to be different. Between periods, there was also Peter Puck, "Showdown," "Howie Meeker's Pro Tips," and more. We'd do features on the players, going to their homes to let fans see a different side of their favourite athletes.

There were some who didn't like what we did—including some of my bosses—but they appreciated that we were trying to keep the show fresh.

Sam Pollock, the great general manager of the Montreal Canadiens, once paid me a great compliment when he said, "Ralph, you have done so much with that show and have improved it so much, even I watch it now."

I laughed.

I had been doing the show for about five years at that point. Coming from him, it was huge because Sam was a straight shooter who would not hide any criticisms of the show.

Sam said he would do anything he could to help me with *Hockey Night*, so I took him up on it. "We would love to get players to come on the show during the playoffs," I said. "We have never had access to them in the post-season before."

Well, Sam hummed and hawed for a while, and then a few days later he called me and said, "You've got it. The only thing is, I want my players to go on during the first intermission."

Deal!

Once I had Sam on board, the other general managers fell right into place. It was just one more way of making the show better.

My career has taken different turns and I've worked on many new projects since I left *Hockey Night in Canada*, but I still consider it my major credit in the industry. People still come up to me, twenty-three years after I left, and ask, "Are you still with *Hockey Night in Canada?*"

It's still a great show, and last year my son, Scott, joined the panel on the Hot Stove Lounge during the second intermission. I was very proud of him and his work. When he got the job, he called me and said, "I didn't know that as part of your severance package I get a job on the show."

In my heart, I still feel a part of the show and watch it every Saturday night.

3

HOCKEY LEGENDS AND FAVOURITE STORIES

When I wrote *Walking with Legends,* which was published in 2007, I mentioned a number of hockey players, coaches and media personalities who touched my life during my many years as executive director of *Hockey Night in Canada.* But there were many others who didn't make the book but were just as important.

When you travel the hockey circuit, as I did for so many years, you never know who you might meet. Or in some cases, not meet.

When I arrived in Atlanta to prepare for work on the 1996 Summer Olympics, it brought back a lot of memories. I soon found out that the guy who was president of the Atlanta Knights of the International Hockey League was Richard Adler. His named sounded very familiar to me.

When I was producing a Stanley Cup final game between the Boston Bruins and New York Rangers at Madison Square Garden during the 1971–72 season, I decided—as usual—that I wanted to prepare a different kind of opening for the show. It turns out that the circus was in town, and as I was making my way around the bowels of MSG, I could see all the animals—lions, tigers, elephants—tied up. It was in the day when the Big, Bad Bruins ruled the NHL and many people who hated them referred to the Bruins as "Bobby Orr and the animals."

I got Bobby, Phil Esposito and a couple of other Bruins on their way into practice one morning to pose with the animals, and then we set it to music—with the song "If I Could Talk to the Animals"—for the opening of our *Hockey Night in Canada* show. I showed it to Scotty Connal of NBC, and he wanted to use it, too. I was very happy with the idea.

I got back to Toronto after the series and I got a call from an executive at Ringling Brothers Barnum and Bailey Circus by the name of Richard Adler. He was very cold and told me he hadn't seen our opening on NBC, but had heard about it and then dropped a bombshell on me.

"I want to inform you we are suing your show, *Hockey Night in Canada*, as well as NBC for $1 million each, and we're also suing you personally for $500,000."

Without batting an eye, I said, "Would you like cash or a cheque?" He wasn't impressed.

As it turned out, I should not have used their animals in my opening segment without their permission. They don't like the public to see their animals tied up, which is understandable. I should have cleared it with the circus people.

The matter was settled out of court, and the solution brokered between Adler and my bosses was to give Barnum and Bailey a couple of free commercials on a few NBC and *Hockey Night* telecasts. Even after it was settled, the incident stayed with me because I was the one who made the mistake and, truthfully, I hadn't made too many blunders in my career. It really bothered me that I could make such an error.

So, the years went by and I moved to Atlanta in 1991 to work on the Summer Olympics. Gene Ubriaco, who coached the Knights at the time and earlier had coached the Pittsburgh Penguins, was showing me around the Omni one day and introduced me to team president Richard Adler.

So I asked, "Are you the same guy who threatened to sue me for using the circus animals as part of my pre-game shoot during the Stanley Cup final in 1972?"

Sure enough, it was. Surprisingly, we became really good friends and still keep in touch.

Although the Knights were only in Atlanta for four seasons, from 1992–93 through 1995–96, they were quite popular. They actually won the IHL championship, the Turner Cup, in 1993–94, but ultimately relocated to Quebec City because of the NHL's arrival in Atlanta.

Selling the sport in a non-traditional hockey market takes lots of ingenuity. One gimmick, if you will, was signing female goaltender Manon Rhéaume to a professional contract. The Knights were a farm team to the Tampa Bay Lightning, and the Lightning actually played Rhéaume in an NHL pre-season game in September of 1992 against the St. Louis Blues and again the following season against the Boston Bruins. She was brought to Atlanta, in theory, to compete for the job as the team's number one goaltender. Truth is, as fine a lady goaltender as she was, she didn't stand a realistic chance of beating out her male competition.

It was a good gig for her, nonetheless. It didn't hurt that she was a stunning beauty, too. Manon kicked around the low minors for a few years, never really establishing herself as a threat to be the number one goalie in a men's professional league, and also helped the Canadian women's hockey team capture a silver medal at the 1998 Winter Games.

During another of my frequent visits to the Omni, Ubriaco asked me if I'd like to meet Manon? Of course I would!

She had her own private dressing room, away from the rest of the team, for obvious reasons. When we arrived, Gene knocked on the door. We didn't hear a sound, so we popped into the room—and Manon was in the shower.

She heard us and screamed, "Can't you guys see I'm in the shower!"

Gene said, "There's somebody here I'd like you to meet."

She yelled back, "I'm not coming out."

And away we went. I never did meet her.

Gene and I still laugh at the experience. He says, "Knowing Mellanby all these years, I expected him to jump into the shower with Manon. Phil Esposito would have!"

* * *

Two of the most memorable men I ever met in hockey were priests, Father Athol Murray and Father David Bauer, both dedicated men of the cloth. I was drawn to them in part because of their religious beliefs, which the three of us shared, but also because of their love of hockey. Both men left their mark on the game—and on Canada. Father Bauer because of his work with Team Canada and Father Murray, because he founded Notre Dame College in Wilcox, Saskatchewan, the school that today is named Father Athol Murray College at Notre Dame in his honour.

I met Father Murray during a flight when Danny Gallivan, the legendary play-by-play voice of the Montreal Canadiens for so many years, and I were making appearances at banquets in western Canada. We had attended one in Calgary, and our next stop was Regina. We got onto this little rented plane that, to be honest, didn't appear to be the safest aircraft I had ever been on. Joining us on the flight was Father Murray. Notre Dame has an amazing hockey program, and many future NHLers—including Rod Brind'Amour, Wendel Clark, Russ Courtnall, Curtis Joseph, Vincent Lecavalier, Brad Richards, and James Patrick.

I had heard of Father Murray, but had never had the pleasure of meeting him and was really looking forward to the chance to get to know him. It turned out he was a great guy, but I noticed before we got on the plane that he was a chain smoker. He was always puffing away on a cigarette.

Prior to the flight, the pilot gave us our instructions, and the one thing he insisted on was that there was to be absolutely no smoking on the plane. Well, we had no sooner taken off than Father Murray, who was sitting with me in the rear of the plane, lit up.

I spoke up right away, saying, "Father Murray, that could set the plane on fire! We could explode."

To which he responded, "Well, my boy, if we do, you'll never die in better company than with me."

He turned and kept right on enjoying his cigarette. He must have smoked ten butts during the trip—kind of gave a whole new meaning to the old phrase "holy smoke"! I was petrified the whole trip.

We didn't crash, so I guess God was looking out for the good father that day.

Father Bauer was the younger brother of Bobby Bauer, who played nine seasons in the NHL, helping the Boston Bruins win the Stanley Cup in 1939 and 1941. Bobby was a four-time Second Team All-Star who won the Lady Byng Trophy as the NHL's most gentlemanly player three times, in 1940, 1941 and 1947.

Father Bauer was a great hockey player in his own right, but chose a life with God over becoming a professional hockey player. He turned down an offer to join the Bruins farm team when he was sixteen years old.

Father Bauer was educated at St. Michael's College in Toronto, and in 1953 he returned to the school, this time as a teacher. He also coached the hockey team, which he led to the Memorial Cup championship in 1961, and was also instrumental in coaching and managing the Canadian men's Olympic hockey team throughout the 1960s. I went to Tokyo to film the "World Hockey Report," which we often aired during intermissions of games on *Hockey Night in Canada*. The Canadian Olympic team was doing a tour of Japan, and I thought it would interest hockey fans back home.

Father Bauer wasn't coaching the team at the time, but was still a part of the team's executive. What stood out for me more than anything, in meeting Father Bauer, was how insistent he was that skill be the determining factor when choosing players for a hockey team. Not only that, he felt it was very important to check out a player's character before making him a part of your team. Sound familiar? All the best NHL teams follow that philosophy today.

Although it has been more than thirty years since I last saw Father Bauer, I distinctly remember him telling me that the NHL needed to put a greater accent on skill and do everything it could to take the hooking and obstruction out of the game. He said he did not like the way the game was going, with intimidation and fighting winning out over speed and skill.

Clearly, he was ahead of his time in terms of the direction hockey would eventually go. When the NHL lockout ended in 2005, the league came back with a solid plan to reduce obstruction and put a greater emphasis on skill and scoring. Father Bauer would be proud. Thank God I met both of them.

* * *

For my money, Jean Béliveau was one of the greatest players of all-time and has been a dear friend of mine since I first moved to Montreal in 1961. Sadly, these days we only seem to bump into one another at funerals. We both served as honorary pallbearers at the funerals of Bernie "Boom Boom" Geoffrion and John Ferguson.

In fact, when I walked into the church in Atlanta at Boom Boom's funeral, Béliveau was already there, and boy, was he happy to see me. Turns out he'd been there a while and nobody recognized him. The hockey people hadn't arrived yet and he had nobody to speak with. That would never happen in Canada.

At Ferguson's funeral in Windsor, a number of us decided to fly in a day early so we could actually spend some time together to talk about old times. At many funerals, you are in and out and don't really get a chance to catch up with old friends. My old friends Marc Cloutier and Serge Savard invited me, and I was thrilled.

If you had a school that young hockey players could attend to learn how to be a great captain, the class would have to be modelled after Béliveau. He was the ultimate leader, a player who inspired others to great heights. You'd never hear him swear, and I can't recall ever hearing him raise his voice. When he stepped on the ice, he was all business. He set such a great example for the other players on the team. He was, for many years, the face of the organization.

I was sitting with Jean the day before Ferguson's funeral, and he turned to me and asked, "Ralph, how is your book coming?"

He was referring to *Walking with Legends*. I told him it was out and selling quite well. Then I told him that I had some regrets in that not all of my close friends made it into the book—people like Bobby Clarke, John Ferguson and, I gulped, Jean Béliveau.

Well, Jean looked at me as only Jean can and said, "I am glad you gave me the list of guys who didn't make it, because I won't be the only one who is pissed off!"

Then he smiled. That was the closest I ever came to hearing him swear.

You could walk to the ends of the earth and not find a more revered gentleman.

Béliveau first came to people's attention as a twenty-year-old playing for the Quebec Aces in the Quebec Senior Hockey League. He was a star in that league, and the Canadiens were very interested in signing him. Béliveau, however, didn't feel any great need to jump to the NHL and was quite comfortable playing with the Aces, an amateur club.

The Canadiens were so desperate to get him they eventually bought the entire league and converted it into a pro loop. Béliveau eventually signed with the Canadiens and enjoyed a wonderful nineteen-year career with the Habs, the last ten as the team's captain. Béliveau, who at six foot three and 205 pounds was one of the bigger NHLers of his generation, was one of the most graceful players to ever play in the league.

Béliveau led the NHL in scoring in his fourth season and was also the first player to win the Conn Smythe Trophy as the league's most valuable player in the playoffs in 1965. He ended his career with 507 goals and 1,219 points in 1,125 games and added another 79 goals and 176 points in 162 playoff games.

Béliveau could easily have extended his career a couple more years, but he wanted to go out on top, and when the Canadiens captured the Stanley Cup in 1971, beating the Chicago Blackhawks in 7 games, he hung up the blades. A lot of players play out the string, grabbing as much money as they can before packing it in, but not

Béliveau. He led the Canadiens in scoring during his final season, with 25 goals and 76 points in 70 games, adding another 6 goals and 16 points in the post-season. Clearly there was gas left in the tank, but Big Jean wanted to dedicate more time to his family. He rode off into the sunset, although he has remained associated with the Canadiens through the years as a much-loved ambassador for the organization.

I played golf with Jean once in Montreal at a Canadiens charity event, and when we went to tee off, I was a little intimidated by the number of fans who turned out for the event and lined the fairway in front of us. Of course, they were all there to see their hockey heroes and didn't really give a hoot about me, but to be honest, I was worried I might hit somebody with my shot. This was not the Masters! I said, "Jean, I'm a decent golfer, but I'm worried I'm going to kill somebody."

Typically, he said, "Don't worry, Ralph. I'll go first."

Now, Jean was not a super golfer by any stretch of the imagination, but he was the guy who could perform under pressure. I believe that is why he was able to score so many big goals for the Canadiens during his illustrious career.

So Jean stepped up and smacked the ball 220 yards straight down the middle of the fairway. Fans roared with approval. I got up next and dribbled it about 120 yards along the ground. Big Jean never failed to deliver. All I can say for myself is I didn't kill anybody.

In 2000, I was at the airport in Montreal, having arrived from Toronto to attend a *Hockey Night in Canada* reunion, and I bumped into Jean in the airport. He had come in on another plane. I knew he had been having some health issues with his throat, so I wandered over to see how he was feeling and to say hello.

Without hesitation—and I still don't know how he knew this—he looked at me and said, "I hear your wife is not doing too well." Janet was terminally ill at the time.

"Give me your address," he told me.

Shortly afterward, Janet received a card with a lovely note from Jean. What a thoughtful gesture. It really made Janet feel special. That's Jean Béliveau.

When everybody picks their all-time all-star team, the majority pick Wayne Gretzky as the number one centre. I always choose Béliveau. Not that Gretzky wasn't fantastic, but Béliveau is my all-time greatest centre. Wayne would be on my second line.

Why? To me, Béliveau did more on the ice than anybody could imagine. He was a hell of a defensive player. I was speaking with the Toe Blake once about Béliveau's prowess as an offensive centre, and Toe said, "That is true, but he is my best checker, too!" Many people look at Béliveau's numbers and think of him as a pure offensive talent. That was not the case. He was no liability out there when he was out against the other team's top offensive centres—all Hall of Famers.

* * *

If Béliveau and Gretzky would centre my first two lines, Bobby Clarke would be my third-line centre. When Keith Allen drafted Clarke in 1969, there were plenty of question marks about him. And despite what people say today, not everybody knew at the time about his diabetes. The fact that he was so small is what scared a lot of people off. You have to remember that that was an era when size mattered. Teams would often pass on a small, skilled player to get a guy with lesser skill but who could mix it up. That was especially true of the Philadelphia Flyers.

What most teams failed to see was that Bobby Clarke fit the bill on both counts. He was small, but he was as tough as nails. Not only that, but he was one of the greatest leaders the game has ever known.

In Bobby's first season in the NHL, he finished fourth in team scoring with a respectable 15 goals and 46 points, and the second year he climbed to the top of the team scoring parade with 27 goals and 63 points. What really stood out more than anything else was how rapidly he became the face of the Flyers. With his stylish, flowing, curly hair and his determination on every shift, it didn't take long for Flyers fans to gravitate to him. He is still loved by them today.

Even more significant, however, was his eye-for-an-eye, tooth-for-a-tooth style of play. Whack him and he'd whack you back twice as hard. He was a fierce as any player in the league and, as it turned out, a heck of a lot more talented than many had thought he'd be, too.

The seventeenth pick in the 1969 NHL draft, Clarke, at five foot ten and just 175 pounds, was not the most physically imposing player by any stretch of the imagination. Yet throughout his glorious fifteen-year career, Clarke developed a reputation for being a player who not only talked a big game but backed his words up on the ice.

He would do anything he needed to do to win. In the legendary 1972 Summit Series between Canada and Russia, Team Canada coach John Ferguson suggested somebody had to do something to slow down Russian superstar Valeri Kharlamov. On his next shift, Clarke got Kharlamov in his sights and, when nobody was looking, he delivered a two-hander to the Russian winger that broke his ankle. Mission accomplished. Anything to win!

In a career that got him elected to the Hockey Hall of Fame in 1987, Clarke led the Flyers to two Stanley Cups, in 1974 and 1975, while winning three Hart Trophies as the league's most valuable player. He finished with 358 goals and 1,210 points in 1,144 regular-season games and another 42 goals and 119 points in 136 playoff games. He was a First Team All-Star twice and Second Team All-Star twice.

Frank Selke, the CBC's vice-president of everything, including marketing, came into my office one day and told me Morgan Estates was building a golf course in Jamaica called Iron Shores (it's still there, by the way). He told me the owners wanted to make a big splash with potential purchasers of homes there—heavy hitters. The idea was to bring a bunch of potential homeowners and sponsors down to Jamaica for a golf tournament, and they were looking for a group of high-profile NHLers to come along for the ride.

Frank and I put together a list—and by the way, it turned out that every player who accepted the offer to join us wound up making Team Canada for the famous 1972 Summit Series. Guess we knew how to pick 'em. It was important for us to make sure that the teams from the big U.S. cities were represented—Philadelphia, the New York Rangers, Chicago, Boston, and so on. I liked Clarke's play in his first two seasons with the Flyers, so even though he wasn't as well-known as some of the others who came with us—Frank Mahovlich, Paul Henderson, Rick Martin from Buffalo—he was my choice. He came along to Jamaica with his wife, Sandy.

We had to share houses, and I put Bobby and Sandy with Janet and myself. When you're down there for a week, you really get to know one another, and it turned out they were a delightful young couple. We'd enjoy a few beers at night and we'd play euchre. It was a great time.

Bobby was just learning how to play golf at the time and, quite honestly, he wasn't very good. He was a lefty and wild. He has improved over the years and is quite good now—a low handicapper.

Doug Sanders, who had just won the Kemper Open, was the resident pro (someone who comes to the club two or three times a year, but whose name is used mostly for marketing purposes). He came down for a day, and the idea was to have him play a hole with each of the foursomes. We started off on the first tee with Doug, who turned out to be a great guy.

Pretty much everybody there was watching us, since we were first to tee off, and Sanders, who had flown in from New York to be with us, smoked one right down the middle. I was up next and I sliced one to the left. Not a great shot, but hey, I'm out there. Well, Bobby got up next, left-handed, and hit it about 80 yards. It dribbled to a stop just in front of the ladies' tee box. Not exactly what you'd expect from a professional hockey player—especially a future Hall of Famer.

Sanders, who shot right-handed, walked over to Bobby and said, "Let me show you how you use that club." He dropped a ball on the tee, turned the club upside down and drilled it about 200 yards down the middle of the fairway.

Everybody applauded except Clarke, who was obviously a little embarrassed about being shown up.

"Why the hell do we need to to be the first ones off the tee?" Clarke muttered under his breath. Couldn't he have hooked up with us on the fourth hole?" Always competitive—that's Bobby. That was his intensity coming through, and I admired that. He was clearly pissed, but he settled down after a while.

When push came to shove, Clarke could really dig in his heels. That didn't change when Clarke retired as a player and became an executive with the Flyers. I know that from first-hand experience because I negotiated my son Scott's first two contracts with Clarke and the Flyers.

Scott was the twenty-seventh-overall pick in the 1984 NHL entry draft and in 1985–86, after his second year at the University of Wisconsin, the Flyers expressed an interest in signing him and having him turn pro. No wonder: Scott was coming off a year in which he scored 21 goals and 44 points in 32 games.

My choice for Scott would have been for him to play one more year at Wisconsin and then join Canada's Olympic hockey team in Calgary, but Scott desperately wanted to turn pro. He didn't want to risk being injured playing college hockey and blow his chance at playing professionally. Since I had lots of experience negotiating contracts, Scott and I agreed I would speak with Clarke, the Flyers' general manager, via the telephone.

Now, I'd say that one on one, there's nobody smarter in hockey than Bobby Clarke. He's not imposing, but he's smart. I had to negotiate a lot of contracts with a lot of smart people over the years, but when it came time to sit down with Clarke to do my son's deals, I told Scott, "This is not going to be easy. Bobby Clarke is a tough negotiator."

Even though we were friends, when we got to the negotiating table, Clarke was going to do what was best for his organization. As it turned out, we got what we wanted from Clarke and the Flyers, so I guess it's safe to say we weren't shooting for the moon—only going for what was reasonable. The biggest thing I wanted for Scott in his first contract was a one-way deal whereby Scott would make the same money if the Flyers decided to send him to the minors as he would if he stayed in the NHL. The Flyers had never given a rookie a one-way deal before.

I guess Bobby liked what Scott brought to the table, because when he became GM of the Florida Panthers, he acquired Scott to play for him there.

Scott used to tell me that when he played with the Flyers, whenever he'd run into Clarke in the Spectrum, Clarke often seemed distant. But occasionally, he would lace on the blades and join the team on the ice. That was when his real personality would come through— he absolutely lit up. He was right in his element. If Bobby had a choice today between being an executive or a player, there's no question in my mind he'd be a player.

To me, Bobby Clarke the person is not the player he appeared to be on the ice. When it came to playing the game, he was ferocious. He was a win-at-all-costs player. Off the ice, he's a class act. Don't get me wrong: he'd still do go to great lengths to win, but he wouldn't kneecap you for 2 points. He's quiet and reserved, although he's very opinionated. Of all the people I ever met in hockey, I'm not sure if I met anybody like Clarke, who has an opinion on everything. That can be a good thing, however—TSN hires him routinely as a guest analyst for his honest opinions. He is still in your face. That's why I love him.

* * *

My dad played baseball with Toe Blake in Hamilton in the 1920s with the Hamilton Tigers baseball team. He and Toe were both pretty close because they also liked to play cards when they were young bucks.

Over the years, I couldn't count the number of times my dad would say, "Toe Blake is a great pal of mine." I was always impressed that my dad knew a national sports celebrity.

When I was directing the Wednesday night *Hockey Night in Canada* games for CTV, we had to pre-tape a segment with Toe. I'd never met him before, so I said, "By the way, you're a great friend of my dad, Edgar Mellanby."

He looked at me, and in a very curt voice said, "Yeah, I knew him."

His nonchalance kind of hurt me. The crew was standing around and was listening, and it was a little embarrassing.

When I became executive producer of *Hockey Night in Canada*, I had to learn about radio, so I took a radio road trip with the team.

As I went into the Forum, I saw a bus parked, not on the main street, Atwater Avenue, but on Lambert-Closse, a side street on the east side of the arena. I assumed it was the bus that would be taking us to the airport for our trip to Detroit, where the Canadiens were scheduled to play the Red Wings.

Remember, this was my first road trip. I was a rookie, and my only two pals were the late Jacques Beauchamp, the legendary sports editor with *Le Journal de Montreal*, and Red Fisher, the most famous English-speaking writer ever to cover the Habs. I didn't really know the players that well, with the exception of John Ferguson, who was a neighbour.

Eventually, the rest of my crew started to arrive, including Dan Kelly and Danny Gallivan.

Toe walked into the hallway of the Forum. As always, he was a frightening character.

"Where the #@$%# is the bus?!" he bellowed.

Without thinking, I piped up, "It's parked over on Closse Street."

"What the hell is it doing over there?" he said. "It's supposed to be on Atwater." And he charged around the building.

Red Aubet, the team's trainer, said, "You should never talk to Toe, Ralph. You're a newcomer. Just keep your mouth shut."

What I didn't know was that the bus was only parked there temporarily, and as Toe was making his way through the Forum, the bus had made its away around to the other side of the building where the players normally boarded. So when Toe got to where I said the bus was, it wasn't there. Yikes!

When Toe got back, he was all over me.

"What is this, a joke?" he screamed.

I felt two inches tall. I wanted to crawl under a rug.

Jacques Beauchamp finally spoke to me and said, "Ralph, you listen to Red and me. We'll look after you. When you get on the bus, go to the back and sit in the middle. Don't sit with the players up front in any seat. Be humble."

Well, you guessed it—the seat Jacques directed me to was Toe's lucky seat. He got on the bus, and once again I was the target of his scorn.

"You again! What is this, another goddamn joke? That's my seat!" I moved to another seat.

Now Red leaned over and said, "Don't listen to Beauchamp; he's putting you on. When you get on the plane, Toe always plays cards and he always sit with me. I'll show you where to sit."

I should have known better.

Toe got on the plane and walked down the aisle to where I was seated and said, "What the @#$#$ is going on?"

"What?"

"That's my seat!"

When we got to the hotel, I decided I'd wait in the lobby until all the players were gone to get the key for my room. In those days, there was no travelling secretary, the way there is today on big-league teams. The coach handed out the room keys. Imagine: here was a guy who had coached five Stanley Cup champions in a row, and he was responsible for handing out room keys.

When all the players had gone, I walked up to Toe, who looked at me and said, "Here's your key."

By this time, I was thinking that all I wanted to do was get to my room so I could hide.

I got on the elevator and pushed the button for my floor, and before the door had closed, Toe walked into the elevator right behind me.

The elevator stopped, and we both got off at the same floor. Not only that, we were headed in the same direction. I couldn't shake this guy!

It turned out my room was right beside his suite. As we put our keys in the door, Toe looked at me and said, "Ralph, have a good night."

And he laughed.

It was right then that I figured out he'd been in on the gag the whole time. This was my initiation. Thank God I passed! Apparently all the players were in on it, too. Looking back at the episode, I'm not sure how I could have been so naive, but this was my first trip with the Canadiens and I was the patsy. I think the same would have happened to a lot of people in my shoes.

Toe was an amazing man. The more I worked with the Canadiens, the more I got to know him. He had been a star in the NHL as a player. He was a member of three Stanley Cup champions—the Montreal Maroons in 1935 and the Canadiens in 1944 and 1946. Toe led the NHL in scoring in 1939 with 24 goals and 47 points in 48 games and was presented with the Hart Trophy as the league's most valuable player that season. He was a First Team All-Star three times and a Second Team All-Star once, and he won the Lady Byng Trophy as the league's most gentlemanly player in 1949. That still surprises me.

One of Toe's habits when he coached was that he would never eat at the same restaurant as the players. He wanted them to have a little freedom on the road. He liked to eat his meals with Dan Kelly, Danny Gallivan, or me.

The first year of expansion, when the league doubled in size to twelve teams from six, there were all these new towns where Toe didn't know where to eat. One of my jobs was to scout any new restaurant we were going to try and see if any of the players were in there. If they were, it was my job to tell them to get the heck out. Can you imagine walking up to an imposing figure like John Ferguson and telling him to get out because the coach wanted to eat there? By the way, they all left immediately. Think that would happen today?

Toe would wait outside for me to come and tell him the coast was clear.

Eating with Toe offered me a great opportunity to get to know his coaching philosophy. He told me he had been treated like crap when he was a player, and he treated players similarly. If you benched a guy or didn't dress them, you didn't tell them why. They sat and kept their mouths shut. That's not the case today, when players—or their agents—demand an explanation for everything.

Toe would bench Ralph Backstrom or Terry Harper and he would never talk to them. And he never taught the game. Toe would say, "When you get up to the Montreal Canadiens, you'd better already know how to play. That's why you have minor league coaches—to teach them how to play. That's where they learn."

What made Toe such a great coach, in my opinion, was his passion and his will to win—his ferocity. Red Fisher wrote a great story about the Canadiens playing at the old Chicago Stadium once. There was a huge dog, a German shepherd, I believe, at the bottom of the stairs that everybody had to pass by. The dog was kept in a cage most of the time, but was let out at night. That was the stadium's security. I could not imagine coming face to face with this creature in a locked building.

The dog's name was Bruno, and trust me, if you ever walked past this thing you'd never forget it. He would charge at you and almost break the bars.

Red wrote about how Toe walked down the stairs on his way to the Canadiens' dressing room and the dog cowered when he passed by its cage. The point Red was making was about how intimidating Toe could be. That column won Red the National Newspaper Award.

As I got to know him, I saw the lighter side of Toe Blake. He had a twinkle in his eye. I guess he figured he had to be a menacing figure to get the most out of his players, and you certainly can't argue with the results. Many people say the Canadiens won the most Stanley Cups because they had the best players. That is not true. The Canadiens won the most Stanley Cups because they had great players that were motivated by great men such as Dick Irvin, Toe Blake, and Scotty Bowman. I know Scotty learned a lot from Toe. Coach Blake was his hero.

What made Toe so great was his emotion and his will to win. He had very simple rules for his players when they were on the ice. For instance, he'd tell his guys, "If you have an option, never retreat.

Never retreat! It's like war. If you get caught and you can go forward, keep going forward." That was the essence of fire-wagon hockey.

As nasty as Toe could be, I always had the sense the players respected him. He wasn't like Scotty, who also got great results, but whose players made no bones about the fact they did not enjoy playing for him. The players loved Toe, and yet he never really made a point of warming up to them.

By the way, as we grew closer, Toe did talk about playing ball with my dad, which really warmed my heart.

My favourite Toe Blake story involved another initiation. We had a young buck on our Montreal staff, André by name, and my producer Jacques Bérubé decided to give him the gears because he was always bugging us to allow him to do more. Now, Toe would often sit in the downstairs press room early before games and have a cup of coffee. At that time, he was always under fire for playing one of the team's rookies, Yvan Cournoyer, only on the power play. So we told André, "Your first big assignment is to go see Coach Blake with a request. Tell him we have an iso camera on Cournoyer, and for TV, could he please use him on a regular shift?"

We let Red Fisher in on the gag, since he always sat with Toe. André went in and made the request. Toe said, "No problem."

Jacques and I were hiding in the hallway, peeking through the door, waiting for Toe to explode. We couldn't believe it when Toe just nodded his agreement. We found out later that Red had changed sides on us and let Toe in on the gag. He got us again! André, meanwhile, was so proud.

* * *

I first met Scott Bowman in the press box of the Montreal Forum when I arrived in Montreal in the early '60s. I got a press pass, back in the days when the press box was located at the end of the arena, to watch the Canadiens play and when I sat down, I had Frank McCool on one side of me and Scotty Bowman on the other.

McCool, who was a writer in Calgary at the time, had been a very good NHL goaltender, helping the Toronto Maple Leafs win the Stanley Cup in 1945, the same year he was chosen the league's rookie of the year. Scotty was coaching the Montreal Junior Canadiens.

As we sat there, I thought to myself what a bright, inquisitive young man Scotty was. Frank wasn't very gabby, but Scotty sure was. Over the years, Scotty and I became close.

The one thing I learned about him was he always wanted to have an edge over anybody or anything he was coming up against. Over the years I often caught Scotty trying to gain a little edge for his team. In the old days, we put little beepers on the linesmen's belts to let them know when we wanted to take a TV time out. In those days we didn't have two two-minute commercial breaks like they do today; there were six thirty-second commercials, and we'd beep the linesmen into the commercial and then beep again when the break was done. We gave one beeper to each linesman, although I learned much later that John D'Amico never turned his on, which is another story.

When we put the system in, Scotty was coaching the Canadiens. He tried to get to my producer—he wanted to be able to send the producer a hand signal when he wanted a TV time out. Scotty wanted to use our system to help his team. I found out about it and put an immediate stop to it. But that was Scotty...he always had to have the edge.

All the players despised him. I can't recall ever meeting a player who liked him. For me, Scotty was simply different. He was interesting, and I like interesting people. And if the players didn't like him, they sure as hell respected him.

Scotty adored Toe Blake, and in turn, as Scotty carved out his wonderful coaching career, others who followed in his footsteps, notably Mike Keenan, worshipped him. Keenan slicks his hair back the way Scott does, holds his chin up high while standing behind the bench and even eats ice chips during games—just like Scotty. Mike is also a successful, Stanley Cup–winning coach, just like Scotty.

The other thing about Scotty is he always likes to be the first to try something new. When I went to work on the Stanley Cup final between the Montreal Canadiens and St. Louis Blues in the first season after expansion, I had the idea that I would like to have Dick Irvin down at the bench to interview the coach before the game. This was Toe Blake's last hurrah and Scotty, at the time, was coaching the Blues.

I approached Scotty with the idea and he said, "Are you crazy? Not a chance."

"I just want to get your comments about what it's like to be in the final against your old team...your former organization," I said.

"No way!"

"You know, Scotty, it's never been done before."

He hesitated for a second and said, "Let's do it."

That was it. He did it and was the first coach we interviewed live before a game. He even gave us his game plan. Of course, that was back in the day before teams had assistant coaches who'd be on the lookout for any tidbit of information they could find on the opposition. Still, Scotty gave us the wrong information.

Scotty actually did a great job in that series. You have to remember that the six expansion teams who made up the Western Division were at a real disadvantage compared to the Original Six (who all played in the Eastern Division) in terms of experience, so even though Toe's Canadiens beat Scotty's Blues in four straight, they were all 1-goal games. It was all down to Scotty's great coaching!

On another occasion, *Hockey Night in Canada* was broadcasting a playoff series between Montreal and Detroit from the old Olympia Arena. Scotty, who by now was coaching Montreal, had the Canadiens on the ice practising while Ted Lindsay, who was the GM of the Red Wings at the time and my old pal from NBC days, was showing me around the rink. I was hoping to find some unusual camera positions.

Well, Scotty saw us walking together and blew his whistle to stop practice.

"You see that?" Scotty bellowed to his players. "You see that guy? He's running *Hockey Night in Canada* and he's from Essex. You know who he's rooting for—Detroit!"

Lindsay looked at me and said, "What the hell is he going on about?"

"He's just trying to get the edge, Ted," I said.

Ted said, "I respect that."

I mean, I'm just a television guy, and here was Bowman trying to fire up his players by inferring we were against the Canadiens. What a guy!

My son Scott played in the NHL All-Star Game in 1996 in Boston and they had a big party on a battleship in the harbour after the game. Scott's team, the Eastern Conference (coached by Doug MacLean, Scott's coach with the Florida Panthers at the time), had beaten the Western Conference, coached by Scotty. The Eastern team carried the play through most of the game, but couldn't score. They hit goalposts and fired just wide time after time. My son set up the winning goal.

What stood out about this game was that the Fox television network, which had the U.S. television rights, introduced the glowing puck. On the TV screen, the puck was encircled with a bluish glow so that viewers could follow it more easily. Whenever it was shot or passed at more than seventy miles an hour, a red tail, like a comet, trailed behind it. It went over like a lead balloon in Canada and was soon scrapped.

Scotty saw me at the party and walked up to me and said, "You know what the problem is with that glowing puck?"

"No, Scotty. What is it?"

"It won't go into the net!"

That was about the closest you'll ever get to Scotty making a joke. At least I think he was joking. With Scotty, you never know.

The only really serious conversation I had with Scotty occurred when he didn't get the general manager's job with the Canadiens after Sam Pollock retired in 1978. It went to Irving Grundman, who won the Cup in his first season using Pollock's players and then struggled afterwards. Scotty wanted the job, and when he didn't get it, he left the organization and joined the Buffalo Sabres as their GM.

I saw Scotty in 2008, and told him I didn't think the current collective bargaining agreement between the NHL and the NHL Players' Association was a good one. My feeling is the salary cap really catered to the high-end players, making the middle and low-end players suffer. I felt the game would start to go downhill because you need a lot of the lower-paid players and only a few of the highly paid players. Lo and behold, Scotty agreed with me.

"I never thought of it that way," Scotty said.

I think it's the first time ever he didn't come right back at me with a point of view that ran counter to mine.

If my son had just one game to play and I was picking the coach, I'd take Scotty. If you want to beat him, then you have to beat him. He'll never beat himself. I can't say that about many coaches.

* * *

If you had to choose the greatest goal in hockey history—just one goal—it would be Henderson's game-winner in game eight of the famous Summit Series in 1972. No question in my mind about that. It is the most significant goal in the game's history and I was there. Closing my eyes today, I can still hear Foster Hewitt calling the action. The puck crosses the line behind brilliant Soviet goaltender Vladislav Tretiak and Hewitt screams, "Henderson has scored for Canada!"

Remarkably, it was the third consecutive game in which Henderson scored the game-winning goal. Who could have believed it?

When I first heard of Paul Henderson, he was a junior player with the Hamilton Red Wings. Before I really got to know him, he had a reputation for being a bit of a party animal. He liked his booze. He didn't do bad things; he just liked to party. That's the way it was early in his NHL career, and he admits it today.

In fact, Paul was one of the guys that came with us for the golf trip to Jamaica along with Bobby Clarke and the gang. By this time he had already played nine years in the NHL with Detroit and Toronto and was coming off back-to-back big years with the Maple Leafs during which he scored 60 and 57 points as one of the NHL's better two-way players. In spite of that, he told me he really didn't expect to make the Team Canada roster. Funny thing, history.

It was in Jamaica I got a first-hand view of Henderson's free-wheeling lifestyle. He and his wife, Eleanor, stayed in the chalet near where we were staying. One night, as things were winding down, my wife and I were in bed reading while Bobby Clarke and his wife were in the other room, and around midnight there came a loud banging at our door. Paul and Eleanor were out with the Hall of Fame announcer Ted Darling and his wife.

We went to the door and there they were, loaded. Henderson, who could barely talk, said, "I want some gin! Let's have some fun!" We didn't have any gin, but as it happened my wife had put fresh water in a gin bottle and put it in the fridge. The gin bottle was the only thing Janet could find to store the fresh water. What a stroke of luck!

Janet poured him some "gin" into a glass of tonic and Henderson sat down to enjoy his cocktail. He looked at me and said, "This is the smoothest #@%$@ gin I've ever tasted in my life!"

From that point on we called the water "Henderson's gin." That became the joke of the trip. I still kid Paul about it.

Although Paul might not have been expected to make Team Canada in 1972, in the end, he, along with Bobby Clarke and Ron Ellis, formed a very effective line that could both score and check. When the tournament concluded and Canada narrowly won the eight-game event by the skin of their teeth, saving face in the process, I walked into the Canadian dressing room and I spotted Henderson sitting motionless in his stall. I wanted to get Tony Esposito's goalie stick and get it autographed by all the players. Paul was stunned—still sitting there in his uniform.

Paul is a very sensitive and interesting man once you get to know him. This was long before he found the Lord and became a born-again Christian. As I spoke with him after the game, it became very evident he was in shock. I was speaking to him, but he couldn't hear me. He was sitting there with his uniform still on, staring off into space, while the rest of the guys whooped it up around him—celebrating. He was exhausted…perhaps even a little confused and overwhelmed about what he had just accomplished.

He was now one of the biggest celebrities in Canada, and I believe he had a hard time handling the notoriety. As much as Henderson did with his late-game heroics, he was still, at the end of the day, just a very good player.

I think perhaps people thought he'd return to the NHL and blossom into a superstar. That, of course, was unrealistic. It doesn't take away from what he accomplished. The small-town boy from Kincardine, Ontario, played the next two seasons with the Maple Leafs, but his production decreased.

Henderson then jumped to the World Hockey Association, playing six seasons for the Toronto Toros and Birmingham Bulls before returning to the NHL with Atlanta for thirty otherwise-nondescript games. He capped his career with thirty-five games in the minors and then retired.

Paul's life underwent an extreme transformation in the years to come. He went from being the party guy to being a Christian who spends a lot of his time spreading the word of God. Today he is a minister of the gospel—and a good one, too.

In 1991, Paul, Eleanor, Janet, and I went back to Prague and Moscow to do a film retrospective on the Summit Series. By that time he had spent a lot of his time trying to save my soul. He nearly convinced me by saying, "Ralph, when you become a Christian, even the love-making is better with your wife." Now that was a great message!

I admire Paul very much. When you see people that can immediately change their life and you look at all the good he has done, it is very refreshing. To me, that trip was one of the most joyful experiences of my life, and being with Paul and his wife made it that way.

They are still my favourite hockey couple.

The most memorable moment happened when I played a bit of a trick on Paul. We were filming in the Luzhniki Arena, where they played the final game, and we were using dry ice, which created a real fog inside the rink. I wanted Paul to skate through the fog toward the net where he scored his monumental goal—and when he burst through it, there was Vladislav Tretiak in net, waiting for him! Paul was very emotional. It was a very moving moment and we captured it on film.

Paul does a lot of speaking as a minister now and he often tells the story about how he made the decision to call a teammate off the ice so he could go on. It was not a coaching decision to have him on the ice in the dying moments of the game. Henderson says he simply had a feeling about what was about to unfold—he knew, deep inside, he was going to score the winning goal and he took matters into his own hands.

I said to Paul, "Maybe it was the Lord telling you to do it."

"Could be," was all he said.

As for me, I don't have any doubt. See, Paul? I am a believer.

Over the years there has been a healthy debate as to whether or not Henderson should be inducted into the Hockey Hall of Fame. To be honest, I am the wrong guy to ask about the Hockey Hall of Fame. I disagree with the way players and builders are selected. I think it's a real clique and I don't agree with fifteen guys sitting around a room voting for their friends. I like the way baseball and basketball choose their inductees—through a vote with many, many more voters.

In any case, the Hall of Fame has honoured Paul and his Team Canada Summit Series teammates, so he will live on in history.

I think so highly of Paul. In fact, he would be the first guy I would ask to speak at my memorial service, and that's saying a lot. And Paul, let's hope that service is a long way down the line.

* * *

I was at the press conference in Montreal in 1964 when Sam Pollock was named general manager of the Montreal Canadiens, and it was a really odd gathering. Frank Selke Sr., who was leaving the post, made it very clear that it was not his idea to step down and he wasn't very happy about the decision. Selke had been the club's GM since 1946, and the Habs won six Stanley Cups under him, including five in a row from 1956 through 1960. I believe Molson's, who owned the team, forced him out, claiming they wanted somebody younger overseeing the day-to-day operations of the team.

I was sitting with Frank Jr., who worked with us at *Hockey Night in Canada*, at the press conference and he didn't look too happy.

Sam Pollock inherited one heck of a dynasty, and I am certain Sam, if he were still with us, would say the same thing.

Sam wasn't one of the more impressive men I had come across, and he didn't present himself very well at the press conference. It was clear the Canadiens had faith in his ability to restore greatness to the franchise, and he certainly came through with flying colours.

When I became executive producer of *Hockey Night*, I didn't know Sam all that well. When you're directing the show, you really don't get to know the team's executives.

The week I was named executive producer, I was told I needed to have a meeting with Sam and Punch Imlach.

Sam called and said, "I really want to meet you. I've got lots to discuss with you."

I have to admit, I was a little intimidated. Here I was, this thirty-year-old kid running the biggest show in the country, and by 1966 Sam had established himself as the most powerful general manager in the National Hockey League.

I went to meet him at his office, and when I walked in, there he was chewing on his handkerchief, as usual, and walking around his office—slouched over. For a guy that I think is absolutely the greatest general manager in NHL history, and will probably never be surpassed, he really didn't make a great first impression. The guy never sat still and was always chewing on a handkerchief—his security blanket that he only used in private meetings, I guess. When I attended board of governors meetings and league functions, it never appeared.

I stood there, waiting to see what was up, and suddenly he turned to me and said sternly, "Who's going to run this show?"

I was a little taken aback, but I managed to say, "I guess you and I, Sam."

It was the right thing to say. Then I told him I had no intention of leaving Montreal, that I was staying put to oversee the show. Plus, I said, I didn't like the power base always being in Toronto. (The real reason for my staying in Montreal was to help the French show.) I think right away Sam knew I would not treat his Canadiens like second-class citizens and there was an immediate comfort level between us. I won him over.

At the end of the meeting, he said something to me that I have never forgotten.

"I'll back you all the way as long as you never hurt the game of hockey," Sam said.

"You have my word," I told him, and I always kept the promise. I often reflect on the executives and owners who have hurt the game by their actions. They know who they are.

As the years went on, Sam and I had a great working relationship. In fact, he called me one day and said Gilles Tremblay, the slick left winger for the Canadiens, had to retire because he had asthma. Tremblay wasn't the biggest star on the Canadiens, but in the nine seasons he played, from 1960 through 1969, he'd helped them win three Stanley Cups. At thirty, he was still a young man.

"I want for Gilles to continue with his career in hockey," Sam said. "Would you put him on *La soirée du hockey?*"

As it turned out, his timing was perfect. I was looking for a hockey player to be part of the French broadcast. Who better than a guy who had been a star with the Canadiens?

I knew I had an opportunity to help Sam, and in the back of my mind I knew that by hiring Tremblay, Sam would owe me one. That's the way he dealt with other general managers—he always wanted to be in a position where they owed him a favour. I know he kept track of all the favours people owed him!

I told him we'd normally have to audition a guy we were thinking of hiring, but we'd hire Gilles. Then we taught Gilles the business and he turned out to be the perfect sidekick for René Lecavalier, who was our premier announcer but not a hockey guy. Suddenly we had a great team that lasted for thirty years.

Tremblay finally made it into the Hockey Hall of Fame, not as a player, but as a broadcaster. I am very proud of him and of my selection. It worked.

When the time came for me to call in my favour, Sam was ready to help. I went to him and said I was sick and tired of not having NHL players made available to us during the playoffs. They were always with us during the regular season, but when the playoffs rolled around, suddenly they weren't able to come on the show. I thought it really hurt our broadcast because it was the most critical time of the year and we had our largest audiences, and now the players weren't on.

I made my case to Sam and I knew that if I got him onside, other GMs would fall into place. He was the leader.

Sam said, "Okay, but the Canadiens have to be on the first intermission and players from the visiting team on the second intermission."

Good old Sam—he always had to win. I said, "Does that mean if we are in Boston I have to put a Bruins player on in the first intermission and one of your players on in the second?"

"No! The Canadiens player always goes on in the first intermission. That's my rule. Don't break it."

After that, and ever since, we've always had access to players. He went to the general manager's meetings and pushed our agenda through.

I learned everything I know at the high level of hockey from Sam. I would often take long car trips with him to games because Sam didn't like to fly, and I'd soak up everything he said. I wish he were still alive. My son, Scott, has aspirations to be an NHL general manager, and I would love for him to have a day with Sam just to learn.

Sam trusted me not to use the information he gave me, and that made me feel good. It cemented our relationship. He said most of the GMs never read the rulebook and didn't know the constitution or the by-laws. He told me how and why he did things, which was wonderful.

I once asked him what made a general manager great and he said simply, "When you look at a hockey player, you have to know he can play. You don't think he can play, you know it."

Sam has his name on the Stanley Cup twelve times, nine as GM of the Canadiens.

Sam had a great mind. He may have chewed on his white handkerchief, but his mind was elegant and well-dressed. He knew the game backwards and forwards and he often gave me tips for our show. Once he said I should isolate the goalies, because that's where all the action is. The next year, I had one camera isolated on the goalies and it worked like a charm!

The last long conversation I had with Sam was at the Olympics in Sarajevo in 1984. Hockey Canada had a house there and Doug Kelcher, who was working for Hockey Canada at the time, brought in Canadian food and beer. Sam asked me about Scott, how he was doing, and then the other guys in the room started to talk about my son.

"You guys shut up!" Sam bellowed. "I want to know about Scott from his father, not you."

He asked me what Scott was looking for, and I said, "A one-way contract."

"You're right on," Sam said.

And I thought to myself, if Sam approves, then I guess I'm on the right track.

I bumped into him over the years when he was on the board of directors with the Toronto Blue Jays, and it was always nice to see him. I felt I owed him a lot. When I left *Hockey Night in Canada* to produce the Olympics in Calgary, Sam was the first person I called to thank him for what he had taught me over the years.

* * *

I had great ties in my life to Leonard "Red" Kelly, one of the NHL's all-time best two-way performers. His cousins, the Furlongs, lived in Essex and were my pals. Once in a while we'd go over to the Olympia when Red was playing with the Red Wings because he'd get us tickets to the game.

My uncle, Arch Mellanby, lived in Simcoe and played golf in the summer with Red, who also lived there.

When you meet Red, it's as though you have known him all of your life. He's not like most hockey players—he's so real. While I was working with *Hockey Night in Canada* I got to know him even better. In fact, for twenty years I would go to George Gross's house on New Year's Eve for a party and the Kellys would always be there along with other couples. George, of course, was the longtime sports editor of the *Toronto Sun*. Those were great parties.

Red was a great hockey player, both a defenceman and a centre over his twenty-year NHL career and he was outstanding at both positions. Red was an eight-time Stanley Cup winner who was runner-up for the Hart Trophy as the NHL's most valuable player in 1954, the same year he was the first Norris Trophy winner as best defenceman. Red also won three Lady Byng Trophies as the NHL's most gentlemanly player.

When he retired from playing, Red stayed in hockey and went on to coach in Los Angeles, Pittsburgh, and finally Toronto. He also became a politician early on and was a Liberal member of Parliament.

As decorated as Red's career was, many will always remember him best when, as coach of the Maple Leafs, he put pyramids under the team's bench and convinced his players it would bring the team good luck. They were up against the big, bad Philadelphia Flyers and they needed whatever edge Red could find.

We opened our show one night with a big pyramid superimposed over the Philadelphia Spectrum. It was a hoot. Red thought it was great.

Red had pyramids in the dressing room and under the bench. The public really ate it up, and so did his players. He didn't believe in it, but it was fun. That was typical of Red Kelly—he loved to have fun.

Through all my years in hockey, I never heard one coach, player or anybody, for that matter, say a single bad word about Red Kelly. And Red never had a bad word to say about anybody. He was universally loved. That was unusual. People in hockey—in all walks of life, I guess—tend to be jealous of one another. But everybody loved Red Kelly. Today, when I meet Red at functions it always gives me a feeling of joy, and it's always fun.

If I could have two people escort me into heaven, I'd have Henderson on one side and Kelly on the other—a Protestant and a Catholic. No use taking chances.

* * *

Marcel Dionne is probably the happiest individual you could hope to meet. He has a magnetic personality. He doesn't live life—he eats it up. Marcel is now my neighbour in Niagara Falls. He owns a memorabilia store, along with a handful of other businesses, and every time I run into him, he makes my life just a little bit happier—except on the golf course, where he beats me up.

When people say to me it was Wayne Gretzky who sold hockey in Los Angeles, I correct them. It was Marcel Dionne and the Triple Crown Line, with Dave Taylor and Charlie Simmer, who first sold the game in California. Wayne did a great job, too, but people involved in hockey when Marcel was in his prime with the Kings insist he did everything in his power to sell the game. He would be out in the community, getting involved, and always had time for the fans. He is a super salesman for the game of hockey.

After a brilliant junior career with the St. Catharines Black Hawks, during which time he scored 154 goals and 375 points in 148 games, Marcel was the second player chosen in the 1971 NHL draft—the Red Wings picked him after the Montreal Canadiens claimed Guy Lafleur first overall.

He enjoyed four productive years with Detroit, but his career really took off after he signed with the Los Angeles Kings in 1975 for what was then the largest contract in NHL history, paying him $300,000 a season. Dionne put the Kings on the map, and while he never won a Stanley Cup in his eighteen-year big-league career, he did make it into the Hockey Hall of Fame based on his terrific numbers—731 goals and 1,771 points in 1,348 games.

When the NHL All-Star Game was held in Los Angeles in 1981, all three members of the Triple Crown Line made the Prince of Wales Conference team. The NHL hosts a big party each year at the All-Star Game for its corporate sponsors, and Marcel was the hit of the party. When he walks into a room, he takes it over. He loves hockey and loves being with people who love hockey. I never saw a player happier to be a hockey star than he was. We need more guys like Marcel Dionne in the game.

A lot of people forget he was a member of Team Canada at the big 1972 Summit Series. He was just a kid and didn't get into any of the eight games, but unlike some of the other players, he did not show his disappointment. Even back then, he was a real pro.

Marcel never lost his passion for the game, and despite being just five foot eight and 185 pounds, was a giant in the game. I can imagine there was no better player to have around in the dressing room. He makes coming to the rink fun.

One thing you can depend on when you are with Marcel: you are bound to have a joyful time.

He is a superstar if there ever was one.

* * *

The New York Rangers have had many stars over the years, but only one Mr. New York: Rod Gilbert. He played with the team his entire sixteen-year NHL career and has been associated with the team throughout his entire retirement. Quite a tribute!

I didn't get to know Rod until he was well into his playing career. One of his best friends turned out to be one of our top hockey producers in Montreal, Michel Quidoz. Michel used to talk about Rod and visiting him in New York. When I worked in New York I used Michel as a bridge to get to know Rod, who wasn't necessarily the Rangers' best player, but unquestionably their biggest attraction. Mickey Mantle and Roger Maris were big stars in New York, but I don't think there was an athlete that shared Gilbert's popularity. He owned the city.

He made the fans feel comfortable. He had movie-star good looks, dressed like a model and, of course, he was the hockey star. I know—I was often with him. All the other hockey players could walk the streets and nobody ever bothered them for autographs. Once they left the arena it was as if nobody knew who they were.

Not Rod. When he walked the streets of the Big Apple he was constantly stopped by the fans. They definitely knew who he was. It was really something to see a hockey player enjoy that kind of stardom in the greatest city in the world.

Even though Rod was not a big drinker, he liked the parties and loved the nightlife. One night we were out on the town and Rod said,

"How would you like to go to Studio 54?" That was the famous disco that was nearly impossible to get into unless you were somebody or were with somebody famous.

"We won't be able to get in there," I said.

"Oh yeah?"

People were lined up for blocks, hoping to get in, but Rod walked right to the front and the guy guarding the door said, "Hi Rod. Come on in."

We got the VIP treatment. And talk about a nightclub!

Emile Francis, the longtime coach of the Rangers, told me Rod was the face of the franchise. There were other great players—Jean Ratelle, Brad Park, and Vic Hadfield—but it was Gilbert's team. Even when Phil Esposito joined the Rangers, Rod was the man.

In 1,065 games with the Rangers, Rod managed 406 goals and 1,021 points. He was a First Team All-Star once and a Second Team All-Star once and also was chosen to play in eight NHL All-Star Games.

After all these years he still works for the Ranger organization. It shows that they value what he did for the team. Mike Richter, the star goalie when the Rangers won the Stanley Cup in 1994, once told me, "In New York, Rod Gilbert is still the king."

* * *

Phil Esposito is a different cat, but also one of the greatest leaders to ever play the sport of hockey. He was often willing to help me out with the things I did for *Hockey Night in Canada* and quite frankly, I think he loved the limelight. What the heck, I know he loved television and he is still on TV today.

They had a special day for Phil and his brother Tony, also a big-time NHL star, in their hometown of Sault Ste. Marie, Ontario, after they retired, and I was the only television guy invited. Actually, it was more than a day. It was four or five days—a big party. The good people of Sault Ste. Marie really loved the Espositos, who, at the height of their popularity, always made sure to mention their hometown when they were interviewed.

Phil was a leader, but he often marched to his own drummer. He was not always keen on taking direction. He felt he knew better and more often than not, he was right. Phil knew he was a difference-maker on the ice and didn't like to relinquish ice time to let others take their shifts. Don Cherry told me the reason the Bruins traded him to the New York Rangers was because he was taking three-minute shifts. It was common back then for players to take long shifts, but really, three minutes? That was pushing the envelope.

I really got to know Phil when we were taping the original "Showdown in the NHL" for *Hockey Night in Canada*. We pitted the best players in the NHL against one another in a series of penalty shot competitions during the summer months and then used them during our intermissions in the following season. When you start a new project, there are always bugs to be worked out, and it really didn't help us that Phil bitched and moaned about the food we served. The thing about Phil is, when he speaks, others take notice and fall into line behind him. He's like the Pied Piper. I knew when I was producing a show that if I could get Phil onside, the rest of the players would follow.

That said, Phil did a lot of things with me—"Pro Tips" and other editions of "Showdown." He was always available. I think Phil loved that stuff, loved being the centre of attention. He was in his glory. I admired his star quality.

Phil is the one guy I met in hockey who really understood how to use the media. I think it's great that after he finished his playing, managing, and coaching days, he joined the media. Phil can be outspoken and controversial, but when he's on the air, you don't dare change channels. He's good for the game of hockey. He is entertaining and damn smart.

One thing I'll never forget is the day he was traded by his beloved Boston Bruins to his arch-rivals, the New York Rangers. I think he would have accepted a trade to Russia more willingly. Phil detested the Rangers. He was devastated.

The Bruins happened to be playing the Vancouver Canucks that day, and we were in Vancouver to broadcast the game. I got a call in my hotel room that Espo had been traded. Like everybody else, I was shocked. Being the TV producer, I needed to act quickly to incorporate the news of the day into our show opening.

I raced over to the rink in hopes of getting Phil on camera to use it as the lead-in to our show—the great Boston Bruins superstar packing his gear and leaving his team. I arranged to get a camera to the rink, but Phil arrived before the cameraman. He came in to pick up his sticks and equipment and he was very upset.

Later, Cherry told me when he went to Phil's hotel room to tell him about the trade, he thought Phil was going to jump out the window. Phil told me he was sure it was another player being moved, not him.

I was waiting for the cameraman to arrive when Phil arrived at the rink. I followed him into the Bruins' dressing room and spoke with him for a few minutes.

Phil grabbed his stuff and said, "I've gotta get out of here and get the #$%#@ away from this team."

Remember how fired up he was after game four of the Summit Series in Vancouver, when he went on TV and pleaded with Canadians to stop booing Team Canada? Well, he was every bit as fired up this day—maybe even more so.

I began to panic. Phil was about to bolt and my camera still wasn't there.

"As a favour, Phil, can you hang in for a few minutes until my camera guy arrives?" I pleaded with him. "I really want to get a shot of you leaving the building with your gear. I want to use it on the opening of our show tonight. This is a huge story for Canada."

Amazingly, Phil waited—for about fifteen minutes! We got our shot and it was a great opening for our show. It couldn't have happened without Phil's co-operation and his understanding of what was needed. I don't think there is a player in the game today who would do what Phil did for me on that day. It struck me that Phil really understood the business he was in—the entertainment business. Most players don't get that.

He understood the role the media played during his early NHL days in Chicago, when he played with the Bruins, at the Summit Series and with the Rangers, as well as in his post-playing career.

I think it was good that he went to New York. He took the Rangers to the Stanley Cup final in 1978–79, where they lost to the Canadiens, and even though he set all kinds of scoring records with the Bruins, it took his profile to an even higher level. Phil was made for the Big Apple.

I wrote it in *Walking with Legends* and I think it is worth repeating: The greatest example of leadership I ever saw during my career was what Phil Esposito exuded during the 1972 Summit Series. Through the entire series, but specifically in the final game, it was Phil's team. I remember saying after the second period of game eight, "Canada needs to score the first goal in the third period if it wants to win this series."

Who got the goal? Espo. Who set up the game-winning goal by Henderson? Espo.

Enough said. A great hockey star and a great person—Phil Esposito.

* * *

When John Ferguson first moved to Montreal in 1963 from Cleveland, where he had played the previous three seasons in the American Hockey League, he became my neighbour. We both lived on the West Island, about a half a mile from one another.

Nobody knew much about him at the time, but it turns out the Canadiens were upset at having been pushed around the year before and wanted to bring a tough guy to town to look after their stars.

I remember Fergy's son, John Jr., traipsing around the yard when he was just a tyke. We used to call him John-John. Who could have known then that he'd grow up to be the general manager of one of the most important franchises in the NHL, the Toronto Maple Leafs?

I liked John Ferguson right away. He was not what people think. Sure, he was an enforcer, but not by today's standards. John Ferguson could also play the game, as evidenced by his 20-goal season in 1966–67 and 29 goals the following year. The Canadiens had a couple of other tough guys already in Ted Harris and Terry Harper, but Ferguson was a guy nobody wanted to mess with—and I mean nobody!

Jean Béliveau once said, "With Ferguson around, we all felt secure."

To me, Fergy was like Dr. Jekyll and Mr. Hyde. On the ice, he was absolutely ferocious, an intimidating force who would do anything to help his team win. He was totally fearless. But we used to share the odd ride into Montreal, and I got to see the other side of Fergy—that of a kind and gentle soul.

On the ice, the one guy who could handle John, calm him down, was his teammate Ralph Backstrom. Ralph knew just what to say—a wisecrack or a joke—when John was about to go over the edge, and always managed to pull him back.

Once, we were in Detroit when the Canadiens were to play the Red Wings. Fergy absolutely hated Detroit defenceman Howie Young, but Young would never fight him. This drove Fergy nuts. It also irked Ferguson that Young had been featured on the cover of *Sports Illustrated* and described as "The Toughest Man in Hockey." "Toughest man in hockey, my ass," Fergy would say.

Fergy went out on the ice for that game determined to set the record straight. We were doing the game on CBC radio that night, and Backstrom warned me, "Keep an eye on Fergy tonight."

Sure enough, Ferguson went after Young, and rather than drop his gloves to fight, Howie took his stick and smashed Ferguson right over the forehead. It cut Fergy wide open—I think it took thirty stitches to close the wound. Not only that, but Fergy got thrown out of the game and Howie didn't. Fergy had gone nuts! I thought, as did Danny Gallivan, that the Detroit police would be called onto the ice.

After the game, we all went out for a beer to a bar the Canadiens and the other visiting teams used to frequent in downtown Detroit, just around the corner from the Leyland Hotel, where we stayed. I have never seen a guy look worse than Fergy that night between the stitches and the swelling. Not only that, but Fergy was still fuming.

Of course, Backstrom couldn't leave him alone. He started joking around in an effort to calm Fergy down. And it was working.

"If I have to tell you one more time, stop it because it hurts when I laugh," Fergy said.

The next thing I remember, Detroit rookie Peter Mahovlich

walked into the bar. There were about twelve Canadiens there, and you should have seen the looks on their faces. The enemy!

Fergy looked like he was going to attack him. Of course, Peter is a jovial guy and wasn't looking for any trouble. Just to be on the safe side, one of the Canadiens went over to Peter and told him he'd better hightail it out of the bar. Wisely, Peter took the advice and left.

The reason I recall this is because it said so much about Fergy. He was battered and bleeding, but he wouldn't quit. He never gave up—never!

I know the only guy John was ever afraid of was his coach, Toe Blake. Funny thing is, Toe loved him. I liked to try to experience first-hand the things I covered on TV, so when I got the executive-producer job for *Hockey Night in Canada* I went to Fergy and wondered if he'd ask Blake if I could join the Canadiens on the ice during a practice. I thought that by skating on the ice with the pros, you could really understand how great they are. That's exactly what I wanted to experience.

You should have seen the look on his face.

"Are you out of your mind? You think I'm going to go to Toe and ask that? Go to Big Jean [Béliveau] if you want, but not me."

I went to Toe and asked, and he said, "You're in television. What the hell do you want to come on the ice for? Besides, the players will kill you."

I told him I wasn't concerned about that, and he reluctantly let me do it.

Turns out Toe was right. Backstrom, Harper, Harris, Fergy—they all went after me. I was lucky to make it through the practice. As soon as I stepped on the ice, one of them tripped me, and it went downhill from there. I was out of my depth. Thankfully, they were friends and were just giving me the business. What Toe said would happen, happened.

Afterwards, Fergy said to me, "I told you that you were nuts!"

Once, we were doing a game in Boston and I was standing at ice level when Fergy got into a fight right in front of me. He cracked this guy right in the face and broke his nose. The linesmen moved in to break up the fight and Fergy spied me standing there. He gave me a wink and pointed to his nose as if to say, "See what I did? I broke his nose!" He was laughing. I realized then how "in control" he really was.

John Ferguson was a tough guy through and through. He really cared about his image. I recall that once I invited him and Backstrom and their wives to our cottage in Ste-Agathe, Quebec, but I forgot to tell them I had also invited a guy I used to work with in the musical-variety field, one of my writers on *Musical Showcase*, Darryl Monroe-Wilson. What a mistake!

Darryl was gay and made no effort to hide it. I had no issue what-soever with Darryl. I loved the guy. He had been a ballet dancer in Britain and was a great idea guy and writer.

There were five cabins and we all shared a pool. The Fergusons and Backstroms arrived first, and after they were settled around the pool, in walked Darryl. He was chatting with the ladies, talking about the ballet days, and they just loved him. He also showed his Royal Ballet moves.

Ralph and Fergy just kept staring at him. Finally, Fergie asked me, "What the $#@%# is that all about?"

"He's a friend of mine, John."

Then I explained his background in England and the Royal Ballet.

Fergy just looked at me. Didn't say a word. Tolerance won out that day. At the end of the day, after a few hours (and a few beers), Darryl and Fergy were fast friends. For years, though, John would say to me, "Boy, Ralph, you really know how to throw a party...how to invite the right mix of people."

As the years went on I moved to Toronto and John and I drifted apart, but we remained pals. When John became GM of the Winnipeg Jets, I looked forward to broadcasting their home games there just so I could see John. When I heard about him tossing a chair from his private box at the top of the rink onto the ice at the referee, I can't say I was shocked.

I thought for sure he'd be suspended. Instead, the NHL caged him in. They made him put Plexiglas around the sides and front of his box.

John was actually quite proud of it.

"Look at this," he said to me. "Nobody has ever had this before."

I was very sad when we lost John. I was an honorary pallbearer at his funeral and I'll never forget standing outside the church after the service and seeing two of his old nemeses there: Bryan Watson and Eddie Shack. What a huge compliment! Fergy and Shack had monumental battles, and yet there he was, paying respects to his old adversary.

It really says a lot about Fergy—a hockey player's hockey player.

* * *

My son Scott has had the good fortune to play for some great coaches in minor hockey, college and in the NHL, but he insists his favourite coach, by far, was Roger Neilson.

Neilson, or "Captain Video," as he became known, was an innovative coach who was always searching for ways to exploit the rules as well as the opposition. But more than that, he was a kind and gentle man, deeply religious, who treated his players like gold.

Scott said, "I've had a lot of great coaches, Dad, and no coach was perfect. I respected them all, even Mike [Keenan]."

By the way, Scott had his issues in the early days of his NHL career with "Iron Mike," but wouldn't say a bad word against him. Might *think* one or two, but wouldn't say them.

Roger, though, was great. He took an expansion franchise, the Florida Panthers, and in his two seasons behind the bench, brought them within a point of making the playoffs both times. That was really something.

Scott said he loved Roger's creativeness and innovativeness. Not only that, "He was a great man...a great teacher."

Roger's big thing was defensive hockey. It has been said of Roger that he'd rather lose 1-0 than win 10-9.

For me, I look at the impact he made on the game. He was the first coach to ever use video as a teaching tool. He started doing that back in his junior days when he was coaching the Peterborough Petes. When you see people waving towels at NHL games, you can thank Roger for that, too. During the Vancouver Canucks' miraculous run to the Stanley Cup final in 1981–82, after taking over as coach of the team from Harry Neale, Roger got upset with the officials. Putting a towel on the end of a stick and standing on the bench, he began waving it in the air. It was his way of protesting calls against his team—"We surrender! We surrender!"

At the next game, all the fans in Vancouver were waving the "terrible white towels," and the tradition remains to this day.

Roger was always after me when he was coaching the Toronto Maple Leafs, trying to get video we had shot from our isolation angles. He used his own video, but he wanted our tapes to show his players their mistakes. Of course, I couldn't give them to him—the last thing *Hockey Night in Canada* needed was to be painted as favouring one team over the rest. Nowadays, with so much tape available to the teams, it wouldn't be an issue.

Darryl Sittler, the Hall of Famer and Leafs captain who also worshipped at the alter of Roger Neilson, once told me, "You'll never find a player that had Roger Neilson as his coach that would say a bad word about him."

Scott thought the only thing Roger might have been better at was to be a little fiery under the right circumstances. I'm certain Roger thought about that, too, but it just wasn't his personality. He'd get mad, just like everybody else, but he didn't like to show it. He was calm and cool—always in control.

That said, Roger had a little bit of a dodgy side to him. He wasn't afraid to push the envelope a little bit—in hockey and in baseball. Some say Roger's first love was coaching baseball, which he used to do in the off-season in Peterborough. Roger once told me baseball was his first love, not hockey.

Once, while coaching in Peterborough, he felt his pitcher needed a rest, so he sent his dog out onto the field. He got the delay his pitcher needed.

Another time, his team was in a tight game and the opposition had a man at third base. Roger called a time out to speak with his club, and during the meeting, handed his catcher a peeled apple. Play resumed and after the first pitch, his catcher stood up and tossed the apple high over the third baseman's head. Thinking the ball had just gone into left field, the runner on third trotted home.

Surprise! Roger's catcher was standing there with the ball.

"You're out!" cried the umpire.

When league officials found out what Roger did, he got royal crap.

That was Roger. Nobody had told him a player couldn't throw a peeled apple into left field.

In hockey, when a penalty shot was called against his team, Roger would pull his team's goalie and put a defenceman in net. As soon as the shooter made his move toward the net, the defenceman would race out toward him and knock the puck away. The Ontario Hockey Association, and all leagues for that matter, soon banned the practice.

Roger never won the Stanley Cup, which is a shame. The year before he passed away, he was inducted into the Hockey Hall of Fame as a builder—a great decision. Roger now has two homes: a penthouse in heaven where he tapes and watches every hockey game from every angle, and a summer home at the Baseball Hall of Fame.

* * *

I first met Dick Duff back in Windsor in the '50s, when I started working in television. I was at a party with a girlfriend that I really liked, and I thought he was going to pick her up. Dick was going to Assumption College, which was later turned into the University of Windsor. He had just joined the Maple Leafs and was finishing his education in Windsor.

Imagine, my first meeting with an NHL star and I was ready to punch him in the nose!

Dick Duff, to me, was the ultimate Toronto Maple Leaf. He wasn't the biggest guy on the ice, but he had the biggest heart. I couldn't believe it when he got traded to the Rangers. I thought he'd be a Leaf for life, and I was shocked when Punch Imlach got rid of him. He won two Stanley Cups with the Leafs, in 1962 and 1963, and later became an integral part of four championship teams in Montreal, in 1965, 1966, 1968, and 1969.

Whenever I took a flight with the Canadiens, I loved to sit and chat with Duff. Dick was a really smart guy; one of the most intelligent players I ever met. He played with a lot of other stars who got way more attention than him, but if you ask his teammates, they'll tell you he was a great contributor. In 2006, thirty-four years after he retired, he was inducted into the Hockey Hall of Fame.

He is one of my favourite people.

* * *

When Jim McKenny turned pro in 1966, he was hailed as the second coming of Bobby Orr. Talk about pressure!

McKenny was a smooth-skating Maple Leafs defenceman who loved to join the rush, and while he had some wonderfully productive years in the NHL, he never came close to attaining star status. That aside, he was a hell of a guy and I really liked him. What a sense of humour!

Jim marches to a different drummer. I'll never forget going to his house one day early in his career to do a film profile on him for *Hockey Night in Canada*, and when I went up to the door with my film crew, this little girl answered. She disappeared for a few seconds, and when she returned she said, "I'm sorry. My dad says he can't make it for the filming today because he says he was hit by a truck last night."

Jim loved to party, so I imagine the truck that sideswiped him came in a bottle.

As we got to know one another, Jim and I used to play a lot of golf together, and I have never seen anybody tee up his ball as high as Jim. He'd use long tees that he'd barely put into the ground. I used to ask him how the hell he hit the ball like that and he would say, "I'm different."

Well, that was certainly an understatement. Funny thing is, he's a pretty damn good golfer.

Once, I was golfing in Florida with my wife, Janet, and two guys in the group behind us kept hitting the ball close to us. After a few holes I got pissed off and jumped in the cart and started heading back toward them. As I got closer, I realized it was Jim and a friend of his. I put my hat down over my eyes, and when I got about fifty yards from them, I yelled, "What the hell are you guys doing hitting the ball at us! Who the hell do you think you are?"

Jim, as only he could do, yelled back, "We're just a couple of assholes from Toronto."

Then I revealed myself to him. Was he surprised!

We laughed about it later over many beers.

Jim never became the great NHL star many thought he'd be. Still, there were some nights, when he was on his game, when he carried the puck with the skill and grace usually reserved for the game's best players. In 604 NHL games he scored 82 goals and 247 assists for 329 points.

When his NHL career concluded, I helped Jim get into television, and he has made a wonderful career for himself as a sports broadcaster at City-TV. When City started in 1972, some of the MacLaren Advertising agency people had money invested in the station. Our office, Canadian Sports Network, ended up doing a favour for two or three of the owners of MacLaren, and became the first sports department for City. I never really figured out why we were doing it, but we did it—and it was fun.

We hired Mel Profit, the former Canadian Football League star, to be a sportscaster. Mel was a bit of a wild guy, but I knew he'd fit right in with the off-the-wall folks at the TV station. They were a little out there, if you get my drift—not my cup of tea.

Mel did a good job as the main sportscaster. After a few years the station actually started its own sports department. When Mel left and they were looking for a successor, I got a call from Moses Znaimer, who founded the station, asking who I thought might be a suitable replacement, and I said Jim McKenny.

I'm proud that I recommended him and I'm proud he's on the air today—although I still don't watch that station. Still not my cup of tea. McKenny today is a TV star and is one of my favourite characters. If you know Jim, you are really lucky.

* * *

When my son Scott played college hockey at Wisconsin, one of his teammates was Tony Granato, who later went on to a fine NHL career as both a player and coach.

When I used to go watch Scott play at Wisconsin, I'd fly from Toronto to Chicago, then hop on a smaller aircraft to fly to Madison, Wisconsin. Quite often, the second flight was bumpy and just a bit frightening.

One day I was talking with Tony's father, Don, and he told me they lived close to the airport in Chicago, and since they drove the family in a van to the games in Wisconsin, why didn't I hitch a ride with them. I was delighted to have a chance to avoid the transfer flight. It was very gracious of Don to make that offer.

I'll never forget the first trip. Don and I sat up front and the kids, including this little girl, were in the back. After a while Don's young daughter, Cammi, and I engaged in conversation. She was a sweet little thing, and when I asked her what she wanted to do when she grew up, without hesitation she said, "I'm going to be a hockey player, just like my brother."

I said, "Women don't play hockey. You have to be a figure skater or a skier."

Shows you what I know. Cammi Granato grew into one of the finest women to ever play hockey and was captain of the United States team that won the gold medal at the 1998 Winter Olympics in

Nagano, Japan, defeating Canada in the final—a future Hall of Famer.

Wrong again, Ralph.

* * *

There are some who call the game between the Montreal Canadiens and the Soviet Red Army on December 31, 1975, at the Montreal Forum the single greatest hockey game ever played. It may have been an exhibition game on paper, but on the ice it had all kinds of athletic and political ramifications. Canada defeated the Soviets in the famous Summit Series in 1972, but by now it was clear the Soviets were gaining in terms of hockey supremacy.

This game had everything you could ever hope for to build a telecast around: Ken Dryden versus Vladislav Tretiak in a rematch of the goaltenders from game eight of the Summit Series; the greatest NHL franchise against the perennial champions from the Soviet Union; not to mention a captive audience on New Year's Eve. This was before there were all kinds of specialty sports channels, and *Hockey Night in Canada* was still where people across the country tuned in to watch hockey on TV. The buildup for this game was tremendous and we knew we'd have a huge audience.

Millions of people were watching that night, and I later found out from a contact I had in the government that the rates of accidents and drunk driving went down 50 per cent across Canada that night. The reason was the game. People had house parties and watched the big game in their homes.

It was a great telecast, largely because of Tretiak. He stole the show. The Canadiens threw everything they had at him, but he was like an impenetrable wall. Dryden, meanwhile, didn't have an especially good evening, allowing two of three shots in the second period to beat him. All told, the Canadiens outshot the Soviets 38–13, but Tretiak was absolutely phenomenal. His performance that night arguably had more to do with bolstering his reputation as one of the finest goalies ever to play the game than anything he did in the Summit Series when, in my opinion, neither the Canadian nor Soviet goaltending was great.

The Canadiens built leads of 2–0 and 3–1, but try as they might, they were unable to squeeze a fourth goal past Tretiak. It was the first international game at the Montreal Forum since the Soviets shocked Team Canada in the first game of the Summit Series, one of Tretiak's best performances of that event.

For a television producer to have the game live up to the hype was really outstanding. We had a great shot of the fans in the Forum giving Tretiak a standing ovation when he was named the game's first star. It was the one international game I can ever recall where the visiting team got such a warm reception from the home crowd.

After the game, we had a gathering upstairs in the Forum, and even Danny Gallivan told me it was the best hockey game he had ever seen. Often when you are broadcasting a game, you don't get a feel for how monumental it is. That night, Danny knew that what he had witnessed was legendary.

Years later, when I did the *Summit on Ice* special celebrating the twentieth anniversary of the 1972 Series, I asked a lot of the old Soviet players about the 1975 New Year's Eve game, and I was pleased to find out they also counted it among the best games ever played. It was a real exhibition of skill and beauty, and the final score really didn't matter. It was a perfect game to have end in a tie.

I have often wondered why the NHL doesn't schedule an annual New Year's Eve game. Sadly, the league has never done it since that night. The NHL has an outdoor game on New Year's Day now, but to me it's not the same.

Bring back the New Year's Eve game, if only for the safety of the country.

* * *

If the Canadiens–Red Army game is remembered for its grace and skill, the January 11, 1976, meeting between the Philadelphia Flyers and the same Red Army team is remembered for blood and guts. It was a battle of championship teams, but it was also a battle of style and courage.

The Soviets proved in the Summit Series that they were capable of sneaky tactics—using their sticks and sometimes even kicking—to get at their opponents. The Flyers? Well, they weren't nearly as subtle. They won back-to-back Stanley Cups by kicking the crap out of their opponents. When it came to settling an international exhibition game with nothing but pride on the line, they weren't about to change their approach.

Ed Snider, the Flyers' owner, came up to me before the game and said, "This will be the first time everybody in Canada will be rooting for the Flyers."

He was right.

Bobby Clarke told me that in the morning skate the Flyers wanted to win the game so badly they could taste it.

I wanted to do something a little different for the opening of our telecast that night, and since I knew the Flyers' coach, Fred Shero, quite well, I asked if he wouldn't mind taping an interview with us from ice level while the teams were warming up in the background. As much as Shero coached a very aggressive style of hockey, I also knew he loved and respected international hockey. He loved Soviet hockey.

I got him at the end of the rink, by the entrance where the Zamboni went on the ice, and I'll never forget what he said: "This game means more to me than you'll ever know. If we lose this game to these guys, to me it will be like death."

I knew we had the greatest opening we had ever done. Talk about a monumental statement! I thanked Fred and watched as he headed back to the Flyers' dressing room. A few seconds later, I got a call from our truck telling me the tape was no good.

"What?" I roared.

I didn't know it then, but it was a sign of bad things to come. It was the hardest game I ever televised.

I had to go running around the rink to grab Shero, who by now was at his team's bench, and ask if he'd do it again.

Now it was his turn.

"What?" he screamed.

Thank heavens Fred Shero was a classy guy; he came back and did the interview again. In fact, he did it better. This time, I was taking no chances—I used two tape machines to record the interview.

When the game started, it was obvious from the outset the Flyers were out for blood. They didn't just want to beat the Soviets—they wanted to beat them up. The Red Army was undefeated against NHL competition in this series, including their 3–3 tie with the Canadiens, but the Flyers were out to change that.

Midway through the first period, Flyers captain Ed Van Impe left the penalty box after serving a two-minute minor for hooking and made a beeline for Soviet superstar Valeri Kharlamov. Van Impe delivered a crushing, but clean, bodycheck that left the Soviet prone on the ice. (After the game, referee Lloyd Gilmour told me, "It was clean, but he could have hit him with an axe and I wouldn't have called a penalty." It was a real us-against-them mentality back then—Canadians against Soviets.)

The Soviets, led by coach Konstantin Loktev, left their bench and headed to their dressing room. They were done.

As our announcer Bob Cole proclaimed, "They're going home! They're going home!" I knew I had a big problem on my hands. The Soviets were leaving the ice and I still had two hours of television to broadcast. We were sitting on a boatload of expensive commercials still to be aired.

What followed was about twenty-five minutes of the toughest production I had ever done because I had to make it up as I was going along. I sent one hand-held camera to stand outside the Russian dressing room just in case there was a meeting between the Soviets and the NHL—which turned out to be a good idea, because a meeting was held. We captured the moment when Snider held up the cheque and told the Soviets if they didn't return to the ice they wouldn't get a penny. It was the final game of the series and they hadn't been paid yet.

That's what got them back on the ice. If they gave out Emmys in Canada, we would have won it for that shot. Thank God for Ed Snider!

Still, I had a lot of scrambling to do. I brought all kinds of guests into the broadcast booth, including Bobby Orr, and sent cameras all over the rink looking for shots. It was tough. I knew I had to produce at least ninety minutes of television just to get the commercials in because they were all paid for. That's ninety minutes with no game! I really thought they were packing it in and going home.

I called one of our runners and told him to go get my boss, Ted Hough, who was sitting in the stands with Frank Selke Jr. I was looking for help on what to do. I started to run some commercials to check them off the list, but it also gave me a little time to think about how I was going to handle this mess. I knew I could come up with enough content, but I was more concerned about how I was to handle dealing with all the commercials we had to air.

Finally, a knock came at the door of the truck and it was Frank Selke Jr., our vice-president of just about everything.

"Ted says to rerun the first period," he informed me.

I won't say exactly what my response was, but suffice it to say I slammed the door shut and got back to work. There was no bloody way I was replaying the first half of the first period. This was live television. You don't start rerunning things on live television. It would have killed our broadcast. We were sitting on a huge story. If the Russians had actually left the building, they could have been suspended from international play.

I said to Ron Harrison, the director, "We're going to wing it. Just keep that camera rolling outside the Russian dressing room."

It turned out to be great theatre. I looked at the tape afterwards and was pretty happy with how we handled it.

When the teams finally came back, I think the first half of the remainder of the game was commercial-free because I'd aired so many during the half-hour the Soviets were hiding out in their dressing room.

The game has been talked about for years. Tretiak has been quoted as saying the Flyers won "playing rude hockey."

Soviet coach Loktev added the Flyers were "a bunch of animals." By the way, the line, "They are going home!" helped Bob Cole's career and has never been forgotten.

Those two games, Montreal and the Flyers against the Soviet Red Army in the Super Series, are my favourite moments in my career.

For me, it was a very memorable night of television. One of the great things about broadcasting live television is there's no script. You might go into it thinking you are just doing another hockey game, but then all hell breaks lose and you have to be prepared to react. That's when you come alive as a producer.

It was great television and the right guys won.

4

TAKE ME OUT TO
THE BALL GAME

If football ruled the day while I was growing up in Hamilton, then baseball ran a close second.

Baseball was the lifeblood of my family; my dad was one of the best players in Hamilton, with the Tigers. My uncle Archie was regarded as one of the best players in Ontario and even had a tryout with the New York Yankees. He was so good that he was paid—under the table, of course—and it led to him getting a job on the railway. In those days, companies would hire you based on your ability to star in sports. That still happens today with good hockey players, who are often gobbled up by police and fire departments.

I was the only boy in the Mellanby family—all my uncles had girls—so I got lots of attention from them. My uncles, that is. It was great, because they really took care of me.

In Hamilton, our house on Chedoke Avenue was a hive of family activity. One year for Christmas, the new big thing was a Ping-Pong table you could set up on your kitchen table to play. I got three of them—one from each of my uncles. My dad swore me to secrecy so there wouldn't be any hurt feelings.

Dad coached the Hamilton Cardinals, so I was always hanging out at the stadium. I grew up around the game. In that atmosphere, it was no surprise that baseball became my passion for years.

Between 1910 and 1930, there was very little radio and no television, so people went out to watch games live, especially local baseball.

You would go to a championship game in Hamilton and there would be thousands in attendance. And a lot of pro football and hockey players played baseball in the summer months. My dad played ball with Edgar Laprade, the great centre with the New York Rangers, and another year he played with Toe Blake, the Canadiens all-star who went on to coach Montreal to eight Stanley Cup championships. The old park was located right behind what is now Ivor Wynne Stadium, where the Hamilton Tiger-Cats play, so when you hit a home run to right field, it would end up on the football field.

In 1945, my dad moved from the *Hamilton Spectator* to the *Windsor Daily Star*. I was eleven years old, and it broke my heart to have to leave Hamilton. My whole life revolved around my aunts and uncles and grandparents, all of whom lived in the area. Suddenly, I was being uprooted—and to me, Windsor might as well have been England. It was devastating.

Before moving the family down, Dad had rented a one-bedroom apartment in Windsor. That fall, he brought me to Windsor to see game three of the World Series in Detroit—the Tigers against the Chicago Cubs. He sure knew what he was doing.

I was put on a train, all by myself—at eleven years old!—and it was off to Windsor. You think that would happen today? Not a chance.

The day after I arrived, we went to the ball game. Dad decided we should go early enough to watch batting practice. He figured that, since I had never been to a major-league game, it would be a thrill for me to see the players whacking the ball into the bleachers.

Unfortunately, Mother Nature was not co-operative. It was raining steadily, so batting practice was cancelled. One thing I'll never forget is how there were servicemen in uniform everywhere because the war had just ended. In fact, a lot of players on the field had recently come out of the service.

Not only was batting practice cancelled, but I didn't get to see a lot of hitting during the game. The Cubs managed 1 run on 3 hits, while shutting out the Tigers, who managed just 1 hit, by Rudy York. Claude Passeau tossed a 1-hitter for the Cubs.

Ralph and famous Yankee pitcher Whitey Ford. —Mellanby Collection

Ralph and Hockey Hall of Famer Marcel Dionne. —Mellanby Collection

From the TV pilot of *Showdown*. Back row, left to right: Jean Ratelle, Art Skov, Ken Hodge, Phil Esposito, Bill Flett, Bill White, Yvan Cournoyer, Dennis Hull, Rick MacLeish, Jim Pappin, Mickey Redmond, Guy LaPointe, Jim McKenny, and Brad Park. Front row, left to right: Jacques Lemaire, Gary Unger, Rick Heinz, Marcel Dionne, Gilles Villemure, Doug Favell, and Tony Esposito. —Courtesy Paul Palmer, creator of *Showdown*

Ralph and Roger Abbott, one of the stars of *Royal Canadian Air Farce.*
—Courtesy CBC

Ralph and Hockey Hall of Famer Dick Duff. —Mellanby Collection

Ralph and the great referee Bruce
Hood. —Mellanby Collection

Ralph and the famous CBC
commentator Terry Liebel at the
Barcelona Olympics.
—Mellanby Collection

Ralph and CTV producer Ed Mercel. —Courtesy CTV

At the Bell South Open Golf Tournament with famous golfers. Left to right: Larry Lefave, Paul Azinger, and Ian Baker-Finch.

—Courtesy Bell South Tourney

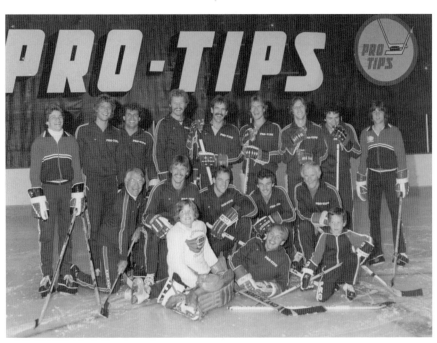

The *Pro-Tips* cast with Howie Meeker. That's fourteen-year-old Scott Mellanby on the far right.

—Courtesy *Pro-Tips*

Promotional shot of the late Grace Meeker and Howie Meeker.

—Courtesy *Hockey Night in Canada*

Ralph and famous pal Celtic singer John Allan Cameron.

—Mellanby Collection

ABC producer Bob Goodrich, CBC director Ron Harrison, and Ralph at the 1984 Sarajevo Olympics.

—Courtesy ABC

Ken Mackenzie, founder and
publisher of *The Hockey News*, and
Ralph.　　　—Mellanby Collection

Ralph and Ron Harrison at Lake
Placid.　　　—Mellanby Collection

Another *Showdown* cast.　　　—Courtesy Paul Palmer, creator of *Showdown*

Glen Sather and Ralph playing golf in Banff. —Mellanby Collection

Scott Mellanby, "The Ratman" of the Florida Panthers, and Ralph. —Courtesy the Florida Panthers

The production crew of the Wayne Gretzky special *Once Upon a Time in Hockey*. —Courtesy *Once Upon a Time in Hockey*

Ralph with François Carignan, producer of *La soirée du hockey*
—Courtesy CBC

Famous singer John Denver and Ralph in Sarajevo.
—Mellanby Collection

Paul Henderson and Ralph on the set of *Summit on Ice.*
—Mellanby Collection

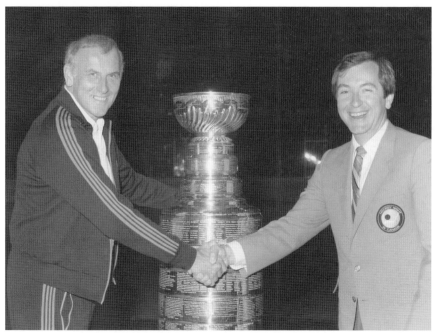

Ralph and John Shannon with the Stanley Cup. —Mellanby Collection

Ralph and Ken Dryden with ABC in Sarajevo. —Mellanby Collection

Pitcher Claude Raymond and Hall of Famer Duke Snider with Ralph on the set of *Baseball Pro-Tips.*

—Courtesy *Pro-Tips*

Good old Peter Puck.

—*Courtesy Brian McFarlane*

Don Cherry with my late wife Janet on vacation in Newfoundland.

—Mellanby Collection

Ralph and Roggie Vachon.
—Courtesy *Pro-Tips*

Ralph and buddy, famous Leaf Ian Turnbull.
—Mellanby Collection

Ralph, opera star Riki Turofsky, and the Zeiglers at celebrity tennis.
—Courtesy CBC

Al Eagleson, Eleanor and Paul Henderson with Ralph in Prague.
—Mellanby collection

At the NHL Slo-pitch Tournament—Ralph tags one.   —Courtesy NHL Slo-pitch

Two pals—Ralph and Don Cherry at the NHL Awards.

—Mellanby Collection

Don Wittman and Geoff Gowan at the Pan American Games.

—Mellanby Collection

On a fishing trip in Labrador. Bruce Hood, Ralph, Harry Neale, and Scotty Bowman—notice, no fish!

—Mellanby Collection

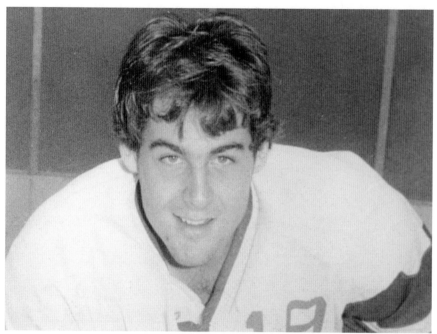

Scott Mellanby at Wisconsin University. —Mellaby Collection

Ralph with famous figure skater Peggy Fleming in Lake Placid.
—Mellanby Collection

Ralph with friend and famed artist Ken Danby. —Mellanby Collection

Ralph and former CFL commissioner Doug Mitchell at Grey Cup party (costumes by Don Cherry). —Mellanby Collection

The volleyball commentators at the 1988 Seoul Games. Left to right: Bob
Trumpy, Ralph, and Chris Marlowe.   —Mellanby Collection

On the set of *The Grapevine*.   —Mellanby Collection

It was a great thrill for me to be there. And I have my dad to thank for the amazing memories. More than sixty years later, I can still see every player on the field—relive every inning. I'm certain that all the players, from Hank Greenberg to Hal Newhouser, have died. I wonder how many of the 52,000 fans at Briggs Stadium are still around.

I went on to play a little pro baseball myself before packing it in to work in the world of television. And it would be television that brought me back to the major leagues.

I worked for a time on the Chicago White Sox and Cubs broadcasts, but I really cut my teeth broadcasting professional baseball with the Montreal Expos. While working in Montreal, I used to play softball with Russ Taylor, the announcer, who worked with me at CFCF-TV. The station was located right behind Jarry Park, and we had a ball team called the Office No-Stars.

One day Russ asked me to join him, as well as Montreal mayor Jean Drapeau and Charles Bronfman of Seagrams, who became the owner of the Montreal Expos. I guess because of my background in baseball and television, I was looked upon as something of an expert when it came to a key question. As we arrived at Jarry Park, Bronfman asked me, "Do you think this could be a major-league baseball park?"

"No way!" I said.

Then he told me he was bidding for an expansion team to play in the National League. And Russ had had the idea that remodelling the little stadium in Jarry Park could provide the team with a home.

"You guys are wasting your time," I told them. "Take another look at Delorimier Downs (where the old Montreal Royals of the International League had played)."

Wrong again, Ralphie boy.

They got the team, and put it in Jarry Park—which I came to think of as one of the greatest ballparks in the world once I started working there. It reminded me of Fenway Park in Boston.

The Montreal Expos made their debut in 1969. As the first

major-league baseball team to be located outside the United States, the Expos were Canada's team. Although baseball ranked well behind hockey and football in terms of popularity in Canada, people were still thrilled to have a major-league team to cheer for.

CBC got the TV rights for the Expos' games, which made sense because they had both French and English networks.

About two weeks before the opening game I got a call from Marc Cloutier, who had previously worked with the Montreal Canadiens in public relations, but was now an executive with the Expos. He said he had a problem. The CBC had forgotten, or perhaps didn't know, that they were mandated by Major League Baseball to provide facilities for the visiting team's broadcast crews, for games that weren't broadcast on CBC. They couldn't supply the alternate trucks and video feed that were necessary to make that happen.

I had a meeting with John McHale, the team president. I knew my old station, CFCF, was located right behind the park, and they had two good mobile units. So I decided to form a company, in conjunction with CFCF, to provide the needed facilities. The company was called REM Productions—as in Ralph Edgar Mellanby. My wife, Janet, became vice-president and ran the business with John Krug, the operations manager for CFCF.

Suddenly, I was in another business. My bosses at *Hockey Night in Canada* gave me the go-ahead because I was investing my own money and time, so there was no conflict of interest, and it was summer, so it wouldn't interfere with my hockey duties.

I supplied cameras to the visiting teams and helped them run their shows out of the mobile unit. I put together a crew of guys I hand-picked from CFCF. Then John asked me who was going to direct the games. That was easy—me! I'd loved baseball all my life and I had finally made it to the majors.

Before long, I got a call from the Hughes Television Network in the United States. They said they really wanted to support my company. This was a huge operation, one I knew well because it had covered NHL hockey. Back in the mid-'50s, the sponsors of the Brooklyn

Dodgers telecasts thought it cost too much to broadcast the team's road games. An ABC television executive, Dick Bailey, found a way to do it for less. Then he thought, "What if I could do this for *all* the major-league teams?" He started his own company, Sports Network International, which provided crews, production facilities, phone lines, and other equipment for just that purpose. It branched out into televising just about every kind of sport and was purchased by Howard Hughes in 1968. In addition to their own units, Hughes also relied on independent contractors, and at that time there were no independent mobile units in Montreal—only those belonging to CBC and to CFCF, the CTV affiliate.

I was in seventh heaven being around Jarry Park during the summer months. I was there so much I became a member of the Expos family. I got to know Duke Snider, who was the team's TV voice from 1973 to 1986. Duke was one of my boyhood idols, even though I cheered for the Tigers and he played centre field for the Brooklyn Dodgers. I appreciated his greatness even though he wasn't playing for the team I cheered for. Of course, the Tigers were in the American League and the Dodgers in the National, so I couldn't be accused of dividing my loyalties.

I didn't work directly with Snider, but I saw him at the park every day, and we formed a lifelong friendship, and when I finally got to produce the CBC telecasts, he was a great supporter of mine. Years later, I did a show with Duke and Tony Kubek called *Baseball Pro-Tips*. It was a sponsored teaching tool for coaches and youngsters. We taped the series in Florida during spring training, and it featured Expo and Blue Jay players.

Duke was one of baseball's all-time great power hitters, and one thing I wanted him to do was demonstrate his sweet swing.

He said, "Ralph, I'm fifty-seven years old…I can't do that."

Well, I knew he could, and I talked him into it.

Wearing the *Pro Tips* baseball uniform that the guys wore for every segment, he stepped up to the plate.

"Who's going to pitch?" he asked.

"I will," I replied.

I told him we might have to shoot ten or twelve takes, but I just wanted to capture his perfect swing—one of the greatest in baseball history—especially in slow motion.

In order to get the perfect shot, I told Duke I wanted to shoot him from a couple of angles. With the camera behind me, pointed at Duke, I grooved one right down the middle and he walloped it right over the centre-field fence.

Boom! Fifty-seven years old, my foot. He crushed the ball. I couldn't believe it. Even the crew applauded.

He dropped his bat and said, "That's it."

"What do you mean, 'That's it?'" I said. "I need to get a couple more angles."

Duke said, "I'm finished. I could swing all day, but I could never do *that* again. I'm finished."

And that was it. I hope we haven't lost that tape—it's a piece of history.

Duke was a wonderful analyst, though he was different from Kubek, whom I consider to be the greatest of all time. Tony would be more critical, but Duke put more colour into his broadcasts. He used his great sense of humour and was a great storyteller.

Duke was a colour analyst on radio and TV for twenty-five years, and he was as well-known to many Canadians for his broadcasting of Expos games as he was to Americans for his brilliant Hall of Fame playing career.

Of all the people I worked with in sports, baseball had the classiest people. And the Expos were most certainly a golden organization. They were so much easier to deal with than hockey people. It wasn't just in Canada, where baseball people knew they had to do a good selling job. Even when I was broadcasting games in the United States, the teams would bend over backwards to see that I had everything I needed. You ask some people in hockey for something when you're on the road and they roll their eyes. It was often as though you were putting them out.

I also became close with John McHale, the Expos' president and general manager. Because of his position, I had to deal with him all the time. When I first met him at Jarry Park, I told him about what a huge baseball fan I had been when I was a little boy. John had played only a handful of games with the Detroit Tigers, but I was at one of them and saw him make two magnificent fielding plays while playing first base. He was a lightweight hitter, but a good fielder—the opposite of most first basemen. When you only play thirty or forty games in the majors, you don't expect a guy to show up and say he saw you play, so he was suitably impressed. I always called him "Slick John," and he loved it.

To McHale, I had credibility. I could talk baseball with him any time. I think that is a mistake a lot of TV people make: They cover sports they don't know a lot about, and try to fake it. Don't try to talk the talk if you can't walk the walk. Whatever sport I covered, I studied it, especially its history—even water-skiing!

CBC's coverage of the Expos in the early days was poor. And that's putting it politely. Their producers were inexperienced, and every American producer I worked with would tell me they were happy they didn't have to share the feed because the CBC had no idea how to cover the game. If there was a routine cut-off play, they'd miss it. That made me proud of my coverage and crew.

I have a soft spot in my heart for the Expos. I had a great three-year run with them, during which I got to work with announcers like Vin Scully of the Los Angeles Dodgers and Jack Brickhouse of the Chicago Cubs. I also met people like Gil Hodges, the manager of the New York Mets. I did more baseball in three years than CBC did in the next ten because they were still only broadcasting one game per week whereas I'd produced several. I was *the* baseball guy in Montreal.

In 1971, when I moved to Toronto, I sold my company back to CFCF because I couldn't service it from Toronto. I have to admit it was difficult for me to leave Montreal. To me, Montreal is very exciting and the people exhibited a great deal of pride. After I moved to *Hockey*

Night in Canada's head office in Toronto, I still felt very welcome in Montreal.

The Expos connection helped my hockey broadcasting career because Sam Pollock, the legendary general manager of the Montreal Canadiens, was a huge baseball fan, too. He'd be at the Expos' games all the time, and I'd even have him in the truck with me during a few broadcasts. Sam loved talking baseball, but when it came to hockey, it was the polar opposite—he was very guarded with his opinions. I guess he didn't want anybody to know exactly how his brilliant mind worked.

I also got to know a number of the players well. While the CBC people were only around the park once a week, I was a regular fixture. I was there nearly every day. One of my favourites was the Expos' all-star right fielder, Rusty Staub. The big redhead was one of the most popular Expos ever, particularly with the women. Rusty was as big in baseball as Rocket Richard was in hockey. He loved the nightlife Montreal had to offer, he learned to speak French and was nicknamed "Le Grand Orange" by the Expos faithful. He had two stints with Montreal, and his number, 10, which he wore during his first few years with the club, was the first number to be retired by the organization.

Another of my favourites was Gary Carter, the chatty catcher who was nicknamed "The Kid" because of his youthful vibrancy. Carter was elected to the Baseball Hall of Fame in 2003, an honour he deserved. Even today, if I were to bump into Carter, he would talk my ear off…and I'd welcome the opportunity to listen to him.

Coincidentally, both players were managed by my old school friend, Gerry Patterson.

Those guys were so popular, it was a complete waste of time trying to get into a nightclub or restaurant with them. Autograph seekers would hound them, and they never turned anybody away. Their popularity was a tribute to Marc Cloutier and his marketing department. The Expos became Quebec's team, and the entire province supported the club.

It broke my heart when the Expos moved to the bigger and more modern (at the time) Olympic Stadium. There was something about Jarry Park that I wound up loving. It was a lot homier. Everybody was close to the field. The fans were knowledgeable. There was one disadvantage, of course: whereas the Olympic Stadium (eventually) had a roof, Jarry Park was exposed to the elements. I remember Dick Irvin saying to me one time, "It never rains in the Forum." As a result, we always needed to have features ready to roll in case of a rain delay. You couldn't just have your announcers sit there, yakking for hours on end, just to fill the time while it rained.

I've never lost sight of what my job afforded me over the years. If I hadn't been a TV producer or director, I never would have had a relationship with people like McHale, Staub, or Carter. To this day, I still maintain close contact with former Expos employees such as Marc Cloutier and Harry Renaud.

My three-year run with the Expos also served me well when I became involved with the Toronto Blue Jays in 1977. John McHale gave me the greatest recommendation, a gesture I will never forget. When the Expos left Canada and relocated to Washington, I sincerely believe that a little bit of me went with them.

* * *

Much of what I have experienced over the years was more about the people I met than the events I was covering. Such is the case with legendary Canadian broadcaster Don Chevrier.

The first time I ever met Don was in 1963, while I was still living in Montreal and he was working in radio at a local station, CJAD. The Montreal Men's Press Club in the Mount Royal Hotel was a haven for us in the media in those days. On any given day you'd rub shoulders with the likes of Red Fisher, the Hall of Fame hockey writer; Jacques Beauchamp, the great French-Canadian writer; Elmer Ferguson, who is regarded by many to be the dean of North American sportswriters; or Baz O'Meara, the famous sports editor for the *Montreal Star*. No lack of great conversation there.

You wouldn't just run into sporting types. It wasn't uncommon to see poet Irving Layton or even Mordecai Richler, one of Canada's best-known authors, sitting on a stool by the bar. Every once in a while, Leonard Cohen would show up.

I loved going there. It was a great place to have a beer and to socialize. It became my home away from home, plus it allowed me to establish great contacts.

I wasn't aware of it at the time, but Chevrier wanted to meet me. I was the major CTV sports producer at the time, and Don wanted an entree into the TV world. I was at the bar, next to Richler. Chevrier wandered over and introduced himself, and right away I was struck by his voice. It stopped you dead in your tracks.

"Ralph Mellanby, I'm Don Chevrier," he said.

"Nice to meet you," I said. "We'd better move." So I said, "Excuse me, Mordecai," and away Don and I went. I looked back at Richler, who had an incredulous look on his face.

"Is that Mordecai Richler?"

"Yes."

"You know him?"

"Sure I do. He's a great pal of mine."

Boy, was Don impressed! To the day Don passed away, he never knew that Mordecai Richler and I had never met. I was just having a laugh.

As a matter of interest, the first time I told that story was at Don's funeral and it brought down the house.

Don was young and ambitious. He told me he wanted to get on CTV. I told him to call Johnny Esaw, but I added, "I don't think you'll ever get a job with Esaw."

"Why?"

"Because your voice is too good. Pretty soon, if you were hired, you'd be doing everything."

I meant it, too. I knew that Esaw loved to be the king of the hill— he was his own top announcer—and I figured he'd feel threatened by this new kid in town.

"Don, your future in network television has to be with the CBC," I told him. How true that turned out to be.

He auditioned for a job at CTV and, as I thought, Esaw wouldn't hire him. Who would have known at the time that he would become one of Canada's greatest broadcasters, if not *the* greatest in history, and that years later we would team up on Blue Jays broadcasts as well as several other events?

When the Blue Jays were born in 1977, I had just signed a long-term contract with *Hockey Night in Canada*. The Jays were owned by Labatt Breweries, while their rival, Molson, was one of the main sponsors of *HNIC*. Still, in my mind I was the perfect guy to produce the Blue Jays telecasts, because of my background with the Expos—not to mention my love for baseball. No one I knew in Canada could do the job as well as I could, but I put it out of my mind because, for several reasons, mostly contractual, I just didn't think it would ever happen.

Then I got a call from John Hudson, who was running CBC Sports. CBC had acquired the TV rights to the Jays—they already had the Expos. He was a great administrator who had worked his way up through the system and was running the ship along with Bob Moir. My office at *Hockey Night* was on the fifteenth floor of a building on Yonge Street, and they were on the third floor of the same building. Hudson asked if I would come down to meet with him.

I figured, why not?

John asked me if I would consider producing baseball for CBC. I said it would never happen, that I was under exclusive contract with the Canadian Sports Network (which owned *Hockey Night in Canada*) and I'd never get their permission—after all, it was Molson versus Labatt.

"Just leave that to me," he said.

I'd heard that line a few times in my career, and until then it had never worked out. The next thing I knew, John was at Maple Leaf Gardens during one of our *HNIC* broadcasts, and he and Bob Moir came up to me and said, "We got you."

"What do you mean? I haven't even negotiated with you."

"Your boss [Ted Hough] has given us permission to hire you. Do you want to produce or direct?"

I told them I'd rather produce, because directing baseball isn't as difficult as producing it. After the *Hockey Night* broadcast, we sat around in the Hot Stove Lounge until about 3 a.m. and discussed everything, including the talent. "As far as play-by-play," John said, "there's only one choice as far as I am concerned, and we already have him under contract: Don Chevrier."

I couldn't have agreed more. In fact, we were on the same page on almost everything, including the crew—to be made up primarily of my people from *Hockey Night in Canada*.

But Peter Bavasi, the president of the Blue Jays, wasn't on the same page. "I don't want a Canadian guy," he told John. "I want a big-name [broadcast] team calling the games for us." As far as I was concerned, Don *was* a big name in broadcasting—in Canada. Luckily, we were able to convince Peter that our way, with Chevrier, was the right way.

At the end of the evening, Hudson said to me, "I want a team of three. I want a guy on the field and two guys in the booth."

Chevrier was our play-by-play man. He was the ultimate pro. He could do anything. He knew when to speak and when to keep quiet. His research was impeccable and he did it all by himself. And I had always liked Tom McKee's work. He later took my job producing baseball, but at the time he was a fine CBC announcer. So he was our man on the field. That left the question of who would be the colour analyst.

"How about Tony Kubek?" John suggested.

I just about jumped through the window. I couldn't believe my ears. I had met Kubek briefly when I was doing hockey at NBC, and we'd taken an instant liking to one another. I thought Tony was the best analyst in baseball. He was intelligent and outspoken and was the number one colour man on NBC's *Game of the Week*, working alongside such gods of broadcasting as Curt Gowdy and Joe Garagiola. Tony would both strengthen our team and give us instant credibility. But it seemed as though it would be easier said than done.

"Are you kidding me?" I said. "We'll never get him."

"I'm not so sure about that," John said. "He works on weekends with NBC, and our games are broadcast on Wednesdays." In the early years, the games were carried over CBC on Wednesday nights. We never did a weekend game. "Besides, we're never going to make the playoffs with this team for years, so I don't see any potential conflict with his schedule."

We flew to New York and met with my old friend Scotty Connal, the executive producer at NBC Sports. Scotty gave us the thumbs-up to hire Tony. The only problem was, as luck would have it, the first game on our TV schedule was on a Thursday afternoon. Kubek wouldn't be able to work the game because of his obligation to NBC—they were due to broadcast their first *Game of the Week* of the season two days later, and he had to attend meetings.

Tony suggested we get Whitey Ford to pinch-hit for him. I wound up having a couple of dinners with both of them, and they were swapping stories about legends like Mickey Mantle and Roger Maris. There I was, a baseball junkie from Essex, Ontario, rubbing shoulders with these superstars and just soaking it up. What a joy! They shared so much baseball history with me. I often wish my dad had been alive to join us. Boy, would he have loved it.

Whitey Ford is one of the finest people I ever met in my life. I didn't get to know him very well, but he made a positive impression on me. He was great for that opening game. We taped a piece with Kubek so that people would know he would be a part of our Blue Jays broadcasting team, but Whitey was a star on CBC for at least one day.

After missing that first broadcast, Kubek worked every game for years after that. Even after he retired from NBC, he still did games on TV in Canada.

Once, when we were in Dallas to do a Texas Rangers game, I wanted to go to Dealey Plaza, where John F. Kennedy had been shot. Tony had never been there, so off we went. The famous school book depository building (now home to government offices and a museum) was closed and boarded up. Luckily for us, the guy who was guarding the building recognized Tony from TV.

We said, "You know, we'd love to go inside and go up to the window where Lee Harvey Oswald took his shots."

"Sure," the guy said. "I'll take you up."

As I looked out the window, I looked at Tony and said, "Oswald couldn't have been the only shooter. When you look out the window, the shot, if you are the only shooter, is obviously head-on as the motorcade approaches, not as it turns underneath you."

Tony agreed with me.

Tony is not the kind of guy who wears his heart on his sleeve. You'd have trouble getting a reaction from him. You never knew what he was thinking. I couldn't get over his size. He's nearly six foot four; I couldn't believe a guy that big could play shortstop. He was such a great baseball player—American League rookie of the year in 1957, a three-time All-Star, a great athlete, now in the Wisconsin Sports Hall of Fame (not too far down the hall from my son, Scott).

I think the trio of Chevrier, Kubek and McKee was the best Canadian team we ever put together to cover baseball—and they were all in the prime of their careers.

Before the season opener, I took my hockey crew and gave them an exhibition baseball game to do. I figured if they could do hockey, a game played at breakneck speed, they could certainly do baseball, which is so much slower. My hockey crew became my baseball crew, and I have always been proud of them.

To make sure we were ready, we decided to hold a seminar and then a rehearsal game at CNE Stadium. On the radio side, Bavasi had hired I guy I'd never heard of, Tom Cheek, as well as Early Wynn, the old star pitcher for the New York Yankees. They came to our seminar.

Early was a great guy, but his broadcasting left a little to be desired. He'd say things like, "It's a long fly to centre field... going... going... no, the shortstop's got it."

I liked Tom immediately, and we became good friends over the years. In fact, I later recommended Don Chevrier and Tom Cheek to ABC for the Lake Placid Winter Olympics in 1980. Don called hockey over the radio, including the "Miracle on Ice" game, while Tom covered speed skating, also for radio. It was really something to see all these Canadians working for ABC Radio at the Olympics. Oh, and it was also fun for me to have them there.

A couple of days before the first game, I had a meeting with Bavasi and asked about the opening pitch. The ball was supposed to go to the Baseball Hall of Fame, so I asked him, "What if the batter swings and fouls it off into the stands?"

"I can tell you right now, Ralph, that won't happen."

"How do you know?"

"Because the batter has been ordered not to swing. The first pitch for a new team in a new ballpark...the batter will not swing. The catcher will take the ball to somebody and it goes to the Hall of Fame."

I was relieved. One less thing for me to worry about. Another lesson and another secret I have kept for years. By the way, it was a strike—right down the middle.

Then the snow came. And came...and came. It was April 7, for heaven sake! It's not supposed to snow in April. My friend, Canada's songbird Anne Murray, sang the national anthem. I saw her on the field rehearsing, so I walked up to her as the sky darkened and said, "Maybe you had better practise 'Snowbird.'"

I make no bones about it: I was scared shitless. I tried to anticipate everything that could go wrong, just so I would be prepared to deal with it. We even brought in a backup power generator just in case. I had a phone hotline from the truck to Bavasi and asked if there was any chance the game would be postponed.

"Absolutely not," he said. "This game will never be postponed!" I found out afterwards that he had bought his dad, Buzzie Bavasi, a gold bracelet on which he'd had the date engraved. How could he give his dad the gift if the date was incorrect?

I had pre-taped the opening for the broadcast: a camera placed in a helicopter "flew" from the site of the old Maple Leaf Stadium, where the Triple-A team used to play, over to CNE Stadium, where the Blue Jays would kick off their season. I had taped it on a sunny day, and here we were in the middle of a snowstorm. I had to tell McKee to tell the audience, "That was yesterday. Today we have a snowstorm, of all things."

Once we got into the ball game, things went absolutely smoothly. From a broadcast perspective, there wasn't one mistake. The crew was so well prepared for the game, they were perfect. During the broadcast, I tried to capture as much of the atmosphere of Exhibition Stadium as I could. We had great shots of the players horsing around in the snow, making snowballs and using the catcher's shin pads as skis.

Brian Wayne, the son of comedian Johnny Wayne, was my production assistant, and he was sitting in the booth with John Hudson and Bob Moir. He told me after the game that they were astounded at how good the broadcast was. He and I were very proud.

Nothing would ever beat Opening Day. The fact that it snowed made it especially memorable. The Blue Jays beat the Chicago White Sox, 9–5, on the strength of two Doug Ault home runs. Of course, the Blue Jays would win just 53 more games to go with 107 losses, but it didn't matter on the day. History had been made!

As a postscript, I found out after the game that my son, Scott, caught a foul ball. What a great souvenir! I still have it in my trophy case.

As always, it was about the people and, with the exception of game one, not about the event. That first year, I wanted to bring legendary White Sox owner Bill Veeck into the booth to speak with McKee. Veeck had been around baseball all his life; his father was a Chicago sportswriter who would often write about how he thought the Cubs should be run. So the owner, Phil Wrigley, hired him as team president. The younger Veeck became the Cubs' treasurer, and it was his idea to build the famous hand-operated scoreboard and plant the ivy that lines the outfield wall at Wrigley Field to this day.

He owned several big league teams, including the Cleveland Indians and St. Louis Browns, and this was his second time as owner of the White Sox. He was always known for outlandish promotions. I boldly walked into his office and said, "I'd like it if you could be a guest on our show."

"Why should I come on your broadcast?"

"Because we're the new team and it would be great promotion for us."

He agreed, and it was a big thrill for me. As usual, McKee did a great job.

It was the same everywhere we went; I couldn't have gotten more co-operation. Baseball was like that; baseball people knew how to sell their game. The Yankees even had a television co-ordinator to help me if I needed it.

There wasn't much pressure on me in terms of producing the games. All John Hudson would say to me was, "I don't care how well you do, Ralph, you just have to be better than the French network."

"Well, that's not tough," I said. "Their coverage is shit!" Still, my intention was to aim a little higher. "Never mind that," I added, "I want to be better than NBC! I'm going to find out how to be better."

Now, NBC was the standard bearer in baseball coverage in the United States, so I'd set out quite a challenge for myself. I went to NBC's baseball seminar and sat in with their guys and got some ideas about how they did things. Then I thought about how I could take their ideas and push them to an even higher level.

I told Tony I was going to use the NBC system, but I was going to add something to it. Then I used the old Roone Arledge line: "Tell me something you have always wanted to do, but haven't done."

He said, "Well, when I see something special I want to be able to talk to the producer in the truck. If I see something happening, regardless of where it is, I want to tell the producer to show it. I don't care if it's in the bullpen or in the stands; I want to be able to say, 'Show the third-base coach's feet,' or 'Shoot the dugout,' or 'Catch what is happening in the bullpen.'"

So I went to Ernie Chilcott, the special head of engineering for CBC Sports, and told them what I wanted. This kind of thing is done all the time today, but at the time we were breaking new ground. We didn't really institute the system until about the fifth game of the season, as we needed time to work out the bugs. The crew nicknamed the new invention the "Ralphie Switch."

Tony was thrilled. A little *too* thrilled, perhaps. After the first game with the Ralphie Switch, I had to tell Tony, "Don't talk so much to the truck—you're not producing the game."

Once I got him calmed down a bit, it was a great addition. Of course, it ended up getting me in trouble with NBC because when he went back to do their games, he demanded the same luxury. Scotty Connal called me, and we had the biggest argument we ever had. I'll never forget it. I had sent Scotty the tape of our first game and asked if we were as good as NBC. He called me back and said, "You're better!" It takes a lot of guts for a guy to tell you that when he's talking about his own network. That made me feel good, even though I still think he was being kind to an old pal. But on this occasion, he wasn't quite as pleasant: "What the #@%$# are you doing, Mellanby? You've got Kubek with his new toy and now we have to do it."

"I'm just trying to be better than you," I said.

At the end of the day, NBC let Tony talk to their guys in the truck, just like he did during our broadcasts. They say *they* were the first to do that, but I know the truth. It's standard procedure today, and it all started out in Canada.

After NBC adopted the new technology, Scotty called me again and asked, "What's next?"

Something else I did that hadn't been done before was to use my low first- and third-base cameras to isolate on infielders when they weren't trained on the batter. This gave me the opportunity for some unusual angles on replays. It's something else that has become a standard part of baseball coverage.

Tony actually became my mentor. Because he was doing the games for NBC as well as CBC, he knew what was going on. He knew the game so well. He'd tell me things like "Isolate on George Brett as much as possible" when the Jays were playing Kansas City, or "Keep an eye on so-and-so" when the Jays were playing another team. He knew which players would be involved in the key plays of the game.

The great thing about John Hudson was he never got in the way. He let me do my thing. And he never messed with the talent. He never messed with *anything*, for that matter. The only thing he ever said was, "Just be better than the French network." The French network still didn't know how to cover baseball. They'd miss plays and had no isolation shots. Baseball just wasn't their game—and it showed.

After that first Jays game, CBC had a party, but I was too tired and didn't feel like going. I never really cared for wrap parties anyway. On my way out of the stadium, I ran into John and said, "Was it better than the French network?"

He just smiled and gave me the thumbs-up.

John later told me the CBC wanted me to produce the Expos games on English television. I commuted to Montreal for those games. Unlike the Jays, they didn't have a set day, but the CBC never aired an Expos game on a Wednesday if the Blue Jays were playing.

Working the Expos' games meant I had to take the weak French feed. Because I didn't have control of the broadcast, it wasn't as much fun. We couldn't do isolations because we weren't in control of the French network's eight or nine cameras. I finally got one extra camera on the field so that I could shoot interviews with it as well as isolate things in the infield. But it was great fun working again with the Expos.

Duke Snider, the colour analyst, was the happiest man in the world to see me arrive.

"We, the English side, don't get enough attention paid to us," he told me. I offered Duke the same thing as Tony, the ability to speak to the truck, but it was really pointless since I wasn't in control of the feed. Besides, he didn't want it. Duke did things his way and he didn't want to change.

I did the Blue Jays' games for two years, but ultimately it just became too much for me to juggle *Hockey Night in Canada*, the Expos, *and* the Blue Jays. I had to be fair to my family. I was spending all my time away from home. After I left, the Blue Jays won two World Series titles, in 1992 and 1993, but my guess is that baseball fans who have been around since the Blue Jays started in 1977 consider their opening game to be the most memorable in franchise history.

Don Chevrier covered just about every sport during his career—especially football, boxing, curling, and horse racing—and worked for ABC and NBC in the States. Brian Williams recalled being asked by Howard Cosell, "Are all Canadian sportscasters as good as Don Chevrier?" Dick Ebersol, the long-time head of NBC Sports, rated him along with Jim McKay as one of the two greatest all-around sportscasters he'd ever worked with. He died in December 2007, but I am happy to say I kept in close touch over the years. In 2005, he was awarded the Sports Media Canada Lifetime Achievement award. I am proud to have been the one who nominated him.

Tony Kubek lives in Appleton, Wisconsin, and I was thrilled to see him win the Ford Frick Award from the Baseball Hall of Fame. I hope Canada's Baseball Hall of Fame follows suit and honours him. He made a great contribution to baseball in Canada.

Tom McKee eventually left the announcer's booth and produced the Jays for years. He did a first-rate job. He's happily retired, and I usually see him at funerals and sports dinners. It is always great to catch up with him.

John Hudson is retired and is my neighbour and friend in Niagara-on-the-Lake. We often get together to talk about the good old days.

Looking back, I wish I had stayed with baseball and dropped hockey. Baseball was my game. I wasn't a hockey player, I was a baseball player. And Hudson was a great boss who left me alone to do my job. I liked adventure and I liked new things, and baseball could have been a nice base for me. Another mistake. But at the time, *Hockey*

114

Night was *the* show on Canadian television. You don't walk away from the number one show in the country.

If I had the chance today to cover one event I never did, it would be the World Series. What a thrill that would be. One thing is for sure today: the Expos won't ever be in it.

5

YOU HEARD (AND SAW) IT
THROUGH THE GRAPEVINE

I have always enjoyed being involved with a new show, building it
from the ground up.

I got that chance in the early 1980s, when Gerry Patterson, the
famous agent whose clients included Gordie Howe and Jean
Béliveau as well as Rusty Staub and Gary Carter of the Expos, came
to me with an idea.

We'd just put together a made-for-TV hockey series called *The
Original Six*. We booked the arena in Markham, just outside of
Toronto, lined up a group of alumni of the NHL's original six teams,
and had them take part in a little tournament over the span of a few
days in the fall. Each team played eight games, giving us enough
action for a twenty-four-week series. Retired NHL referees officiated.
We charged admission and filled the arena with hockey fans who
were delighted to have the opportunity to see recently retired
NHLers in action once again. It was a huge success.

My kid brother, Jim, produced the series for me, and Ron
Harrison directed. I would have done it myself, but I was still under
contract to *Hockey Night in Canada*, which put me in a conflict—
Labatt sponsored *The Original Six*, while *HNIC* was a Molson property.
In fact, no *Hockey Night in Canada* personalities were connected with
the *Original Six* show.

I never went near the rink during the tapings. Instead, I hid out in
a hotel in Markham. The crew would record three games each day and

then bring the tapes back to me at the hotel so I could work on them.

The games were a riot. We wanted the players' skills and creativity to be demonstrated to their fullest, so we had them play under non-contact rules. If a game was tied at the end of regulation time, we decided the contest with penalty shots. It wouldn't be until years later, following the lockout in 2004–05, that the NHL finally instituted the shootout to decide regular-season games that were tied after sixty minutes of regulation time and five minutes of four-on-four action.

My relationship with Patterson dated way back to my high school days in Essex. I just happened to be the quarterback of the varsity football team, and Gerry was my backup. After a while, it became very apparent that Gerry was never going to get any playing action, so he went to the coach with an idea.

"I'm never going to beat out Mellanby, so I think I'd like to be a cheerleader," he said. The coach agreed and Gerry became the head cheerleader.

When he started to manage guys out of Montreal we re-established our relationship. We formed a company together, Special Event Television, which was a sideline for me, but was his main company, through which he wanted to generate television and radio vehicles for some of his clients.

With the success of *The Original Six*, Gerry and I started talking about what we could do as a follow-up. By this time, Don Cherry—or "Grapes," as he was commonly known—had been on *Hockey Night in Canada* for about six years, and I told Gerry my dream was to show people that Don could do more than spout off about hockey. I thought his personality was larger than life and that his "Coach's Corner" segment limited what he had to offer. A lot of people saw some of the *HNIC* personalities as one-trick ponies that couldn't do anything else. I disagreed.

As I got to know Don over the years, I realized that he was a huge boxing fan and was a friend of world middleweight champion Marvin Hagler. And I learned about Don's interest in sports in general. He was a big baseball fan and he also loved the Canadian Football League. There was more to this guy than people saw in a few minutes each Saturday night.

I also had always wanted to do a talk show about sports that was set in a bar. The amazing thing is that nobody had done it before and nobody has done it since. You have all these sports bars scattered all over North America, and you'd think somebody would do a sports talk show from one of them.

Gerry loved the concept, so *Don Cherry's Grapevine* was born. The title came about because Don had always dreamed of owning a bar. And of course, he would call it the Grapevine. We signed a deal with CHCH-TV in Hamilton, which had also been involved with the *Original Six* show, to produce a half-hour syndicated program with Cherry as the host. (The show moved over to TSN in its final days.)

In those days, every major city had a local station that wasn't affiliated with CBC or CTV, which made it easy for us to syndicate the show. It wasn't hard to sell them on the idea of a television show featuring one of the country's most recognized personalities.

I made one major mistake with *Grapevine* from the outset. I thought Grapes would need a support cast because he had never done anything like this before. Doing a short segment once a week for *Hockey Night* was one thing; carrying a half-hour TV show was quite another. So I hired a singer, John Allan Cameron (at a reduced rate) to sing a few songs on each show, and had two actor friends of mine sitting at the bar. Also, I hired a writer for the show—*that* was the mistake. The last thing Don Cherry needed was a script. He thinks on his feet, and ad-libbing has been his bread and butter for years. Cameron's songs were short, maybe two minutes long, and the first would always be dedicated to our guest on the show that day. John Allan would sit there and strum his guitar and sing away. I loved it, but it was a little too much for a half-hour show.

One smart thing I did was to hire Don's son, Tim Cherry, to research the profiles on our guests. Tim was a great help, both to his dad and to me.

We built the set in the old CHCH studio on King Street West. CHCH had an old theatre there that they were about to close because they were rebuilding their studios, so we took it over. We shot the show in that facility for the first couple of years, which was fine because it allowed us to keep our set there permanently.

Our goal was to tape three shows a day. We had to get an audience, and even though we only had room for twenty people, that was pretty difficult at CHCH. We weren't exactly in one of the nicest parts of Hamilton. We'd go out into the street and just pull people in off the sidewalk to fill the seats at the bar—boy, were they disappointed when they found out this was a bar with no booze, just coffee and donuts!

When you work within a very limited budget, you have to find creative ways to get things done. For instance, we hired a limo service to run our guests from Toronto to the studio in Hamilton, and in exchange for their services, we gave them a credit on the show. Most of our guests were put up for free at the Valhalla Inn in Toronto, also in exchange for a credit.

I was happy with the first season, but despite our efforts it still proved to be a little too expensive. Cuts had to be made. John Allan Cameron—one of my best friends and a Canadian legend—was dropped from the show. I also dropped one of the actors and made the other guy, Jimmy Loftus, the bartender. In so doing, I believe we really got down to the true essence of what the show was supposed to be: a chance for Don Cherry to spread his wings by himself.

I didn't book athletes from other sports besides hocket at first, because I wanted to make Don feel as comfortable as I could and help him get established. (By the way, Don loves to tell the story about the first show and how I held his hand backstage to calm his nerves.) The first *Grapevine* show even had Wayne Gretzky as the guest, and the second had Bobby Orr. You can't do any better than that! The third was colourful referee Bill Friday, who jumped from the NHL to the World Hockey Association. He was a real character.

It was the only show I ever produced in my career where I was always on the studio floor. I wasn't in the control room, where a producer would normally be. I was a soothing presence for Don, and I just felt he'd need me around. I was his confidence builder. I'd also go to his house and we'd talk about the shows so he'd be prepared.

Our crew was made up mostly of the guys who had done Wednesday-night NHL hockey on CHCH. Our director was Paul Starkman, who used to do the *Wayne and Shuster Show* for CBC. Sadly, Paul committed suicide during the run of the series. Ron Luciano, the famous major-league baseball umpire, was one of our guests, and he took his own life the same year. At that point, Don came to me and said, "Is the show that bad that guys are killing themselves to duck us?"

I loved the show. It was a mixture of variety, which I had always loved, and sports. Of course, Don would always get most excited when we had hockey people as guests, and quite frankly those were our best shows. When I told Don we had booked Gordie Howe, he just about went through the roof. Same thing when we booked Phil Esposito.

By that point I figured he wasn't going back into coaching again, so I hoped to turn him into a full-blown entertainer. While I tried to make Don as comfortable as I could, I must admit that sometimes I'd throw him a curve.

He'd say, "Who do we have next?"

"Virginia Wade, the famous tennis player from England."

"Holy shit! What the hell am I going to talk about with her?"

"Hey, this is a very interesting woman, and a lot of people that play tennis will love her."

Don did a beautiful job, thanks in a big part to Tim's research and Virginia's wonderful personality.

We'd have golfers, such as Arnold Palmer, and our audience loved it. Not Don, though—he wasn't keen on golf. We'd have the great skier Steve Podborski or Olympic high-jumper Greg Joy on the show, and the research always came to the fore. I stuck a lot of other celebrities with him and he did a damn good job.

Don wasn't just nervous at the start; he nearly had a breakdown. I told him not to bother worrying where the cameras were—he wanted to use just one camera, as on "Coach's Corner," but we used three— and to just imagine he was sitting in his bar and the people around him were just visitors. I told him to have fun with it. It helped that I was on the floor with him. During a commercial break, I might remind Don of a few questions he'd forgotten to ask, and when the next segment began he'd open with those questions. From the first show on, he fully grasped the concept, and as it turned out he loved doing the show. He even stayed on for several years after I stopped producing it. *Grapevine* really helped to raise Grapes' profile across the country—it was CHCH's top-rated show in the Toronto market, and thankfully, we got huge ratings all across Canada.

After I left, the producer didn't work the same way, but Don was just as good because by that time he was well trained and was comfortable. What many people don't realize is that the producer and director can make or break a show. They make a real impact. They're not there to be mechanics.

Norman Jewison, the famous Canadian film director, producer, and actor who had produced *The Judy Garland Show* for CBS in the early '60s, once told me, "You have to get the people you are working with to trust you, Ralph. You don't have to tell them how to sing or how to dance, just get them to trust you."

I asked him how he did that.

He said it was always about the lighting. Judy was like most stars—when she walked into the studio, she immediately looked at herself in the monitor to see how she looked. She didn't think she looked good and told Norman the lighting was at fault.

"I could have told her she was wrong, but I wouldn't do that. I always had a deal with my lighting man. I would say, 'Move this' or 'Move that.' He'd go up the ladder, but he wouldn't change a thing.

"She'd say, 'That's better.'"

The lesson was that performers have to trust that you'll take care of them. It's not easy to walk out there and perform, but if you trust that your producer and director will take care of you, it gives you a real comfort zone.

That advice from Jewison really helped me years later with the *Grapevine* show, because I had never worked with anybody that wasn't a professional entertainer or broadcaster before. But I told Don never to turn professional—"Just be yourself, Don. You'll do fine." And in that regard, Don never let me down. Given his ascension to one of the most recognized stars in Canadian television, I'd have to say he has done just fine.

Don really developed nicely as a performer. That said, his costumes—er, suits—that he wears today might have been tough to pull off on the old *Grapevine*.

My role wasn't limited to just producing the show. I'm a hands-on executive who liked to make our guests feel as comfortable as I could. I'd always be in the limo to pick up the first guest at the Valhalla, and then I'd ride back in the limo with the final guest to the hotel. If I didn't know much about the guest, this process could yield insights into topics we might ask about on the show. In fact, some of those trips back and forth were better than the shows!

One of our guests was my old pal Ken Dryden, the Hall of Fame goaltender who played just eight seasons in the NHL with the Montreal Canadiens and won an incredible six Stanley Cups. I think Dryden could have won another six if he had remained in the game, but he was a real intellectual who wanted to do more with his life than play hockey.

Dryden is also the author of one of the most highly regarded hockey books ever written, *The Game*. I had the limo pick him up at his dad's house, and while we were driving to Hamilton from Toronto I admitted to him that I just didn't get *The Game*. I am a college-educated man, but I just didn't understand the point he was trying to make in his book.

He talked about his book all the way to Hamilton, an hour-and-a-half drive. Just as we were arriving at the studio, I said, "Wait a minute...the forward pass ruined the skills of the game?"

He said, "You got it!"

I said, "That only took you an hour and a half to tell me." Ken is a brilliant man, but man, can he ramble.

One of our regulars on the show was the late, great Dick Beddoes, an outspoken and controversial sportscaster who worked at CHCH. He would fill in at the last minute for any guests who were unable to make it. He was probably on the show more than any other person. He loved the show and loved the fee—which was $500. That was pretty good money in those days. Dick was one of Don's favourites, so they always had good shows.

Come to think of it, I don't think we ever had a really bad show.

One of our most memorable guests was "Smokin'" Joe Frazier, who won the gold medal in heavyweight boxing at the 1964 Olympics in Tokyo on his twentieth birthday and later went on to a very distinguished career as a professional boxer. He defeated Muhammad Ali on March 8, 1971, in a bout that was dubbed the "Fight of the Century," and finished with an impressive 37–4–1 record. Twenty-seven of his victories were by knockout.

It didn't happen too often, but on this day the limo was late and we were holding up production of the show while we waited for our guest. The driver had gone back to Toronto to get Joe, who was to be on the second show we were taping that day. These were the days before cellphones and text messaging, so we had no idea what the reason for the delay might be.

Finally, I got a call from the limo driver, who told me the car had broken down on the highway.

"What's happening?" I enquired.

"Frazier's fixing the engine."

"Are you serious?"

He was. And when Joe finally arrived, we had to allow him some time to get cleaned up because he was covered in grease!

"I love cars," Joe told me. "It's one of my hobbies."

Right away, we had a subject for Grapes to lead with.

Ron Luciano, the former major-league umpire, was the best

guest. His stories were interesting and entertaining, and they were real—real stories about real big-league baseball players. He was a bit of a showboat whose personality finally got him drummed out of the game. But he was willing to talk about what guys were really like. You'd ask him, for example, about Bill "Spaceman" Lee, the pitcher for the Expos and Red Sox, and he'd tell you what an out-there guy Lee was. He didn't pull any punches. It might not have made him popular in the baseball community, but in terms of being a guest on a television show, he was pure gold. When I heard that he died, I was very sad.

Don was a star, but that didn't mean everybody in the country liked him. It remains that way to this day.

One day, I booked the Olympic pentathlete Diane Jones-Konihowski to be on the show. Don was not thrilled.

"Cripes, Ralph, I can't even say her name," Don said. "Why the hell would I want her on the show?"

It turned out the feeling was mutual. I was driving in the limo with Diane on the way to Hamilton, and she said, "Ralph, I can't figure out why I'm on this show. I hate Don Cherry. I think he's an idiot."

I told her, "Say that on the show!"

She didn't say it exactly that way—she had too much class for that. She said, "Don, I'm not exactly your biggest fan. I don't understand what you are saying half the time."

Well, I had given Don the heads-up about this and he responded, "Diane, you are a woman of good taste."

One of our biggest coups was getting Muhammad Ali to appear on the show. I had met him before when I directed the telecast of his bout with George Chuvalo at Maple Leaf Gardens in 1966. It was one of the most memorable fights in Canadian boxing history. Ali won, but was unable to knock the tough Chuvalo down. I bumped into Ali and his entourage at the Royal York Hotel after the fight, and when I went to shake his hand he pulled it back and said, "Sorry, I hit that sucker so many times I can't shake anybody's hand."

Ali had no idea who Don Cherry was, and didn't know a thing about hockey. So I told him. *Grapevine* was a boxing show. Sometimes you have to bend the truth a bit when you are trying to coax big-name stars to appear on your popular, but low-budget, show.

The thing that surprised me was how he and Grapes hit it off. Ali wasn't a show-off on the show. And Grapes got a lot out of him. They talked about Howard Cosell, and I got the distinct feeling Ali didn't care for him. He had made Cosell a star, and Cosell would always say his best friend was Ali, but I got the impression that the friendship ran just one way and it wasn't really reciprocated by Ali. Cosell seemed to have used his relationship with Ali to climb the ladder of fame.

I worked on *Grapevine* for five seasons, and then left, ultimately selling my interest in Special Event Television. After I left, the staff only booked guests from the hockey world. I must say I was flattered when they had me come back one day to be Don's guest on the show. The show did a lot for Grapes. It gave him credibility and proved he could do more than he'd been doing on *Hockey Night*. Some people had suggested that Grapes would never be able to pull it off, and I would tell them he'd be able to do it with me.

Of course, he eventually realized his dream of opening a bar—many of them, in fact, right across Canada. He came to me one day after he'd got his restaurant chain going and started franchising them. He offered me a piece of the action, but I turned him down.

When he asked me why, I explained that it would put me in a conflict of interest. I was his boss at *Hockey Night* and might have to fire him one day. How would I be able to do that if we were business partners?

"You're crazy," he answered. "You would never fire me, business or no business."

This year, I'm working with Tim and Don on a new series featuring the great hockey guests from the *Grapevine* archives. It's running on the NHL Network, with future shows to appear on the Internet and home video. It's great the have the old team back together again.

The CBC is currently turning Don Cherry's life into a movie. When I heard about that, I told Don I'd like to have Alec Baldwin (my favourite actor) play the role of Ralph Mellanby. That would be cool! However, Tim Cherry said Martin Short would be better casting.

What Grapes learned, perhaps more than anything else, from that show was the importance of discipline and preparation. He had to write his own opening. The writer did that job the first year, but I didn't think he was capturing the essence of Grapes, so from then on I got Don and Tim to write them. I felt the openings were much better after that.

Most of the guests, when they left, told me Don was really great. And all of them seemed to love the concept of the show. Pat Gillick, the baseball executive who led the Toronto Blue Jays to two World Series titles and won another with the Philadelphia Phillies in 2008, once told me, "Ralph, the only problem with the show is there's no beer in the damn bar."

He was right!

6

THE BUSINESS OF SPORT

I was told a long time ago that professional sports is the best business in the world, but it is often run by some of the worst businessmen. In my experience, that proved to be quite true. There were some exceptions, but not too many.

I have been very satisfied with my life in television covering all sports. But there were times over the years when I wondered what it might be like to cross over to the other side—instead of televising sports, to run a pro team. Without trying to minimize what it takes, I can say that I have seen a lot of people with less talent than myself build championship teams.

One day in 1991, I got a call from my friend Glen Sather, who was running the Edmonton Oilers at the time. He told me the New York Rangers were in the market for a new team president, having just fired Jack Diller. Glen was feeling me out to see if I'd be interested, because if I wasn't, there was no point in him suggesting me for the post. Naturally, my interest was immediately piqued.

Slats told me they were looking at a couple of other guys, including their general manager, Neil Smith, who eventually got the job. Nevertheless, Glen had given my name to Dick Evans, the president of Madison Square Garden, who was heading up the search. Evans was renowned for having rescued Radio City Music Hall. He was well known in show business as an innovator.

Evans called me and arranged for me to fly to New York for our initial meeting. I was really pumped at the thought of running the Rangers, who were an Original Six team and one of the NHL's marquee franchises. By this time, I had finished work on the 1988 Winter Olympics in Calgary and was busy with my own company, Ralph Mellanby and Associates. I loved my TV work—I was at the peak of my career—but this would present a completely new challenge. It would also allow me to sit on the NHL's board of governors and perhaps help change hockey—or at the very least upgrade the game with new ideas. People in the league's inner circles had received many of my ideas warmly over the years, but my role in television meant I didn't have the necessary clout to see any of them put into play. I viewed it as the chance of a lifetime, and I was perfectly willing to change my career path to see it through. Besides which, the job would bring me back to New York City—a place I loved.

So, I flew to New York where the Rangers put me up at the Plaza Hotel. Talk about doing things first class! I called all my New York friends to say hi, but couldn't tell them specifically why I was in town. If I didn't get the job, I didn't want to hurt my reputation.

I met with Dick, and he treated me like gold. We had a two-hour conversation and then he showed me around the Garden. I knew a lot of the television people at Madison Square Garden Productions, including Pete Silverman, who had also run the Philadelphia Flyers' telecasts and was now the boss at MSG Productions. During the tour, I avoided all of them.

Evans didn't offer me the job, but did promise to get back to me soon after a decision had been made. He assured me I was more than qualified for the position, and that he felt we had instant chemistry and would get along great. I felt the same way. He was very impressive.

From there, I went to stay with my son Scott, who was playing for the Flyers at the time and had a place on the Jersey Shore. Evans called me for a second interview a week later, so I took the train into the city. As I got onto the train, Scott said, "Get that job, Dad. You can trade for me and then pay me a lot of money to play for the Rangers."

"Sole purpose of my visit," I replied.

With each passing day, I could see myself more and more as the president of the Rangers. I was doing my best not to put the cart before the horse, but damn, it was exciting to think about running this team. Evans told me to make sure I wore a jacket and tie for the second interview. About five minutes into it Evans, stood up and said, "Let's go."

"Where?"

"We're going to Paramount Communications' head office on Columbus Circle to meet Stanley Jaffe." Paramount owned Madison Square Garden and its teams. Jaffe, the newly installed chairman of Paramount, was an award-winning producer who had made films such as *Goodbye, Columbus, The Bad News Bears, Kramer vs. Kramer,* and *Fatal Attraction.*

I wondered what the heck I was doing meeting with this man. Above all, what qualified a great movie producer to be an executive of a huge conglomerate?

"You'll find out," Evans told me as we got into a cab. "Don't be surprised if you are disappointed."

We walked into Jaffe's office. The walls were covered with all kinds of Hollywood memorabilia. I always felt you could measure a guy's ego by the size of his office, and Jaffe's office was gigantic!

The first ten minutes went by just fine. Jaffe had done his homework and knew who I was. Then, suddenly, Evans got up and left.

"You're on your own now, Ralph."

I just about fainted.

I found out later that Evans wasn't getting along with Jaffe, which was his reason for leaving. He wanted me to make it on my own merits and didn't want his presence to influence Jaffe. Dick wanted to let Jaffe think I was his—that is, Jaffe's—choice.

Jaffe asked me about my plans for the team. I gave him my usual ten-point plan, which included many new ideas. I also told him I felt I could get Mark Messier, one of the biggest stars in the NHL, to sign as a free agent. The fact is, Sather and I had talked in confidence and he'd told me that the Oilers, for which Messier was currently playing, would not be able to afford him when his next contract came up. They were a small-market team and simply didn't have the money to keep him. Given the fact that Wayne Gretzky and Paul Coffey had left Edmonton for similar reasons, this would come as no shock to anybody. (As it happened, Messier ultimately wound up in New York, and in 1994 he led the Rangers to their first Stanley Cup championship in fifty-four years.)

After I gave my spiel, Jaffe talked. And talked. And talked.

I have to tell you, I wasn't very impressed with him. He talked about what he was doing and what he expected, and about the only thing he said that I agreed with was that New York fans deserved the best teams in the world. And that Paramount's teams, the Knicks and Rangers, needed to get back on the local sporting map. The football Giants had just won a Super Bowl. In baseball, the Mets had won the World Series in 1986, and were aggressively bidding for superstar players. The Yankees were in the doldrums but were laying the groundwork to become a dominant team, and their first baseman, Don Mattingly, was revered as a god by New York fans.

The Knicks had already cleaned house. Dave Checketts was their new president, and he in turn recruited Pat Riley, who had won four NBA championships as coach of the Los Angeles Lakers, to be their coach. Jaffe told me he was flying upstate after our meeting to watch Riley's first practice with the team. He made it clear he was very hands-on.

"I want to make one thing perfectly clear," he told me. "If I want to speak with the players or make changes with the team, I'll do it."

"Not if I'm president," I replied, although I don't believe I said it quite so politely.

Well, that put an instant chill in the air.

The final fifteen minutes of our meeting were brutal. I continued with my sales pitch, telling him I felt it was important that I live right in New York and outlining how I would line up sponsors and work with the television people. But I knew when I left the room that I was in trouble.

I went back to meet with Evans and told him I didn't believe things had gone very well with Jaffe. I told him I was off to Cuba to cover the Pan-American Games and that I'd be gone for about a month. I also told him he'd have trouble reaching me, but he assured me I shouldn't worry and to call him when I got back. Which is exactly what I did, six weeks later, when I landed at the Miami airport.

I called Madison Square Garden and asked for Mr. Evans.

"He's no longer with the company," the voice on the other end of the line told me.

My heart sank. Evans had been rooting for me to get the job, and I felt my fate was in his hands. I called him at home to find out why he no longer worked for the Garden, and he told me *I* was the problem—or at least, my bid to run the Rangers. Evans had never gotten along with Jaffe, and when he insisted he wanted me to be the president of the hockey team, it was the final straw.

I asked Evans if it would help if I went back to see Jaffe.

"I wouldn't if I were you," Evans said.

That was the end of my dream.

As I said, the job ultimately went to Neil Smith. Every now and then when I bump into Smith, I jokingly say, "You're the guy who took my job." By the way, Neil was a sound hockey man, and I would definitely have kept him on as GM had I been given the job as president.

I didn't have many disappointments in my career, but that was certainly one of the biggest. Needless to say, Scott was disappointed, too.

Not long before that, I had been recommended for the position of president of the Toronto Maple Leafs—right after Harold Ballard, the longtime owner of the Leafs, died. I wanted the job and got along very well with Donald Giffin, who was then running the organization. I figured if Harold could run the Leafs, then *I* certainly could. I had one interview for the position, but Giffin got pushed out of the picture by Steve Stavro, who had launched a successful takeover bid of Maple Leaf Gardens. There never was a follow-up meeting. Giffin died shortly afterward. I believe that if Giffin had continued to run the Gardens, I would have had a great shot at the

Leaf job. I often look back and wonder what might have been.

Another opportunity came along in 1996, when I met with Harley Hotchkiss, who was looking for a new president of the Calgary Flames. They loved me in Calgary, and I had a great reputation out there from my work at the 1988 Winter Olympics, but things didn't really get too far. I had one meeting in Boston, during the NHL All-Star break, but Harley got back to me a little later and told me I wasn't the right guy for them. Apparently, I was too old. I kind of expected the verdict, so I wasn't overly disappointed. They hired Ron Bremner, who was a friend of mine and a good choice.

One organization that did hire me was the Global Hockey League, in 1990. The GHL was the brainchild of Michael Gobuty, a former owner of the Winnipeg Jets, and Dennis Murphy, who had co-founded the World Hockey Association back in 1972. The idea was that there would be teams in both North America and Europe. Gobuty approached me because he knew I was a big advocate of the NHL expanding into Europe. (I also felt the Stanley Cup final might one day become an international event.) NHL president John Ziegler agreed with me, but the owners hated the idea, plus Ziegler didn't want to step on the International Ice Hockey Federation's toes. It strikes me as funny that, many years later, there is again talk of the NHL introducing a European division, and teams are playing regular-season games overseas each year.

Despite my misgivings about the concept, I went to Switzerland with Gobuty to watch the World Hockey Championships. One reason was that my old pal Marc Cloutier, from the Montreal Expos and Canadiens and Winnipeg Jets, was involved, so I agreed to serve as a consultant. At the Worlds, I ran into a bunch of hockey writers I knew, but I wasn't at liberty to tell them why I was there. They all thought I might be one of the owners of the new league. No one could say they lacked imagination!

I stayed with the Global league for about eight months, until it fell apart because of a lack of financing. Another lesson learned. It was just as well; at that time I didn't know whether I would ever get back into televising pro hockey, and I wasn't really interested in burning any bridges with the NHL by being associated with the rival league.

By the time I got to Atlanta in 1992, I had a lot of experience running my own businesses (two of them) and had learned a great deal from my associations with people who ran successful organizations. And after I finished work on the 1996 Summer Olympics in Atlanta, I received a call from Ted Turner, the broadcasting magnate who also owned the Atlanta Braves of Major League Baseball and the Hawks of the NBA. His company had just been granted an NHL expansion franchise, the Atlanta Thrashers. Truthfully, I could never figure out why Atlanta was given another NHL team. The Flames, who had played there from 1972 to 1980, had failed and moved to Calgary. I later found out it was because Stan Kasten, the president of the Braves and Hawks, had a relationship with NHL commissioner Gary Bettman, which had apparently paved the way for the new club being placed there.

Kasten was a fixture on the Atlanta sporting scene, having become the Hawks' GM in 1979, at the age of twenty-seven. Seven years later, he became president of both the Hawks and the Braves. I think he also wanted the top job with the Thrashers, but it went to Dr. Harvey Schiller, who was president of TBS Sports.

I knew Schiller a bit because he had been the head of the U.S. Olympic Committee. He had also risen to the rank of brigadier general in the U.S. Air Force, and was a professor who had been head of the chemistry department at the Air Force Academy in Colorado. He called me at my home in Atlanta and said he was looking for somebody who was already in the hockey family to help the team. He told me they didn't have anybody in their organization who knew a thing about the game, especially not Ted Turner, the owner of the team. "Ted doesn't even *like* hockey," he told me.

Quite frankly, I had my business, a partner in Toronto, and a successful hit in the *Royal Canadian Air Farce* TV show. I wasn't looking to play a major role with a team at this point, and besides, I had been stung by the Rangers, Leafs, and Flames. But Harvey wasn't looking to hire me as team president—he and Kasten would fight over that job. I told Harvey, "What you need is a consultant—a guy to come in for a year or two and help set things up, and then be gone."

So, we met at the Atlanta Athletic Club downtown, and again I felt myself getting excited about being part of a new venture. The team hired me in a consulting capacity, and I was with the organization for eighteen months. The fact is, I became the hockey consultant nobody listened to.

I was also consulting on the construction of their new home, the Philips Arena. That was another story—they listened to my every suggestion. I was the reason why they put the press box and broadcast facilities on one side of the rink and the private boxes on the other. I also placed all their camera locations for them. My old friends who had run the old Omni Arena when the Flames were still in town, were now in charge of building the Philips Arena (on the former site of the Omni) and they treated me like gold.

What the Thrashers also needed was a general manager who was firmly entrenched in the old boys' club, one who had a lot of favours he could call in. A guy like Sather would've been perfect.

They did meet with Sather, and I knew he was ready to make his move from Edmonton and the multiple ownership partners—more than thirty of them—who took over from Peter Pocklington. I thought Atlanta would have been great for him—he had the necessary flair to get people talking about the team—and vice versa.

The team set up a second meeting with Glen, but instead of flying one of the top brass out to Palm Springs to meet with him, they sent a middle-management type. Glen was not happy about that, and with good reason: If they were serious about signing the most established executive in the NHL, they should have sent Ted and Harvey, not the B Team. When a candidate is looking for a big salary and shares in the company, they ought to be negotiating with the big guys, not someone halfway down the ladder.

The Thrashers ended up hiring Don Waddell from the Detroit

Red Wings organization. Waddell was a rising executive, but wasn't yet part of the NHL "club." And Waddell didn't want anything to do with me—I believe he saw me as a threat. I wasn't consulted about his hiring, and I think he knew I was pushing for someone of the calibre of a Glen Sather or Cliff Fletcher. Remember, Cliff had been the GM of the old Atlanta Flames and had won a Stanley Cup with the organization after it relocated to Calgary.

I mentioned the old boys' club. Who's in it? I'd include the likes of Sather, Fletcher, Harry Sinden, Bill Torrey, Ed Snider—the NHL's longtime power brokers. These guys can pick up a phone and get things done. *And* they stick together and exert a great deal of influence over what goes on in the NHL.

Look at what Bill Torrey did with the Florida Panthers. Three years in, they were in the Stanley Cup final. Torrey had connections. I think that proves why expansion teams need an established executive. It always surprises me when they fail to see the value of bringing in someone with experience and connections.

There were other guys lobbying me for the Atlanta job, including Brian Burke. Burke, who was then the league's vice-president, who has since proven himself to be a great GM, but I didn't feel his personality was right for Atlanta. I don't think people in the Old South would have bought his gruff style. You have to know how to fit in with the community. I think Brian, who was working in the NHL head office in New York at the time, has probably never forgiven me for not backing him.

The Thrashers have been a dismal failure in Atlanta, making the playoffs just once in nine years. I don't mind telling you that my son was captain of the only team to make it into the post-season. And the year after he retired, the Thrashers were back on the outside, looking in. Many NHL insiders have told me that when Scott was with the Thrashers, it was his team. When he retired, I think they should have kept him in the organization, the way the Detroit Red Wings did with Steve Yzerman, the Boston Bruins did with Cam Neely and the St. Louis Blues did with Al MacInnis.

* * *

Ted Turner was an interesting dude. What stands out about him for me is that he never, ever remembered my name. I always got a laugh out of that. I did get to see his office one day (another *big* office, I might add) and got to see the MGM lion, which he had had stuffed and kept on display there. Needless to say, as a movie buff I was suitably impressed.

I had met Ted before, at the Goodwill Games in Washington State in 1990 (the games were Turner's idea, and of course, were broadcast over Turner Network Television). Hockey was one of the events, and I was producing the games for TNT. Turner and his wife at the time, actress Jane Fonda, came out to the hockey venue in the Tri-Cities area. Jane was the first one I met; I told her if I had known she was coming, I would have asked her to sing the national anthem. I was surprised when replied, "I would have done it." Then Ted came over and said, "I'm Ted Turner," as if I wouldn't know who he was. He had seen me talking to several big shots at the pre-game cocktail party, so perhaps he thought I was somebody important. The head of the Goodwill Games, Don Baer, was there and he introduced me.

"This is Ralph Mellanby and he's producing hockey for us," Don said.

Turner turned and walked away without saying so much as a word. Suffice it to say, I wasn't very happy. In fact, I was pissed off. After all, I was freelance and not an employee of Turner.

I will say, though, in future meetings I loved speaking with Ted. He was a good ol' boy, and every time I saw him his shirt seemed a little wrinkled and his tie askew. He always called me "Mr. Hockey," so I guess I had his blessing—even if it was just to cover the fact that he never knew my name.

* * *

The business side of sports also has a political dimension, as I found out when I was asked by Otto Jelinek, a fellow Conservative who was Canada's minister for fitness and amateur sport in Brian Mulroney's cabinet, to serve on two government commissions: the Fair Play Commission and the Sports Marketing Commission.

The Fair Play Commission wanted to get fighting banned from all levels of hockey, and they knew I was against fighting in hockey— I have been quoted as saying fighting is holding the game back, preventing it from gaining traction in the United States and elsewhere. Whenever I would ask Otto why I'd been asked to sit on the committees, he would tell me it was because I was the most powerful guy in hockey on television. We didn't get fighting out of the NHL, but we brought a lot of attention to the issue, and I am proud to say you don't see the sort of brawling in hockey that we did in the 1970s. At most levels of hockey, players are now automatically ejected for fighting. Most leagues have made it nearly impossible to carry a "goon," but not the NHL. That said, with the death of twenty-one-year-old Don Sanderson in a senior men's hockey league during the 2008–09 season, there has been a resurgence of anti-fighting sentiment.

I used to tell John Ziegler all the time, and I told Gary Bettman the first time I met him, that the NHL will never get a major television contract in the United States unless it is viewed as a family sport, not as roller derby. A number of high-ranking hockey guys, including some in "the club," have agreed with me.

Alas, fighting and strategic match-ups between goons, have returned. There was more fighting in the NHL in 2008–09 than there had been the past few years. The NHL brass, unapologetically, sees it as a vehicle to sell the sport. But from my standpoint, the NHL will never be a credible, big-time professional sports league until fighting is banned.

When I worked in the glory days at NBC, CBC, and ABC, the presidents of those networks felt the same way. As Roone Arledge once put it to me: "We have Olympic hockey—it's classic—but we will never bid for the NHL rights. Games are too long, there are too many breaks, and two intermissions are one too many. But above all, the fighting hurts its image. Until they get rid of fighting, they will never get the big bucks football, baseball, and basketball get."

I agree. Are you listening, Gary?

7

GOIN' TOE-TO-TOE: MELLANBY AND BROPHY DEBATE FIGHTING IN HOCKEY

My co-writer, Mike Brophy, and I share a lot of similar opinions when it comes to the game of hockey, but one area where we differ significantly is over fighting.

In a nutshell, I believe there is no place in the game for it. More than anything else, fighting has stood between the game being a niche sport and enjoying mass popularity, particularly in the United States. Mike, obviously, disagrees and, like so many others, believes there is a place in the game for fighting. That's why we decided to drop the gloves, so to speak, split this chapter in half and offer our separate points of view. Read on!

RALPH SAYS:

The two people in hockey I admire the most are my son Scott, who was a pretty good fighter during his nineteen-year NHL career, and Don Cherry, who promotes fighting in hockey more than anybody on the planet. Both of them totally disagree with me when I say there is no place in the game for fighting.

By the way, as far as watching the NHL and hockey is concerned, I go back to the 1930s and '40s. That gives me tremendous experience on the subjuct.

I did a piece once for the Society for International Hockey Research on fighting in the game. I looked at game sheets and found that in the 1930s, '40s, and '50s, there was only about one fighting major issued every three games. That's because fighting, back then, was reactionary. Unlike today, it wasn't a tactic.

I also noticed that the toughest guys were also the best players— for example, Maurice "Rocket" Richard, Gordie Howe, Milt Schmidt, and Ted Lindsay. They were elite players, but they stood up for themselves. They had to. If a guy cross-checked you in the face, there wasn't a resident goon sitting on the end of the bench just waiting to fight your battles. Similarly, everybody had to be able to play the game. Even John Ferguson, who is often referred to as the first "policeman," a player who was at the cutting edge of being an enforcer, was a 20-goal scorer.

Even into the 1960s, players took care of themselves. Bobby Orr is unquestionably the best defenceman to ever play in the National Hockey League, and he was also a great fighter. Nobody dared try to take advantage of Orr because he'd drop his gloves in a heartbeat. Late in his career, Bobby Hull spoke out against fighting and even staged a one-game strike, refusing to play, while he was in the World Hockey Association, but in his prime nobody messed with him. He was built like a Greek god, could look after himself, and often did retaliate.

So when they say fighting has always been a part of the game, it must be acknowledged there have been two distinct eras: one in which fighting was a reaction and a second where fighting became a tactic intended to intimidate the opposition.

I have talked to the older players and asked them what it was like playing back in the "good old days." Newsy Lalonde, who was a great player from 1917 to 1927, told me that in his day players looked out for themselves. If a player was accosted by an opponent, he'd take care of business himself. That era came to an end in the 1970s with the arrival of Fred Shero and the Philadelphia Flyers. It was "Freddie the Fog," as he was called, who initiated tactical fighting.

It had actually started earlier with the Boston Bruins, but they never really fought as much as they were given credit for. The "Big Bad Bruins" of the late '60s and early '70s were a tough team, but they were also very skilled, unlike the Philadelphia Flyers who wanted to beat you up.

The Flyers' game plan was simple: beat the crap out of the opposition and try to scare them into submission. Shero's "Broad Street Bullies" made a mockery of the game. His feeling was that referees would call only so many penalties against his team, and if tormenting the opposition made it easier for his team to win, so be it. And it worked, to a degree. The Flyers won back-to-back Stanley Cups in 1974 and 1975 and the likes of Dave "The Hammer" Schultz, Don "Big Bird" Saleski and Andre "Moose" Dupont—players with limited ability, but willing fighters—became cult heroes in the City of Brotherly Love.

Fred Shero told me, "I want players from other teams to come into the Spectrum and to be terrified to play there." It was said that many players came down with an affliction called the "Philadelphia Flu." Teams hated playing in Philadelphia because, quite simply, they were scared. Toronto Maple Leafs defenceman Jim McKenny, who later became a popular sportscaster, summed things up when he said, "We would get off our team bus and start walking toward the Spectrum. If you stopped and looked back at the empty bus, it was still shaking."

I believe that is when the other teams started carrying designated fighters. They needed to have somebody on the bench who was willing to stand up to the Flyers. It grew from there to the point where just about every team started carrying one or two players whose only job was to fight.

In my opinion, you'll never get fighting completely out of the NHL. Physical intimidation has always been, and will always be, an ingredient, and players will always cross the line. When that happens, fights will erupt.

However, I just think the NHL should be like every other league in the world—if you fight, you are ejected from the game. NHL players don't fight in the IIHF World Championship or Olympics, because they know if they do, they will be ejected. You get to the playoffs each season, and fighting all but disappears. Why? Because teams don't dress their goons. You don't need to have fighting in the game.

Even Scott didn't fight during his two years at the University of Wisconsin because he knew that if you fight in the NCAA, you get booted from the game. When he played in the World Junior Championship he didn't fight either. He played in the World Championship after turning pro and again, it was the same thing— no fighting. He abided by the rules.

When Scott played in the NHL, I was terrified every time I watched him fight. He never took on the little guys—he always tangled with the likes of Bob Probert, who for years was the heavyweight champion of the NHL. He always said, "When I fight a guy like Probert, I'm at least strong enough to hang on." And Scott was a pretty good fighter. He usually won or at least fought to a draw. Still, I was always concerned when he dropped the gloves.

The tactical fight must be eliminated from the game. I am sick and tired of watching two guys line up for a faceoff and fight for no reason other than to justify their existence. Strangely enough, following the lockout in 2004–05 when the NHL shut down for an entire season, fighting began to trail off significantly. In fact, *The Hockey News* did an in-depth feature on fighting and titled it "The Death of the Goon." The story was based strictly on the number of fighting majors that were issued per game. The NHL had done a great job in eliminating brawling, and now it looked like there was a greater emphasis on speed and skill.

Well, fighters may not be able to score goals, but they can read. When a guy earning upwards of a million dollars a year reads that he may become redundant, you can guess what his reaction will be. Fighting took off again. The Anaheim Ducks won the Stanley Cup in 2008 and, not coincidentally, also led the NHL in fighting majors. Thankfully, the Detroit Red Wings, one of the league's cleanest teams, won the Cup the following year.

If it were up to me, players that take part in staged fights would be suspended and their teams fined. If two players are sent off for fighting, their teams should be forced to play four on four for the duration of the penalties. I don't care how many goals are scored. That would get rid of fighting in a hurry.

The other thing that scares me is that a player might someday be killed during a fight in the NHL. It happened already in the winter of 2009 when a young man, Don Sanderson, died after hitting his head on the ice during a fight in a senior amateur game. With the size of players in today's NHL, especially the big thugs who only fight, it is inevitable that somebody is going to be killed. And when that happens, the NHL will react by making visors mandatory and they'll likely ban fighting then. Why wait for the inevitable?

It's just like the mesh the NHL put up in its arenas to protect fans from pucks that leave the ice surface. I covered hockey in Europe for years and this mesh was a feature of rinks over there. I used to ask NHL president John Ziegler why the NHL didn't follow suit, and he said it would obstruct the fans' vision. But when a little girl was killed after being struck by a puck at a game in Columbus, the NHL didn't hesitate to put up mesh in all its rinks.

Over the years, I have grown tired of hearing people say fighting is kept in the game because it drives TV ratings and it's considered entertainment. That is bull. I worked for the big three networks in the United States, ABC, NBC, and CBS, and I can state categorically that fighting, more than anything else, has *prevented* hockey from getting the major television contract it so desperately covets. Hockey will never be able to compete with football, baseball, and basketball, and one of the big reasons is fighting. The majority of American viewers despise it, and the sooner the NHL realizes this, the better. It is a negative in television, and hockey will never be considered a family-friendly sport as long as fighting exists as an acceptable part of the game. Some major television executives still feel hockey falls in the same category as wrestling, roller derby, and mixed martial arts.

Those who support fighting like to say nobody ever gets hurt. That, of course, is utter nonsense. Of course players get hurt in fights—more often than the NHL would care to admit. They break fingers, knuckles, noses and orbital bones, and suffer concussions. People *do* get hurt in fights—and teams lose man-games as players sit on the injured reserve list.

What's worse, in my mind, is that the spectacle of the game is damaged because fights interrupt the flow of the game and are major time-wasters. Fighting hurts the entertainment value.

MIKE SAYS:

I can see a day coming when a player who fights in the NHL is tagged with an automatic game misconduct. It is inevitable. But when a young man dies in a hockey game as a result of being engaged in a fight and the NHL reacts by saying, "We'll continue to discuss the state of fighting in our league," then I don't see that day coming anytime soon.

With the death of twenty-one-year-old Don Sanderson, the distaste for fighting in hockey reached its highest peak. Sanderson, who played for the Whitby Dunlops of the Ontario Hockey Association Senior AAA league, lost his helmet and hit his head on the ice in a fight with Corey Fulton of the Brantford Blast on December 12, 2008. He was knocked unconscious, and although he came to, he ultimately slipped into a coma and passed away on January 2, 2009.

Many in the hockey world reacted as though they were shocked when the truth is that they had been sitting on pins and needles, just waiting for the day to arrive when a player would die as a result of a hockey fight. You used to hear "Nobody gets hurt in a hockey fight" all the time, but in recent years, as hockey fighters have become more specialized thugs, you don't hear it very often.

I happen to think there is a place for fighting in hockey. Call me a dinosaur—you certainly won't be the first—but I believe the majority of faithful hockey fans don't mind the occasional scrap. I say that, however, with a new-found hesitation. I do not like the way fighting has gone in recent years. As Ralph suggests, fighting used to be mostly a result of something that happened in the game. One player would take exception to something an opponent had done to him, they'd drop their gloves and away they'd go.

But that is not always the case these days. Now, most teams carry a designated fighter (or two) whose only job is to fight. And you should see the size of some of these monsters.

Derek Boogaard of the Minnesota Wild stands six foot seven and weighs 258 pounds. He can barely skate, and in his first 198 NHL games as the Wild's enforcer, he had a mere 2 goals and 10 points with 439 penalty minutes. In that same span of 198 games, Boogaard had taken just 35 shots on goal. Mitch Fritz of the New York Islanders also stands six foot seven and weighs 242. In his first 18 NHL games he had no points to go with 38 penalty minutes while averaging just 2 minutes and 53 seconds of playing time. Of his 38 minutes in the box, 30 minutes were for fighting majors. Zack Stortini of the Edmonton Oilers is on the small side compared to Boogaard and Fritz, at just six foot four and 220 pounds, but with a week left in the NHL's 2008–09 regular season, he led all fighters with 25 majors.

To his credit, Stortini can also play the game a little. He had 6 goals and 11 points in 51 games, 10 goals and 24 points in 146 career games.

Most teams have to hide their fighters. Boogaard, for example, averaged just 4 minutes and 59 seconds of ice time per game. When the Wild played against one of the NHL's elite teams, you could find him munching on popcorn in the press box. The same goes for most of the league's one-dimensional players who can only fight.

Andrew Peters has played five years for the Buffalo Sabres, yet has never dressed for a playoff game. The six-foot-four, 226-pound enforcer once mocked the Toronto Maple Leafs, who were destined to miss the playoffs, by making a golfing motion with his stick to indicate the Leafs would soon be hitting the links. It was actually kind of funny, but the Leafs got the last laugh: Peters's Sabres made the playoffs, but he didn't get into a game.

As Ralph points out, things started to go off the rail in the 1970s with the birth of the Broad Street Bullies. The Philadelphia Flyers used intimidation as a tactic and won back-to-back Stanley Cups in 1974 and 1975. But even their tough guys could play the game. Dave Schultz, for example, terrorized the league for nine years, but even when he was racking up huge numbers of penalty minutes, he was also scoring and setting up goals.

In 1973–74, Schultz registered a whopping 348 penalty minutes, but still found time to score a career-best 20 goals and 36 points. In fact, over a four-year period from 1973–74 through 1976–77, Schultz averaged 31 points a season while averaging 362 penalty minutes.

Brawling also became popular in the '70s, when it became commonplace for both teams to spill off their benches onto the ice for a melee. Those were dangerous because a fighter would often get paired up with a non-fighter. Over the years, the NHL did a tremendous job of ridding itself of bench-clearing brawls. The league instituted severe fines and suspensions for participants, and they have all but disappeared. You might see the occasional line brawl nowadays, when all five skaters on the ice drop their gloves, but rarely will you see more than two fights take place at a time.

And in the wake of those changes, there were still some pretty good fighters, but they could also play the game, too. Dave "Tiger" Williams is the NHL's all-time leader in penalty minutes with 3,966, but in 962 games he scored 241 goals and 513 points. Bob Probert is probably the greatest example of a fighter who could also play. In 935 NHL games the six-foot-three, 225-pounder scored 163 goals and had 389 points to go with 3,300 penalty minutes.

Even a little guy like Tie Domi, who at five foot ten and barely 200 pounds fought every heavyweight in the NHL, scored 104 goals and 245 points with 3,515 penalty minutes in 1,020 games.

As Ralph says, when the league returned to action following the labour war of 2004–05, it seemed for a while as though fighting was completely under control. Based solely on statistics from the first half of the 2005–06 season, fighting majors were down significantly. It should also be noted that when the league returned to action following the lockout, it was more determined than ever to reduce obstruction (holding, hooking, interfering with players who don't have the puck) and make room for the game's most skilled players to show their expertise. This was done in an effort to increase both scoring and scoring chances.

And when word got out fighting was down in the NHL, enforcers around the league became very aware that they needed to get busy or risk being made redundant. Fighting quickly started to soar, and within a few years the numbers were up significantly.

The fact is, even in a salary-cap world, players who can't do anything but fight can still earn big bucks. Boogaard earned $750,000 (U.S.) in 2008–09, and his contract called for a raise to $1.25 million in 2009–10. George Parros, who graduated from Princeton University, but figured out in a hurry that he could earn more as an NHL fighter than he could climbing the corporate ladder on Wall Street, signed a three-year contract extension during the 2008–09 season that will pay him $875,000 a year through 2011–12.

I have no issue with a fight that breaks out as a result of something that has happened within the game. And to those who point out there is very little fighting during the playoffs and virtually no fighting in international competition such as the World Championship and the Olympics, I say you are comparing apples and oranges. The NHL regular season is eighty-two games long, and teams can afford to use—and even lose—those games to establish themselves as a tough squad to play against, thereby sending a message to the opposition.

In the playoffs, as well as international competition, every game is important. There is still plenty of room for toughness, but teams generally don't want to waste a roster spot on a player that can only fight.

That is not to say you *need* fighting for it to be a good game. That is not the point I am making at all.

While Ralph would eliminate fighting completely from the game, I would concentrate more on getting the staged fights out of the game. These are the fights that start immediately after a faceoff for no apparent reason. I believe players must earn the right to fight.

My answer to ridding the NHL of goons who only fight is to institute a rule whereby if you fight, but your average ice time per game is under ten minutes, you are automatically ejected from the game. So, if you're a Derek Boogaard or Mitch Fritz, you're booted out of the game. If you're Jarome Iginla, the wonderful superstar for the Calgary Flames who has been known to participate in the odd scrap here and there, you're issued a five-minute fighting major, but you are allowed to stay in the game.

The NHL could give newcomers to the league a three-game grace period during which they can fight and not be ejected from the match. But if a player fights in his fourth game, he needs to have averaged at least ten minutes of ice time through his first three to avoid being ejected. Alternatively, the NHL could draw a hard line in the sand and make every player start from zero. If you fight in your first NHL game and you haven't yet played ten minutes, say goodbye.

I believe this would go a long way toward eliminating staged fights from the NHL.

That said, the minute an NHL player dies as a result of a fight, you can bet the league will act fast in making fighting an automatic game misconduct. Let's hope that day never comes.

8

THE CONSTANT VARIETY
OF SPORT

Hockey Night in Canada and my work at the Olympics unquestionably brought me the most attention throughout my career, but a lot of people don't know that I was involved in many other high-profile sporting events. In fact, many of my most enjoyable experiences in television occurred in these venues.

My favourite sport to televise was horse racing. I think a big reason was the people associated with it. I hobnobbed with some of the classiest people I have ever met in my life while working at the track.

I got my start in 1963 in Montreal, working on a show called *Saturday Night at the Races* on CTV. Dick Irvin, who would later join *Hockey Night in Canada*, was the host and Albert Trottier, who was "Mr. Horse Racing" in Ottawa and Montreal, was the analyst.

The show took place at two big Montreal racetracks, Blue Bonnets and Richelieu Park. Blue Bonnets was located in the west end of Montreal and featured only thoroughbreds. Richelieu was in the east end and was for harness racing only. I had never done horse racing before, nor had I even been involved in it, even though my dad was a man who loved to bet on "the ponies," as he called it.

As a little boy, my grandfather used to take me to a track in Hamilton back in the 1930s and early '40s and, as you might imagine, it was a magical place for a young boy to be. My grandfather loved the horses, too. We'd go to the track on the odd Saturday morning to watch the jockeys put their mounts through their paces.

Thinking about those special moments with my grandfather still puts a smile on my face.

So when I got the opportunity to televise the races, it was almost like I was able to relive my youth. And through the years, I grew to love horse racing. I even got the opportunity to produce a couple of Queen's Plates, the biggest race of the year on the Canadian calendar.

When I started out, the seasons were split; one part of the summer was for the trotters and the other for the thoroughbreds. Each Saturday night, we would telecast two taped races and one live feature race. It wasn't the toughest assignment in my television career, but unquestionably one I thoroughly enjoyed.

I got to meet some great French-Canadians during this chapter of my life. Ray Benoît was a legend in Quebec and he called the races in both languages—a feat no other announcer could accomplish. I also got to know Jean-Louis Lévesque, the man who owned the tracks, and he was a real class act. Raymond Lemay, who was the president of both tracks, became a friend and supporter of mine.

One fellow I already knew quite well, but who assisted me with plenty of information, was Montreal Canadiens legend John Ferguson. He owned horses and was always hanging around the track, and he introduced me to several jockeys and drivers. At one Queen's Plate, Elizabeth, the Queen Mother, attended and I got to meet her (with the appropriate bow, of course).

Prior to the first episode of *Saturday Night at the Races*, the crew came to me and said they wanted to make a bet. Not only that, but they wanted me to talk to Albert Trottier to find out which horse they should bet on. I guess they were looking to pick up a few easy bucks. I said what the heck and I chipped in $5 myself. Hey, if there was some easy cash to be made, I wanted a piece of the action.

I found Albert and asked him for a few tips.

He said, "There is a saying in horse racing, 'It's a jockey's race,' and this is not a jockey's race."

"What does that mean?" I asked.

"It means this is not fixed," he said.

Fixed races?

It turned out the jockeys or drivers—or so it was rumoured—often got together and decided to put a few bucks in their own pockets by rigging the races. Albert said there were no jockey's races on this particular night, but mentioned, "There is a horse that is at 10-to-1 odds to win, and I think it can't miss in the featured race." Then he gave me a little wink.

Naturally, we put all our money on that horse.

Of course, the featured race was the one that was telecast live. Well, the horses broke out of the gate, and suddenly I could hear voices through my intercom saying "Shit!" and "Damn!" and "Hell!"

"What the heck is going on?" I said. "Shut up, you guys!"

"The jockey fell off our horse!"

We lost our hard-earned money.

I looked for Albert after the first show to congratulate him, but he had already disappeared. I guess he didn't want to face the music that night!

I'm sorry to see horse racing has been so negatively affected by the tough economic times. It is a great and classy sport—truly the sport of kings.

* * *

It's funny how you have an idea about something based mostly on other people's perceptions, yet when you give it a try, you wonder why you didn't try it much sooner.

Everybody who knows me knows that tennis is a great love of my life. But when I was growing up in Essex, tennis was perceived as a sissy sport. There weren't any courts, so nobody played. Fact is, I didn't pick up a racquet until I was in my late thirties.

One summer day, I got a call from Ron Ellis, the star right winger for the Toronto Maple Leafs, who told me he and teammate Tim Ecclestone were going to a tennis camp to train for the coming hockey season and wondered if *Hockey Night in Canada* would be interested in shooting a feature to be used during an intermission the following year. Ellis told me a lot of hockey players used tennis to get in shape during the summer.

I thought it sounded like a great idea.

The camp was at the Inn at Manitou, a few hours north of Toronto, near Parry Sound. I tracked down the inn's owner, and was pleasantly surprised to find out it was Ben Wise, who used to be a director at CBC. The host pro was Peter Burwash.

Burwash was actually quite a good hockey player for the University of Toronto Varsity Blues, but tennis was his true love and that is the sport he elected to pursue professionally. He never established himself as one of the world's best players—his highest world ranking as a singles player was 240th in 1974—but he did represent Canada in the Davis Cup. Upon retiring as a player, he formed Peter Burwash International, a successful tennis management company that operated in thirty-two countries.

He has also worked with tennis stars such as Serena and Venus Williams, Daniel Nestor, Greg Rusedski and Sébastien Lareau. Today he is the number one tennis commentator on TV in Canada.

I decided to take a little scouting trip to the camp, just to see what I would be facing when I taped the intermission piece with Ellis and Ecclestone. I always liked to check out the facilities when I was doing a remote. It was during my scouting mission that I first met Burwash. He told me, "If you're going to shoot this feature on tennis, then you should learn how to play the sport."

I replied, "It's funny you should say that, because it has always been my philosophy to learn how to play the sports that I shoot for TV—especially sports I have not played." If I had to televise bowling, I learned how to bowl. I went on the ice with the Montreal Canadiens to see what it was like to practise with an NHL team. You get the idea.

I said, "When I come back, I'll take a quick lesson with you and try to learn a little bit about the game." Then I told him that I had always considered tennis something of a sissy sport. It wasn't my cup of tea. I'm not sure how he took that, because it was clearly an insult to a sport that was not only his passion, but provided him with his livelihood.

When we finally went up to the Inn at Manitou to shoot the feature, I arrived a few days early. Peter got me on the court to teach me, and right away I fell in love with the game. This was no sissy sport. Not only was it a great workout, but to play the game properly took unbelievable co-ordination, strength, and concentration. I knew that very day that I had found a sport that would be a big part of the rest of my life. It ultimately led to me joining the Boulevard Club in Toronto.

The shoot was wonderful, although we did run into all kinds of technical difficulties. In the end, we shot the guys fishing, golfing, and hiking, as well as playing tennis. When it was edited down, it turned out to be a great piece. That was the goal, but it wasn't all I got out of that particular assignment. What I remember most fondly was being introduced to a great sport that really got my competitive juices pumping.

I wound up taking lessons, as did my wife, Janet, and I now have a shelf full of tennis trophies—reminders of some of my accomplishments on the court.

Some of my fondest tennis memories involve playing in an event called *Celebrity Tennis*, a CBC show that featured the likes of musical stars Hagood Hardy, John Allan Cameron, and Guido Basso, as well as famous movie producer and director Norman Jewison. It turns out many celebrities like to play tennis, and I became close with many of them.

When CBC took over the Canadian Open for men's and women's tennis, they asked me to produce it. I wound up doing it for many years.

My initial crew included Tom McKee as the host and Don Fontana and Jane O'Hara as the analysts. Fontana had been a top-ranked Canadian tennis star in the 1950s and '60s, and while he was never the top-ranked men's player in Canada, he did manage to reach number two on six occasions and was a three-time Canadian doubles champion. He won the Ontario singles championship twice and was inducted into the Tennis Canada Hall of Fame in 2000. Fontana had been the tournament director for a number of years before joining our TV crew, so he was well acquainted with the event.

Jane O'Hara had been a brilliant tennis player who won every major Canadian title before embarking on a successful international career, during which time she played at Wimbledon four times and in the U.S. Open six times. O'Hara advanced to the round of sixteen in 1972. She was inducted into the Tennis Canada Hall of Fame in 2002.

Without question, my biggest coup was getting tennis superstar Virginia Wade to be an analyst, our third person in the booth. As accomplished as our Canadian talent was, I really felt we needed a name to join the team. Virginia was the best British female tennis player of all time, and I had heard her work on the BBC and thought she was very talented. When I approached her to join us, she flew to Toronto, listened to our proposal and readily agreed.

Virginia won three Grand Slam singles titles (the U.S. Open in 1968, the Australian Open in 1972, and Wimbledon in 1977), as well as four Grand Slam doubles titles (Australian, French, and U.S. in 1973 and the U.S. Open again in 1975) in her illustrious career. Virginia brought us the credibility I was looking for, and not only became a great TV personality for us but also became my close friend. She was a great gal!

We brought some innovations to the telecast, such as putting a camera under the net for isolation shots and moving the cameras closer to courtside. I also devised a way to isolate on each player—a practice that continues today. Many tennis aficionados prefer the men's game because of the brute strength with which they play. Not me. Given my druthers, I would rather watch women's tennis. I prefer the longer rallies.

Not surprisingly, I had the good fortune of meeting many of the top tennis stars in the world, both current and past. I even got to play Roy Emerson, the great Australian champion, at the Boulevard Club in Toronto once. Emerson had won twelve Grand Slam singles titles and sixteen doubles crowns. By this time I was something of an accomplished amateur player myself. It was memorable because Emerson was half in the bag when we took to the court. We were slated to play against tennis legend Rod Laver and another member of the Boulevard Club, but Emerson had been pounding back the beers.

I said, "Can you play? You've had about ten beers."

He said, "Actually, I've had twenty." And away we went.

Emerson was unbelievable. He was hitting lob shots sixty feet in the air, which really pissed Laver off. He was magnificent.

I also got to play against Bobby Riggs at the Toronto Lawn and Tennis Club. Riggs was a strange little man best known for his celebrated match against female champion Billie Jean King in the Astrodome in 1973. It was a charity event, and when he found out I was a TV producer he was all over me with ideas for wacky TV shows involving him. I couldn't get rid of the guy. Quite honestly, he was a pain.

He was getting on in those days, but he was still a pretty good player. I asked him about the famous match against Billie Jean King, but he didn't want to talk about it. All he wanted to talk about was this idea he had for a new show in which he would take on the world's best athletes, but with a handicap system.

Over the years, I also played tennis with a number of hockey players, and one of the best was goalie Glenn "Chico" Resch. It was late in his playing career, when he was my son's teammate with the Philadelphia Flyers.

The best hockey player I ever came up against on the tennis court was Pavel Bure. One of the most gifted goal scorers in NHL history, I truly believe Bure could have been a professional tennis player if he had been so inclined.

My son was also a good tennis player in his youth. Scott was ranked in the top five in Ontario in the twelve-and-under division when he came up against future pro Andrew Sznajder in the final of the provincial championships. Sznajder beat Scott 6–0, 6–0, and when Scott walked off the court, he said, "Dad, that's the end of my competitive tennis." Today, on the odd occasion that he picks up a racquet, he still beats the hell out of his old man.

The late George Gross, a brilliant newspaperman, was also a tennis buff who arranged for me to play against the likes of Sam Sniderman (late owner of Sam the Record Man) as well as actor and singer Jan Rubes, who was in the movie *Witness* among his many credits.

George preferred to play doubles, and one day he called me to come down to the club for a match. My partner was to be Cardinal Gerald Emmett Carter. I was the best player in the foursome and Cardinal Carter was, well, not a great player, so we were teamed together. Being a man of faith, I relished the opportunity to play with a man of the cloth.

I'm as competitive as the next guy, and when you get engrossed in a game, you sometimes forget your surroundings. I missed a shot that I should have made, and without thinking, I yelled, "Oh shit!"

Well, right away, I knew what I had just done. But I looked over at Cardinal Carter and he was laughing. I apologized, to which he responded, "I absolutely agree with your comment." Then he looked me in the eye and added, "As long as you don't take the Lord's name in vain, you'll have no problems with me, Ralph."

I once participated in a rather interesting media charity event in which teams could be purchased. The person who purchased the winning team got a free one-week vacation in Bermuda. My partner was the actor Alec Bollini and I must say, we didn't think much of our chances in the event—we weren't ranked in the top ten for the event—so we didn't buy our own team.

As it turned out, we made it to the final and were matched up against a team that included tennis journalist Tom Tebbutt, who was a former pro, as well as another really good player. Alec and I figured we were toast. They beat us badly in the first set, 6–1, but we eked out a 7–5 win in the second. It came down to a 12-point tiebreaker.

Tom is a friend of mine and Alec's, but what the heck, it was a competition. Somehow, we managed to beat his team 7–5 in the tiebreaker. The look on Tom's face when we won was painful. The guy who had bought our team was some shoe manufacturer who promised Alec and me a new pair of shoes each if we won him the trip to Bermuda. We had no idea who had bought Tom's team, but we found out quickly enough when the tournament was over.

We got to the locker room, and I said, "Tom, what's up? You look like you are going to cry."

"We bought our own team, Ralph."

Now I understood why he was so down.

Alec piped up and said, "Why didn't you tell us? We would have thrown the tiebreaker!"

Tom said, "Really?"

"Damn right," I said. "You're our friend."

By the way, the guy we won the trip for? Never saw him again. We won the guy a week in Bermuda and he stiffed us on the shoes. Oh well. Sorry, Tom.

I used to play a lot of tennis at the Rosethorn Club with former Toronto Maple Leafs defenceman Mike Pelyk. He played nine years with the Leafs during a very lean time in the organization's history, and the fans were quite often relentless with their shouts of disapproval.

We were in the men's doubles final once when, in the middle of the match, with a lot of the club's members watching us, I turned to him and said, "Mike, you're playing great."

"I love playing tennis," he answered. "At least here nobody boos me."

I laughed.

My favourite tennis story takes me back to Virginia Wade and the Canadian Open at the National Tennis Centre in Toronto.

Virginia and I developed a tradition whereby we would meet at 8 a.m. on the morning of the final to play against one another. Actually, we didn't really play games, we just rallied, but it was an incredible feeling to play a champion.

Virginia used to joke about the fact the only people hanging around at that time of day were the maintenance crew. Here I am with one of the greatest tennis players in history, and we're rallying in front of ten thousand empty seats.

The last time we got together for our friendly little game, we looked at one end of the court, where there was a drainage hole where the water would go if it rained. We noticed that a muskrat had just emerged from the drain. It sat there for about fifteen minutes and watched us as we rallied.

Virginia smiled and said, "Ralph, we finally got a spectator!"

* * *

I am the worst golfer in the Mellanby family, and I'm actually not all that bad—about an 18 handicap. My dad, on the other hand, was a good golfer, and when I was a child he used to take me along with him to ride in the cart when he'd play at Chedoke Golf Club in Hamilton. I was too young to actually play, but I liked being along for the ride.

As I grew up, I took up the sport. Back in the 1930s, '40s, and '50s, golf wasn't as popular as it is today. Arnold Palmer, Jack Nicklaus and a kid named Eldrick Woods—you know him as "Tiger"—have helped bring the sport to the mainstream.

When I started working at CKLW in Windsor, I found out that the station had a golf club membership for two and anybody at the station who played golf was welcome to use the passes.

I went to Art Laing, our director of sports, and said, "Does anybody use the golf passes at Roseland?"

"No."

"Well, give them to me."

Now I could play for nothing and take a guest. Remember, I was very young and had no money to spare, so I played a lot of golf on those passes.

When the word got around that I was golfing, some of the lighting guys at the station who used to moonlight at nightclubs would find partners for me to play with. One day, one of my pals came up to me and said, "Dean Martin is looking for a golf game."

"*The* Dean Martin—of the Rat Pack?"

"Yep."

Turns out Dean was appearing at the old Elmwood Casino in Windsor and really loved playing golf. He and his partner Jerry Lewis had just split up, and he was playing the nightclub circuit all over North America as a solo act. I was in my early twenties at the time and wound up playing with him twice, and it was a great pleasure. I have never met a looser guy in my life. His manager would drive him to the club, and away we'd go. He just loved to play the game, and he didn't take it too seriously. He had fun and he provided me with a wonderful memory.

One day I was golfing with a friend, and things were moving pretty slowly. We came up behind a twosome. One of them asked us if we'd like to form a foursome and we said, "Why not?"

Imagine my surprise when I discovered I was now golfing with Joe Louis, the former heavyweight boxing champion of the world! Louis was 69–3 in his career, winning 55 of his fights by knockout. He was a great golfer and a really friendly man. Despite his great fame, he was just like a regular guy.

I asked him after the round, when we were in the clubhouse having a beer, why he chose to play in Windsor. He told me he wasn't welcome in Detroit country clubs because he was black. I was dumbfounded. I mean, this was Joe Louis—the great American hero! That was racism at its worst in the '50s.

Like most boxers, Louis's career ended with a loss. On November 26, 1951, he was knocked out in the eighth round by another legend, Rocky Marciano. Louis was well past his prime and probably shouldn't have ever taken the fight. I asked him about the Marciano fight, but Louis set me straight.

"I don't talk about the losses." Fortunately, with only three losses on his record, that left a lot to talk about!

Many hockey players are passionate golfers in the off-season.

Some of the best I ever golfed with include Gary Dornhoefer, Stan Mikita, Dale Tallon, and Vic Hadfield. Another great golfer is Dick Irvin, who won his club championship at Beaconsfield in Montreal numerous times. Frank Selke Jr. was no slouch, either. I never beat either of them.

Without question, the best hockey player I ever had the good fortune to golf with is Marc Savard, the Boston Bruins scoring ace who was a teammate of Scott's with the Atlanta Thrashers. Not a big guy by any stretch of the imagination, Savard is one of the best passers in the National Hockey League. In my opinion, he also could be a professional golfer if he decided to go down that path.

Keith Tkachuk was a great hockey player and golfer, and he was definitely a lot of fun. Keith, or Walt as he is called by his teammates, used to play with Scott in St. Louis with the Blues. They were also great golfing buddies and used to play a game called Bingo-Bango-Bongo which, to this day, I have no idea how to play.

There would be some pretty big money bet on the outcome of each hole. I wasn't in on the betting, but my shots still had an effect on the outcome of the game. Keith and Scott would play from the back tees, where the pros hit from, because they were both big hitters, but I would play off the middle white tees, putting me a little closer to the greens. Since I could use my handicap, I usually got a shot on each hole.

Keith had no problem with that. "Fine, we'll beat you anyway."

On one occasion, with my handicap I started out birdie, par, par, and I couldn't believe my good fortune. I looked at Scott and said, "You know I'm not going to be able to keep this up."

Of course, Scott knew how crappy I usually was.

"Dad, you don't have to do another thing. You've already won me some big bucks."

The next time we played with Keith, he made me shoot from the back tees with the rest of the gang. Still, they were giving me a stroke per hole. Damned if I don't start out par, par—which is birdie, birdie with the handicap they were giving me.

"Next time," Keith said, "you get no strokes!"

When I was asked by CTV to produce the Canadian Open, as well as the Skins Games, I jumped at the opportunity. It wasn't because I needed the money; it was because I loved the game. What I didn't know then, but learned very quickly, is that golf is the hardest sport to cover on TV.

Think about it: You have golfers spread out over acres of land, and your job is to bring the action to the viewer. So who do you concentrate on? Well, nowadays if Tiger Woods is in the event, you focus on everything he does—from showing up to the club in the morning, to his practice shots, to every shot he takes during his round.

Obviously, once the tournament is in full swing, you keep an eye on the leaders. But that doesn't mean some guy 15 shots behind isn't capable of making a fantastic shot that the viewers would like to see—or, heaven forbid, a hole in one.

You have to have a battery of spotters, one for every golfer on the course. They're not in contact with the director in the truck—they have their own truck, and they report to a co-ordinator who lets the producer and director know who is shooting for par or an eagle or bogey. So, even if the broadcast is focusing on the leaders, we still get a chance to switch to other golfers who are making important shots. I also used my brother Jim as the isolation director—he'd get stuff on tape that we could replay when we didn't get the live shot.

Frank Chirkinian invented golf TV coverage, and I got to know him a bit when we worked together at CBS in the United States. I spent a day with him in hopes of learning his system, and the biggest thing he told me was to use the spotter system.

I was doing the Canadian Open in Montreal once, and Frank was in the other truck working for CBS, but taking our feed. I'll never forget what a volatile guy he was. He was a legend in the United States, owned a cottage outside the gates of Augusta National, where they play the Masters, but he was on our turf now.

It was clear he wasn't very happy with our coverage. I was just stepping into my truck when he screamed, "There's too many fucking French-Canadians here! They don't know golf."

I pulled him aside and said, "Frank, you're in Quebec. You can't scream and yell about the French." He got the message and settled down.

It was important to have Canadian talent on the CTV crew, and two of my favourites were Jim Nelford and Sandra Post.

A two-time Canadian amateur champion, Nelford played on the PGA Tour for ten years, but was seriously injured in a water-skiing accident in 1984. One of his arms was badly sliced by a propeller blade. He never regained his top form and eventually lost his playing status on the PGA Tour. Post was a three-time Ontario and Canadian junior champion who went on to win eight LPGA events, including the Dinah Shore Open in back-to-back years, 1978 and 1979.

My biggest thrill in golf was when we did the Skins Game in 1989 at Glen Abbey in Oakville, Ontario, and all the Mellanbys worked on the broadcast. My wife, Janet and son were spotters, my daughter Laura was the unit manager, and my brother Jim was the isolation director.

Talk about some great golfers. The event included Arnold Palmer, Jack Nicklaus, and Lee Trevino.

Palmer is one of the most popular golfers in the history of the sport. In fact, his popularity is punctuated by the hordes of fans that follow him hole to hole, hanging on his every swing of the club. They are known as "Arnie's Army." He has rewarded his faithful with an amazing sixty-three victories on the PGA Tour, including seven majors. He won the Masters in 1958, 1960, 1962, and 1964, the Open Championship (a.k.a. the British Open) in 1961 and 1962, and the U.S. Open in 1960.

Jack Nicklaus was the Tiger Woods of professional golf long before Tiger burst on the scene. A big hitter, Nicklaus won two U.S. Amateur championships, in 1959 and 1961, before seizing the PGA as his own. The blond bomber won a whopping seventy-three PGA titles, including eighteen majors—eight Masters (1963, 1965, 1966, 1972,

1975, and 1986), five PGA championships (1963, 1971, 1973, 1975, and 1980), four U.S. Opens (1962, 1967, 1972, and 1980), and three Open Championships (1966, 1970, and 1980). While others golfers threatened the king of the hill, Nicklaus held onto his crown as the game's number one player for more than two decades.

Trevino, meanwhile, was never the most dominant golfer on the tour, but gained notoriety for his showmanship. He did capture twenty-nine PGA titles, including two Masters (1975, 1985), two U.S. Opens (1968, 1971), two PGA titles (1974, 1984), and two Open Championships (1971, 1972).

What an amazing trio of golfers to have on Canadian soil!

It was a two-day event, and Scott was assigned to spot Palmer. He was part of Arnie's Army.

Scott wanted to get his picture taken with the golfers, so he asked Palmer if that would be possible. Palmer said sure.

When the event ended, I was going into the clubhouse and Palmer came up to me and said, "Where's Scott? We're ready for the picture. I'm looking all over for him."

Here's Arnold Palmer, a golfing god, going out of his way to find my boy to have his picture taken. Talk about a great guy! A lot of guys would have promised to take the picture and then hightailed it out of town at the first opportunity. But Palmer kept his word. Scott still has the picture hanging in his office at home.

George Knudson, one of the greatest Canadian golfers of all time, called me one day to say he was working on an instructional video and wondered if I'd like to be involved. I jumped at the opportunity.

The 1955 Canadian Junior Champion, Knudson went on to record eight PGA Tour victories to go with five Canadian PGA titles and a second-place finish at the 1969 Masters. In ten Masters appearances, Knudson had three top-ten finishes—quite a remarkable achievement.

I learned a lot about the game from working with him on his video, and he had one of the best lines about me I've ever heard.

George was introducing me to some people and he affectionately said, "Ralph knows more about golf than anybody I have ever met who can't play the game."

Oh well, I still enjoy playing golf, and today I can still lose to my son and my brother, Jim, the good Mellanby golfers. Now that I'm getting on, my daughter Laura beats me, too. Such a great game! Turns out Knudson was right about me.

9

OUR MAN IN HAVANA

One of the fondest chapters in my career took place in 1991 when I accepted the job as co-host broadcaster for the Pan-American Games in Cuba.

Over the years, I have worked at a lot of international events, but just because you are there doesn't mean it will wind up being a memorable experience. I did the Commonwealth Games in Edmonton in 1978 and Victoria in 1994, the Pan-American Games in Mexico City in 1975, plus the 1990 Goodwill Games for Turner Broadcasting in Seattle. Actually, the bulk of those games were held in Seattle, but I produced hockey, which was based out of the Tri-Cities region of Washington State.

In any case, the point is that sometimes it is just work—you just go in and do the job. For instance, the most memorable thing about the Pan-Am Games in Mexico was when I arrived at my hotel and had to step over a dead horse to enter the building. That certainly was not a great start.

The Pan-American Games in Cuba in 1991 were different. This was a once-in-a-lifetime assignment and an experience I never expected to even be a part of. I had sold my company, Ralph Mellanby and Associates, to CTV in 1990. John Cassaday had become president at CTV, and at one of our first meetings he told me he wanted his sports department to be made up of outsiders. He offered to purchase my new company and my people.

Part of the deal was that CTV would also employ me as well as my five partners. I didn't want to hang my people out to dry. One of my staffers, Doug Beeforth, now runs Rogers Sportsnet. Another member of our staff at the time was my daughter, Laura. Since we were struggling financially in spite of our success, the offer was intriguing. And since CTV was my biggest client, it made sense for me to sell the company to them when they showed interest.

It was a somewhat unusual experience for me because I was now basically at CTV as a consultant. The funny thing is, I had turned down the opportunity to be the head of CTV Sports earlier—but the timing hadn't been right.

One day, I received an unexpected call from Roone Arledge, my old boss at ABC. He told me they had run into trouble with the State Department and we couldn't live up to their contract with the Cubans to help broadcast the Pan-American Games. ABC was to be the co-host broadcaster along with Turner Sports in a three-way deal. But the U.S. government would only allow one hundred people to go to Cuba, and Roone said they needed me to represent ABC and Turner as the co-broadcaster. Because of Canada's friendlier relations with Cuba, Roone and his colleagues at ABC and Turner felt I was ideally positioned to take over. "We trust you and based on the job you did in Calgary we know you, and only you, could do the work. We need your help."

I was very flattered. Since I had worked for all the American networks, I knew I had a solid relationship with them, but this was to be a monumental task and it was comforting to think ABC had confidence in my ability to pull it off. Not only did Canada have very good diplomatic ties with Cuba, but Arledge knew that Canada had the production and technical resources.

I was immediately interested, but I had to say, "I cannot make this decision because I am now with CTV. I have sold them my company."

Roone then told me he'd have his business manager at ABC, Steve Solomon, call me, and when he did, I basically told him the same thing—"You're going to have to talk to John Cassaday, the president of CTV, to get permission. I can do the job, no question about it. We can get the mobiles and get the crews to work with the Cubans. I can be the lead guy, but I sold my company and now I need permission from my president. CTV must make the deal."

Fortunately for me, Cassaday jumped all over it. I was going to Cuba!

John assigned Peter Sisam, who was vice-president of marketing at the time and later became head of sports at CTV, to head the project and had Gary Maavara, the legal vice-president at CTV, to draw up the contract.

We then flew to New York and sat down with Arledge and his brass and laid out our game plan. Working with a couple of my guys from the Calgary Olympics, Doug Beeforth, and David Rhines, who were with the network now, we applied pretty much the same business plan that we used in Calgary. Hey, why not? If it works for an Olympic Games, there's no reason to think it wouldn't work at the Pan-Am Games. They listened and gave the go-ahead, just like that.

They wanted us Canadians to cover the major sports—track and field, swimming, aquatics, volleyball, basketball, and gymnastics—with our mobiles. Most of it would be taking place in Havana, but some of the action would be in Santiago de Cuba, five hundred miles away. We faced a tight deadline—we only had a year before the Games were to be held. Usually, this is a two- to three-year project, especially when the event is being held in a foreign country.

One of the first things I said to ABC and Turner was, "I'm not trusting the Cubans to pay us. If we're going to do this, the money has to come from Turner and ABC directly." They agreed.

We also told them we wanted to be compensated for the loss of any of our equipment, because I wasn't convinced the Cubans wouldn't abscond with our stuff. In the end, they didn't take a thing, but I couldn't be sure of that going into the project. ABC then agreed to pay insurance on all shipped equipment.

A while later, I flew to Atlanta to meet up with the Turner and ABC people. I was pleased to be working with Don McGuire, the executive producer of Turner Sports, and Jack O'Hara, the top production guy at ABC, both of whom I knew very well.

From there, it was on to Cuba—on ABC's private jet. I had begun the Great Adventure, as I like to call it. I couldn't know it at the time, but this was to be the highlight of my fifty years in television.

I was the executive producer and producer. I needed to get the lay of the land to start preparing. Until I got down there, I had no idea of the scope of what was to unfold. There are always surprises when you do an initial survey mission, and this trip was certainly no exception.

When we arrived in Cuba I met with the head of television, General José Ramón Fernández. In the Castro government, the general was the head of arts, television, health, sports—and about five other ministries. He had been one of Castro's key men.

General Fernández was nearly seventy when I met him. He didn't speak English and I didn't speak Spanish, yet there was a real chemistry between the two of us, which I felt immediately. The first thing he did at our meeting was to thank me—and Canada—for coming in. I felt proud and honoured. He also made it very clear that he had checked me out very carefully. Smart guy!

General Fernández was the chairman of the Pan-American Games committee, so we would be working closely together for a long period. In our first meeting, he assured me Cuba would cover all our health-care needs. That was very comforting.

The first few days in Cuba were indescribable. I'm not exactly sure what I was expecting, but I was pleasantly surprised, especially by the Cuban TV people, who were very accommodating. The guys from ABC and Turner were there, too, and we had to go around and inspect all the venues to make sure they were up to standard and usable. I didn't realize at the time that I'd be going back every few weeks. In fact, as the Games drew near, I was in Cuba as often as I was in Canada. Essentially, it was my bailiwick—CTV couldn't afford to keep releasing key staff to run back and forth to Cuba, and the folks from ABC and Turner were there sometimes, but not always.

During the first visit, they took us to their broadcast centre. It was like a little local TV station. I was shocked! Mostly, they were using old Russian TV equipment that was out of date, and they had two or three mobile units that were like little bread trucks. They also had just a handful of cameras. It was as though I had walked back in time to the '50s.

I wondered how the hell they expected to televise an international competition with this junk. On the flight back home on the ABC jet, I told their executive producers, "This is a lot bigger job than we anticipated. I'll devise a plan and tell you how much it's going to cost. We're going to have to bring all the mobiles out of Canada and ship them to Cuba from Miami. This is a huge risk."

I was relieved when they responded, "Ralph, whatever it takes, do it." The money didn't matter to them—it was the prestige. This was the first major American television venture in Cuba since Castro took over, so it had to be first-rate.

I came home and devised a plan with Rhines and Beeforth. We decided we'd use all of the mobile units we had used in Calgary, along with some independent mobiles. We would need about three hundred people, so we went through our crew lists and decided we'd be wise to lean on many of the people we had used in Calgary. They knew how we worked, and how we liked things to be done.

Two weeks later, I was back in Havana, but I didn't go with ABC. I had to take what they called the "Freedom Flight" out of Miami on American Airlines—the only regular flight between the U.S. and Cuba. It was kind of weird—you never knew exactly what gate the flight was leaving from at the airport, right up until the end. They'd keep that a secret for security reasons. And the departure time was different every time. Sometimes I'd have to sit in the airport for three or four hours, and there were rarely more than two or three people on the flight going to Cuba. Coming back was a different story. It was always packed with elderly people who had been given permission from Castro to visit relatives in Miami if they were old and (probably) near death.

With all the trips I made, I eventually got to know the flight crew—it was always the same one. Since there was rarely anybody seated in first class, the crew would move me up to make my trips more enjoyable. I was usually alone with a full bar and two flight attendants. I was grateful.

General Fernández was huge, about six foot four, and to me, he really looked the part of a general. He didn't much care for the ABC or Turner guys, but he really took to me. One day, I asked the head of Cuban television, "What does General Fernández like? Is there anything I can bring him from Canada?" I knew I certainly couldn't bring him cigars or rum.

He said, "General Fernández loves peanut butter—Kraft peanut butter." Turns out they don't make peanut butter in Cuba, in spite of the great supply of peanuts. So on my next trip to Cuba, I brought him six jars of Kraft peanut butter. Well, you would think I had given him the world! He was overjoyed. He was so happy I could have gotten anything from him.

Every trip I went—and there were many—I made sure I brought General Fernández his peanut butter. The one time I forgot, he was so upset, I thought he as going to shoot me! Just kidding—General Fernández became like a father figure to me; he treated me like gold. To be honest, I could not have accomplished this project without that relationship.

He asked me if I was, like him, a great hero in Canada. I said, "No, I'm just an itinerant producer." I'm not exactly sure what the Spanish translation is for what I had told him, but he laughed like hell.

On another trip, I brought him a certificate that made him an honourary Canadian. More joy!

When I was rounding up the equipment we would need to broadcast the Games in Cuba, Peter Sisam and I went to Doug Bassett, the head of CFTO, and he said, "I'll give you our mobile and crew on one condition—you sell the mobile to the Cubans."

He didn't want it anymore and was looking to get rid of it. We said sure, and although we tried to sell it, we didn't succeed. So much for Canadian-Cuban relations.

Part of the deal I made with the Cubans was to integrate their people into the crews. I was actually quite pleased about this—I felt it would be a good experience for our Canadian crewmembers to work with the locals. We came up with an extraordinary plan: on every crew, my unit managers would be bilingual, able to speak Spanish, and we would include Cubans on every crew as well. I took some people who had no TV experience but who I knew could speak Spanish. One woman we chose, Julie Osborne, was very smart. I was convinced I could teach her what she needed to know to be a production manager and run a crew. Julie was a rookie, but she did a fabulous job.

A unit manager is responsible for running the unit, making sure everybody is doing their job and things are running smoothly. Julie worked on my major venues, and we became a great team in spite of the fact I am a tough guy to work with.

Some of the Cubans worked as cameramen, some were cable pullers. They didn't get any of the main jobs, though, as most of them couldn't speak English. If I used a Cuban as a cameraman, I had to make sure he could speak at least a little bit of English and keep his functions to a minimum.

There were other considerations. For starters, we weren't just in Havana, we were also in Santiago de Cuba, five hundred miles away, doing gymnastics. It is an important sport at any athletic competition, and we needed a separate crew for that. The good news is I had a year to get things prepared. It's not like I was under the gun and had to do it in three months. I was thankful for the time. I placed my top engineer, Jim Eady, in Santiago along with a top crew.

On one of my preliminary trips, we went to the main stadium, where the opening and closing ceremonies, as well as track and field, were to be held. Once again, I was shocked. There were cracks in the big concrete walls all over the stadium. The swimming pool also had cracks in it. We were with the guy who ran the facility—his name was Castro, also—and through my translator, Julie, I said to him, "There are cracks everywhere!"

He replied, "Well, it only has to make it through the Games." He wasn't joking.

I expected people in Cuba to be different—perhaps more down-trodden, with deplorable living conditions. But that was not the case at all. I went to a couple of their homes and it reminded me of going to my grandparents' home back in Hamilton in the '40s. They had no doors on the inside of their homes, just curtains separating the rooms—just the basics.

Yes, it was a very poor country, but they had free health care, free education, and free dentistry. Everybody went to school. It wasn't at all what I expected.

The Cubans seemed to me very contented people. I kept waiting for them to knock the country's political system and tell me how unhappy they were, or how they'd like to escape, but it didn't happen. What I had experienced in Russia and in Eastern Europe was that people there were always bitching about not having anything.

Yes, it was a dictatorship. Yes, it was only Castro's party that got elected, but the people I met didn't seem to care. They all said it was better now than in the old days. "Better than Batista!" they proclaimed.

There was a large house where we used to meet on the outskirts of Havana—because there were no large meeting rooms at the TV station or the hotel—that was like a halfway house. I was thrilled to find out Fidel Castro often held meetings there, too.

I actually quite enjoyed going to that meeting house. One day, about two months before the Games were to begin, I was there with General Fernández, and without warning, Fidel walked in. I was stunned.

He wasn't alone; he had a huge entourage with him. He walked over and shook my hand. Through the translator, he said, "I wanted to meet you, and on behalf of the Cuban people I want to thank you for coming in and working with us to do our Games. We are very proud of our relationship with Canada and we love doing business with Canadians."

And then he said something I'll never forget: "General Fernández says you are going to do a fine job, and if there is anything you need from me, just let me know."

I thought, "What the hell could I need from Fidel?"

Fidel Castro was a very striking man—much taller than I had imagined. He had a real presence. He made me happy and made me feel I was really doing something worthwhile.

I didn't say much to Castro, other than I was pleased I could be of service.

I did, however, collect on his offer to help me. Just before the Games started, Barbara Walters at ABC wanted to do an interview with Castro, and I was the guy who set it up through General Fernández. I called in my favour, and ABC was thrilled.

I went to the taping, which was held in the same house where I met Castro—the meeting house. It was quite a moment for me.

When we arrived at the hotel just before the Games, there was plenty of preparation work to be done, and knowing that, I promised the crew two full days off before the Games started. They had worked so hard—long, long days—and they were really excited about getting a little downtime to enjoy themselves.

At the same time, I kept working at the Cuban mobile parked beside us—this little bread truck that was supposed to be the base of operations for the opening ceremonies—and I said, "Are they kidding?"

One day, about forty-eight hours before the scheduled two days off, I heard a knock at my mobile door. There were Steve Solomon, Jack O'Hara (the ABC executive producer), Don McGuire (the executive producer of Turner Sports), plus the rest of the TV brass. I thought they had come to see our setup and check on how we were doing. I was wrong.

They said, "Ralph, we have to talk with you."

Uh-oh. "What is it?"

"You're going to have to do the opening and closing ceremonies."

"What?!"

"Well, we know you helped do it in Calgary and you did a great job." It was clear they were trying to butter me up.

I said, "My guys are tired. They have been setting up for days and this will be a huge undertaking. I have promised them two days off and they have earned it."

"Well, Ralph, the Cubans can't do it."

"Why?"

"They can't get their mobile to work."

Deep down, I was not surprised to hear that. I knew all along they were in over their heads; I just didn't know it would be up to me to bail them out.

I called the crew together and said, "Listen, I know you have been anxiously waiting for these two days off, but they need our help. It's completely up to you whether or not we do this. I won't force you into it. I'll be happy to produce if you want to do it."

The crew said, "Ralph, if you want to do it, we'll do it."

I was blown away by their dedication. Talk about professionals!

Now, I had no idea what the organizers had planned for the opening ceremonies, so we were starting from scratch. I met with the woman who was in charge of producing the opening and closing ceremonies and she walked me through the plan. She also said, "Don't worry, we are having a rehearsal tomorrow."

That put me at some ease.

The next day, though, the biggest rainstorm I have ever seen hit Havana. You guessed it: no rehearsal, and the opening ceremonies were the next day. Now the pressure was really on. Instead of enjoying two days off to gear up for the Games, we had our backs against the wall.

Before the opening ceremonies, we arrived early in the morning and I was informed by the head of security that we'd have to leave the mobile to allow a police dog to check it—for bombs, I presume. I envisioned a great big German shepherd, but instead they showed up with the smallest dog I have ever seen. I laughed!

I really had to be on my toes that day. I put up a big piece of cardboard up beside the monitor walls and I drew a diagram of the stadium on it. Then I got a pointer and I was able to show what was happening and where. I could point to a place on the stadium I had drawn and could tell the director, Garth Fowlie, "There are going to be five hundred dancers coming in here," and so forth. We were winging it.

We also had great support in the mobile from the our associate producer and field director Cecil Browne and from our production manager Len Chapple, who kept us organized.

The hardest part of the ceremonies was at the end, when the speeches began. Castro spoke for ninety minutes and General Fernández spoke, too. The amazing thing is there were fifty thousand people there and nobody left. That said, my guys were wiped. It was a long three hours. Staging the Pan-American Games was Cuba's coming-out party, and as a Canadian I was proud to be a part of it. Thank God we could tap into their audio system—so the sound was no worry.

After the show, boy, were we relieved! I recall we drank a few beers that night in celebration of our efforts. The executives, the same people who asked me to pick up the ball on the opening ceremonies, got a hold of me afterwards and said they couldn't believe how well it went with no rehearsal. There wasn't a mistake. I was sure proud of the crew. Our hand-held guys were running all over the stadium, picking up shots that I didn't know were there. The whole crew pulled together. It was a great achievement.

Once the Games actually got under way, I can't explain what a great thrill it was to do track and field, basketball, and volleyball. I wasn't only the guy in charge of the proceedings, I also produced those sports, too. It was great to be back in the trenches. It was a whirlwind experience, since I had crews all over the place. I only went to Santiago de Cuba once during the Games, on a private plane. During the trip, Peter Sisam and I went swimming in the ocean in our underpants—just like a couple of kids!

Our Canadian guys were fabulous, even though the working

conditions were tough. It was as hot as hell, but the crew never complained. The hand-held cameramen had it especially hard because they were out in the baking sun all day long. They were real troopers.

I also renewed my friendship with the great American announcer Jack Whitaker. When the Games started, we got to stay at the famous Tropicana Hotel. We asked General Fernández, "You guys were weeks sitting outside the city with Fulgencio Batista, Cuba's U.S.-friendly dictator, still in power and you never went in. Why would you wait?"

He said, "We were waiting for Meyer Lansky to finish building the Tropicana."

We laughed! Some strategy.

The Tropicana had the amazing nightclub, the Copacabana, in it, and some of my Cuban crew took me there one night. It was like stepping back in time. The show that night was just like it was in the 1950s, showgirls and all. In fact, much of what we saw in Cuba during our stay reminded me of the 1950s, especially the cars.

Donna de Varona—the American swimming star who was now an International Olympic Committee member—and I took a tour of the network television executives' houses. They were just one step up from my grandma's house.

De Varona was born to be a star. At thirteen, she was the youngest member of the 1960 U.S. swim team that competed at the Olympic Games in Rome. At the next Olympics, in Tokyo, she won two gold medals, and by the time she was eighteen she had broken eighteen world records.

When her swimming career ended she became an ABC broadcaster and we became great friends. It wasn't all work during the Games. One day, Donna and I decided to have a battle between Canada and the United States at the pool at the Tropicana. The public-address guy was my buddy Brent Musburger, who was best known for his work on *The NFL Today* on CBS. He'd just joined ABC.

Brent used to hold court at the pool every day. He was happy to do the announcing of our swim meet. It was a hoot. By the way, Brent is Brian Williams's hero and role model, and I told him so in Cuba. He felt quite honoured.

A bunch of my Canadians also did a little exhibition of synchronized swimming, and in case you were wondering, a substantial amount of beer was consumed before the show. It was hilarious—I wish we had taped it.

The days were long, but the spirit was great. We'd always end up back at the hotel at the end of the evening, sitting on the balcony, sipping beer. The Cuban people who worked for me also enjoyed the socializing.

As another aside, my daughter Laura arrived with the great cameraman Peter Allies. She was to shoot all the special features for CTV—quite a job for a young producer. Typical of CTV, she had been assigned no car, which made it impossible for her to work in Havana. As a good father should, I gave her my car and English-speaking driver—problem solved. Laura did a super job and I was very proud of her.

We did the closing ceremonies, during which Castro spoke for two hours, but that was no problem because this time we were prepared.

Hosting the eleventh Pan-American Games was a huge deal for President Castro and his country. "We have a sacred commitment to the Pan-American Games and we will honour it," Castro told a group of Western journalists, as reported by Michael Janofsky in the *New York Times*. "So the Pan-American Games have been given high priority and they will continue to enjoy a high priority."

All in all, it was a great Games for us. With the ABC and Turner guys, we stuck together and pulled it off without a hitch.

All told, some 4,519 athletes from thirty-nine countries participated in the Games in thirty-one different sports. Cuba emerged as an athletic powerhouse at the event, winning 140 gold medals, compared to 130 for the United States, and 22 for Canada. The Games will always be remembered for the friendship offered to visitors. Cuba really did itself proud.

When I saw how little people in Cuba had, I asked our crewmembers to consider helping them in any way they could. We had given each of the Canadian crewmembers a uniform to work in, and all of them gave the uniforms to the Cuban crewmembers. It was a small gesture, but the Cuban workers loved it. Each of the Canadians gave a Cuban a gift package—including all their clothing. I had brought my baseball glove with me, just in case we had an impromptu game against the Cubans, and I gave it to one of my Cuban production workers along with just about everything else I had with me—including all my clothes, my underwear, shaving stuff and toothpaste. He was married to one of the most famous television personalities in Cuba—the weather girl. I met her a couple of times. After the closing ceremonies I was about ninety minutes late getting back to my hotel, and she had been sitting there the entire time, waiting for her package.

That night, we had a closing party with the Cubans, and one of the boys who attended was the kid who had worked the end-zone camera for me. He was hilarious; a great kid named José, but he couldn't speak a lick of English. The guys in our crew said, "Don't worry, Ralph; we'll teach him."

Some teachers. He'd walk up to women and say, "Hello, do you want to see my monkey?" and a few other questionable things, too.

When we left, and gave them all the stuff we had at the party, José broke down and cried. He came over to me and hugged me and cried and cried because we were going home. Laura was there and said, "Isn't that something, Dad? José had lost his father just before the start of the Games, and I guess you have become like a father to him."

I was very touched.

When you do an event in a foreign country, it's always tough to leave, especially the people on your team that you know you'll probably never see again. I still think about José every now and then, and I wonder if he still walks around and asks tourists if they want to see his monkey.

Another thing I'll never forget about the trip to Cuba was this little three-legged dog that hung around outside the Tropicana. Every time we'd enter or leave the hotel, we'd see this mutt. He was always there, and our guys would feed him. The guys nicknamed him "Tripod." Jack Whitaker had brought his boat to Cuba and parked it at the Hemingway Marina, and when he left after the Games, he took Tripod with him. Everybody was delighted.

I said, "How can you take him? You don't have papers."

"Screw the papers! He's coming with me."

That's the type of guy Jack Whitaker is—one of a kind.

I'm not sure if Tripod was a defector or a victim of a kidnapping, but I am certain he was happy to be leaving. He finally found a home—with a legend.

Of all the Games I did, I'd say the Pan-American Games in Cuba were the most satisfying. It really proves that if you choose your crew carefully, you can accomplish anything. I knew going into the Games that I had to have amazing Canadians working for me, and I was proven right. Even in a strange land with another language, the crew came through brilliantly. I know we couldn't have pulled it off without them. Everything came off spotlessly.

Just before the 1996 Olympic Games in Atlanta, I was at the broadcast centre when the news came that Jack O'Hara, the ABC executive I worked with in Cuba, had been killed, along with his wife and family in a horrific air crash in Paris. They were on their way to a vacation in France.

Jack and I had shared many wonderful experiences at ABC, and the best, unquestionably, was Cuba.

Sadly, I have never been back to Cuba since. I did read about General Fernández as recently as the winter of 2009, so I presume he is alive and well. When Raul Castro took over running Cuba, General Fernández's name was mentioned as one of the cabinet. He'd be eighty-six years old now. Amazing man—I miss him.

I wonder if he ever found another source for peanut butter.

10

TALES FROM
THE WINTER OLYMPICS

There were times during my association with *Hockey Night in Canada* when I couldn't imagine myself doing anything else. I loved hockey and I loved my job. Life couldn't be any better.

But life can throw you a curve ball. And when it was time for me to leave *Hockey Night*, there was only one thing that could pry me away: the Olympic Games.

I had worked on hockey broadcasts for NBC and CBS in the United States, but I had never worked at ABC, so when I got a call from them telling me they needed somebody to do hockey at the 1976 Winter Olympics in Innsbruck, Austria, I was a little surprised.

It was about eight months before the Games and Geoff Mason, who later became ABC Sports' executive producer, told me they had their own producer, but they were looking for somebody to direct. I told him I had a lot of great directors working for me, but they were all busy with *Hockey Night in Canada*. I didn't like the idea of lending them out for two or three weeks to go and do the Olympics.

I told him, "It's helping you, but it's not helping me if I give you one of my top directors." Then I suggested, "I'll tell you what: I'll give you a hell of a hockey director."

Geoff asked who.

"Me."

I told him I had the directorial background to do the job and besides, I had never worked a Winter Olympics and the idea of working on the biggest sporting stage in the world really intrigued me.

I needed *Hockey Night in Canada*'s permission to direct for ABC, and there was no problem. Since ABC was the king of the hill in terms of sports broadcasting, Ted Hough and Frank Selke, my bosses, felt it was a feather in their cap to have one of their guys working the Games for an American network—but not CTV.

Of course, ABC wasn't going to hire me without checking me out. They called the NHL—Don Ruck, the vice-president of marketing for the league, and Bill Jennings, president of the New York Rangers—wondering if I could do the job. Thankfully, the reviews that came back were positive.

When it came to covering sports, ABC was the leading network in the world, and of course no expense would be spared if it meant putting on a top-notch show. In preparation for the Innsbruck Games, I was sent to a seminar in New York with some of the biggest names in the business—the likes of Frank Gifford and Curt Gowdy and Chris Schenkel. Howard Cosell, the biggest star at ABC, was also there. To be honest, it was quite a thrill for me to be rubbing shoulders with such stars.

Cosell, at the time, was arguably the biggest name in all of television. I walked up to him, and I could see the other guys in the background looking at me as if to say, "What the heck are you doing?"

I said, "I'm Ralph Mellanby from Canada and I'll be directing hockey in Innsbruck. In spite of the fact you have many detractors, you are the greatest thing on television."

He turned to me and very curtly said, "You name them! Name my detractors!"

I said, "The press."

"The press doesn't count."

A little stunned by this candid conversation, I turned and walked away. I never cared for him after that. His ego was too big. All I was trying to do was pay him a compliment. I think what ultimately led to his demise was the fact he got to thinking he was bigger than the network, and no network likes it that way.

I went to Innsbruck early, two weeks ahead of the start of the Games, to make sure things were being set up properly. It's a good thing I did, because a couple of the camera positions for hockey had been set up incorrectly. You really don't want to have to deal with things like that at the last minute. I made the appropriate changes.

Now, you might think that making adjustments to two cameras is no big deal. We were told it would cost $10,000 per camera, which in those days was a lot of money. ABC didn't blink. There's no way a Canadian broadcaster would have paid—we would have fought day and night to avoid paying such a high fee. I knew I was in the big time.

Furthermore, I was paid $25,000 for those three weeks of work, and that was enormous money. I was making around $50,000 a year in those days for my job at *Hockey Night*, and I certainly didn't tell *them* how much I was getting for the ABC assignment!

I had met Roone Arledge, the president of ABC Sports, at the seminar, so when I saw him in Innsbruck (I was the first director on site), I wandered up and asked him if there was anything I could do to help out before the Games began. I was eager to learn and just as eager to please—sometimes a little too eager, as it turned out.

He said, "I'd love you to do the helicopter shots. I need a director up there to get the aerial shots."

I smiled and said I'd do it, but inside I was asking myself, "What the hell have I gotten myself into?"

The helicopter was open on one side. I felt as though I was literally taking my life in my hands—I'd never been so scared. I had a list of things to shoot—old Innsbruck, the various venues, things of that nature. There was just me, the cameraman and the pilot, and as we zipped through the air, I was scared out of my mind. Every time the cameraman would go to take his shot, the pilot would tilt the helicopter to that side and I'd think I was going to fall out.

The cameraman, on the other hand, was great. He'd done lots of work for ABC and was a real cowboy in terms of tackling the assignment head on. His name was Pierre de Lespinois, and he won four Emmy Awards as a TV producer and director.

The next day, I was back at the broadcast centre and I bumped into Arledge, who put his arm around me and said, "Great job, Ralph, on those helicopter shots."

I was thinking to myself, I didn't do a damn thing except direct the cameraman what to shoot. Still, even though I had very little to do with them, I would go to the broadcast centre during the Games to watch the feeds go out, and every time I saw one of our helicopter shots I was really proud of them.

The nature of producing an event like this for television has really changed. Nowadays, you have a crewmember for just about everything. But back in 1976 there were just eight directors to work the entire Games, and I was one of them. There were just six producers. Today, there would be nearly thirty of each.

Because we were short-staffed, you often found yourself doing things you'd never done before. Arledge walked up to me one day and said, "Oh, by the way, I forgot to tell you: you're also doing speed skating."

I had never worked on speed skating in my life, and there I was splitting the chore with another director, Andy Sidaris, who admitted to me he didn't know a thing about directing the sport, either. The speed-skating oval was right outside the arena where I would be directing hockey, so we went over there and got a feel for what would be happening. Our announcer was Warner Wolf, who also didn't know a thing about speed skating. As it turned out, it wasn't too difficult. We survived.

The only problem we encountered was that Warner was so much shorter than his female colour commentator! When he was on camera, he had to stand on a box—and often fell off.

For hockey, ABC gave us Curt Gowdy as our play-by-play voice, and Brian Conacher was hired as colour analyst. Brian had done a marvellous job of broadcasting the 1972 Summit Series between Canada and Russia. Gowdy had done some play-by-play for the Boston Bruins many, many years earlier, though he was better known for baseball and football. I knew I'd have no problems with his work.

Not everybody on our crew was well versed in what we were trying to do. We had a rookie producer named Bobby Goodrich, who grew up in Texas and was a great high school and college football player. He had never produced the Winter Olympics and was a little unsure of what to do—and he knew *nothing* about hockey.

Bobby said, "I don't know anything about this fucking game so you're going to have to help me."

I said, "Okay, you can look after the replays."

He turned to me with a puzzled look on his face and said, "I wouldn't know *what* to replay!"

So I used him on the goalie isolation cameras and I picked all the other replays. I think Bobby picked three replays that actually made it to air. Boy, was he excited when he got that first one right.

When I met with my crew at the broadcast centre, I found out none of them had done hockey—they were the *Monday Night Football* gang—so I had to educate them. I thought, boy, am I in trouble here, but they were a great bunch of pros, so it all worked out.

The good news is we weren't covering every hockey game at the event. We only did the ones involving the United States, along with other important games. And in the early going, they weren't broadcast live. The network wanted to air hockey during specific time slots—not prime time, because the game wasn't big in the States, and besides, the U.S. team wasn't very good. The network would air five-minute segments of the games, and the announcers would record new voice-overs, using notes they had taken during the match.

One thing I'll never forget is the way Gowdy would pick Conacher's brain during meetings. He really respected Brian's knowledge of the game and would lean on him for information. Conacher was only too pleased to help. However, Gowdy would ask Brian about something specific from the game and then, when we went back to tape one of the segments, he would take the information he'd gotten from Conacher and present it as if it was his own. Conacher was caught with his pants down, having to react to Gowdy, who was spewing *his* thoughts out over the airwaves.

Brian was livid, but I told him, "Gowdy is the ultimate pro. He doesn't care how *you* look, he just wants to sound knowledgeable." Then I added, "If it bothers you, stop giving him your 'A' material."

So that's what he did. When we finally got to the live games, I told Conacher, "You know, Brian, you're getting better and better and Gowdy is getting worse." We both laughed.

One night, I went out one night for dinner with Schenkel, Gowdy and an American ski jumper named Art Devlin. Devlin had made five Olympic teams, but is best known for his heroics during World War II, when he flew fifty combat missions over Europe in a B-24 bomber, winning three Purple Hearts.

Devlin starts telling us a story about how he escaped from a prison camp during the war and ended up in Innsbruck.

"I walked into a little Austrian restaurant and they hid me and took care of me," he said.

I asked if he remembered where it was, and even though it was thirty-two years later, he said he did. So off we went to find the restaurant. We went down by the railroad yards to the worst part of town— the red-light district.

"There's the restaurant," Devlin said, and we all went in.

It turned out to be a whorehouse! We had one beer and we left. The funniest thing was when he looked at us and said, "Wow, it really hasn't changed much."

Another night, I went to watch Arledge work with the feeds going back to the USA, hoping to pick up some tips from a master. Innsbruck is, like Hamilton, Ontario, an industrial city, and there is a place in the mountains outside the city called Seefeld in Tirol. Every time Roone would show a scenic shot, you'd see either Seefeld or the old part of town, which was quite historic, but you never really saw Innsbruck downtown. On about the third night I asked Roone why he never broadcast any shots of the city itself.

"Perception is reality, Ralph," he said to me. "This is *my* Innsbruck. And this is the Innsbruck people back home want to see—not the factories and the mills."

From that I learned that it's all about pleasing the audience, and if you stretch the truth a little bit, it's not always as bad thing.

I got more than a paycheque for my efforts; I learned the ABC way of doing things, and it served me well when I went back to work in Canada.

There are some directors who are yellers and screamers. I think those people make crews nervous and unable to do their jobs to the best of their ability. Me, I lay out my instructions before we get started, making my expectations very clear, and I let the people I have hired do their jobs.

Julius Barnathan, the vice-president of engineering for ABC Sports, came up to me after the Games and told me I was the first director he'd ever had whose voice required him to turn the volume on the intercom up instead of down—because all the other directors yelled!

As for the hockey, it really wasn't very memorable. Canada didn't send a team to Innsbruck—these were the second consecutive Olympics in which Canada refused to compete, having pulled out of international competition in 1970 to protest not being able to use professional players. Canada always insisted that while the powerful Russians were considered amateurs, the reality was that playing hockey provided them with their livelihood, which made them de facto pros.

The Russians won their fourth consecutive gold medal, winning all five of their games in the medal round by a combined score of 40–11. The United States, meanwhile, placed fifth, after winning just two of five games and being outscored 21–15. Bob Dobek was their leading scorer, with 3 goals and 4 assists for 7 points. Be honest: have you ever heard of Bob Dobek?

The Soviet Union won the most medals at the Games, claiming thirteen gold, six silver, and eight bronze. Austrian skier Franz Klammer, who won the men's downhill, defeating the favourite, Bernhard Russi of Switzerland, dominated the headlines. Dorothy Hamill of the United States captured the gold medal for figure skating, and at the same time made quite a fashion statement with her "wedge" haircut.

Within weeks, girls all over the world copied her look. Meanwhile, Soviet speed skater Tatyana Averina won four medals.

I was very fortunate to be nominated for my first Emmy Award for our coverage of the Games, so when the Stanley Cup playoffs ended in Philadelphia that season, I hopped on a plane for Los Angeles, where the awards ceremony was being held. This is something most people in television only dream of, but rarely have the opportunity to experience, so it was a little surreal for me. Janet was all dolled up in a long dress and I was wearing a tuxedo as we joined the others from ABC at a cocktail party before the ceremony. This was before the sports Emmys were spun off into a different show, so everybody was there. I must say, as a Canadian kid I felt pretty special.

Roone Arledge walked up and told Janet, "I'd like to welcome you to Los Angeles and the Emmy Awards. Thank you for lending your husband to us." What a wonderful gesture on his part, recognizing the sacrifice Janet had made while I was away for five weeks.

Janet made no bones about the fact she wanted her hubby to win. She had her legs, feet, *and* fingers crossed when it came time for our category to be presented. It worked!

When they announced that we were the winners, everybody jumped up from their table in an effort to be first to get to the stage. I was the first Canadian to ever win an Emmy for sports, and the guy who handed me my Emmy was O.J. Simpson. It kind of creeps me out thinking about that now. He was working for ABC at the time, and ABC broadcast the Emmys. Years later, I was at a convention in Miami. I was sitting on the porch at a golf course, having breakfast, and who should be sitting beside me but O.J. and some of his friends. This was long after the murder of his wife, Nicole, and her friend Ronald Goldman.

My daughter said, "Why don't you go over and say hello to him?"

"I wouldn't say hello to that son of a bitch if you paid me," was my response.

He was limping and looked to be in pretty bad shape, which actually made me feel kind of good. But I digress.

After we were presented with our awards, we were whisked back-stage, and before I knew it, there was a charming young woman standing there with her hand out, demanding I give the Emmy back to her. I was shocked, and totally unaware that this is just part of the procedure. They hand out the same Emmys over and over again, and later they engrave the "real" ones and simply send yours to you. Talk about taking the wind out of my sails. I didn't want to hand it back—but ultimately I did.

Next, we were taken to an elevator that would hoist us to the next floor, where we met with the press, who were watching the show on TV monitors in a huge room. Naturally, my American cohorts bar-relled into the first available elevator, leaving me stranded behind. No worries, I thought to myself, I'll just catch the next ride. Besides, who the heck is going to want to interview me?

As I waited, the cast from *The Mary Tyler Moore Show* came over because they had just won their Emmys, so I got to ride with them. There I was, in an elevator with Ed Asner, Ted Knight, Gavin MacLeod, Valerie Harper, and Mary Tyler Moore herself. Sometimes it pays to be left behind, especially when, in close quarters, you are squeezed up to Mary Tyler Moore.

To top things off, when I finally got to the interview room, the other ABC guys were standing around with nobody talking to them—and the Canadian media descended upon me! I looked at the other guys and said, "See, it pays to be Canadian." I don't think Chet Forte and Don Ohlmeyer, two top directors at ABC Sports, were too impressed.

Later, I went to the after-party, where they seat you with anybody and everybody. If you are nominated for an Emmy, regardless of whether you win or not, you get an invite to the party, and it lasts until about four in the morning. It just so happened that Scotty Connal, my pal and executive producer at NBC Sports, sat at my table, a table for twelve. He had been nominated many times, but this was his first Emmy win. We laughed because I won my first time out. I got one of the biggest thrills of my life when I got to dance with Dorothy Hamill. She didn't know who the hell I was, but it was a dance I'll never forget. We met in 1980 in Lake Placid, where she was a special guest, and she pretended to remember our last encounter. Thanks, Dorothy.

I was emotionally wiped, having just covered the Stanley Cup final. Janet, on the other hand, was wide-eyed, loving every second we spent in La-La Land. In those days, I was always working, so she was home and watching a lot of entertainment television. Now here she was mingling, with the stars. It was a thrill beyond belief for her.

I found myself sitting beside this guy I didn't recognize, and he asked me what I'd won for. I told him it was for my coverage of the Olympics, and he seemed genuinely thrilled for me. He then told me he was nominated for best supporting actor, but he didn't win. We kept talking, and it was clear he was quite a sports fan. Typical of me, I was focused on myself and not really clueing in to whom I was speaking.

Finally, I said, "I'm Ralph Mellanby from Canada."

"Hi, Ralph, I'm Henry Winkler."

There I was, sitting beside the biggest star in television, "The Fonz," and I didn't know it! But my wife, Janet, did. I had never seen his show, *Happy Days*. But Janet was all over him afterwards, as she and the kids were huge fans.

As Janet and I were leaving, he gave me his business card and said that if we were ever in Los Angeles and wanted to attend a taping of the show, he'd arrange it for me. The next year I took our kids, Scott and Laura, to L.A. and Disneyland during a baseball trip, and I called Henry at home.

He treated us like gold. He introduced us to everybody backstage, and we were put in the front row of the grandstand while they taped. You know the old story—how people say, "We'll keep in touch"? Well, I've never seen him since, but I can say he was absolutely marvellous to us. Today, I am still his biggest fan.

* * *

Shooting the CFL for CTV with Alouettes Jim Andreotti and George Dixon.

—Courtesy CFCF-MTL

My favourite building—the Saddle-dome in Calgary. —Mellanby Collection

My doctorate from the University of Windsor. —Mellanby Collection

The *Pinbusters* show with Al Shaver.   —*Courtesy CFCF-MTL*

Saturday Night at the Races with announcers Albert Trottier and Al Shaver.

—*Courtesy CFCF-MTL*

Ralph and George
Stroumbolopoulos on *The Hour.*
—Courtesy CBC

Scott Mellaby, at age five, with my friend
Jean Beliveau on Scott's first trip to the
Forum in Montreal. —Mellanby Collection

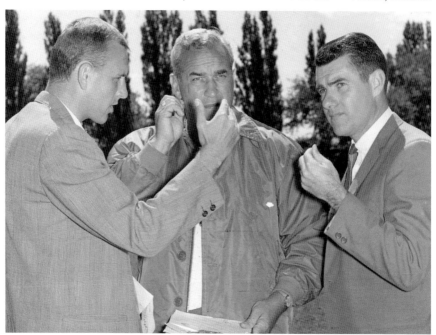

Directing the *Jim Trimble Show* with Dick Irvin and the legendary football
coach. —Courtesy CTV

Scott Mellanby playing for Canada at the World Junior Tournament in Hamilton.
—Courtesy Hockey Canada

The great Canadian all-star team of producers and directors for the 1988 Calgary Olympics.
—Courtesy CTV

The *Hockey Night in Canada* brass at an NHL function. Left to right: vice-president Frank Selke Jr., Ralph, president Ted Hough, and senior producer Dan Wallce. —Mellanby Collection

Howie Meeker coaching at *Pro-Tips*. —Courtesy *Pro-Tips*

The first Calgary Flames game at the Corral. This promotional shot has Danny Gallivan on the horse.

—Courtesy the Calgary Flames

Ralph and Bobby Orr.

—Mellanby Collection

Ralph at the base of the downhill in Kananaskis, Alberta.

—Mellanby Collection

The 1985 Stanley Cup finals production crew. Left to right: Ralph, Chris
Cuthbert, Don Wittman, John Davidson, director Larry Brown, Howie
Meeker, associate producer Steve Lansky, and producer John Shannon.

My great baseball team, Don
Chevrier and Tony Kubek with the
Blue Jays.

Ralph and Calgary '88 president,
the late Bill Pratt.

NHL tennis team. Left to right: John Ziegler, Ralph, Frank Mahovlich, and Václav Nedomansky.
—Mellanby Collection

Ralph being interviewed by Brian Williams.
—Mellanby Collection

In the announcers' booth at the Forum: Dick Irvin and Jean Beliveau.

Famous Chicago Cub pitcher Ferguson Jenkins with Dick Irvin.

In Hollywood—my first Emmy with my buddy, the executive producer of NBC Sports, Scotty Connal. —Courtesy ABC

My family at Expos' spring training with Rusty "Le Grand Orange" Staub.
—Mellanby Collection

Another *Pro-Tips* gang. Left to right: Larry Boschman, Guy Lafleur, Bobby Smith, Larry Robinson, Kevin McCarthy, Dave Christian, goalie Don Edwards, Al McNeil, and Howie Meeker. —Courtesy *Pro-Tips*

Frank Selke, Ralph, and Danny Gallivan. —Courtesy *Hockey Night in Canada*

Ralph and Hall of Famer Steve Shutt after playing tennis at the Boulevard
Club in Toronto. —Mellanby Collection

Another tennis friend, Frank Mahovlich. —Mellanby Collection

A favourite player—Captain Kevin McCarthy of the Canucks.

Shooting the *Bobby Hull Story* in Jamaica.

Ralph in the Olympic control centre in Atlanta.　　　　　　—Mellanby Collection

A *Grapevine* publicity photo.　　　　　　—Courtesy Don Cherry

The French (Radio Canada) production team for *La soirée du hockey*. Left to right: Bert Vinson, Neil Leger, Ralph, François Carignan, and Jacques Berube.
—Courtesy Radio Canada

Doing a dinner gig with my pal, former great Leaf, Jim McKenny.
—Mellanby Collection

Ralph and 1980 Team USA captain, Mike Eurizone in Lake Placid.

—Mellanby Collection

NHL fantasy camp game day. Our group included (far left) Jim McKenny, (centre) Mats Sundin, (third from right) Wendel Clark, and (far right) Doug Gilmour.

—Courtesy Bob Lavelle

It's widely regarded as the greatest sporting accomplishment of all time: Team USA's astonishing gold-medal victory in hockey at the 1980 Winter Olympics. And it happened on home ice, in Lake Placid, New York.

Even *Sports Illustrated*, which doesn't cover a lot of hockey, bought into the hype. "It may be the single most indelible moment in all of U.S. sports history; one that sent an entire nation into a frenzy," the magazine wrote of the Miracle on Ice.

In my first book, *Walking with Legends*, I wrote in detail about my exploits as a producer for ABC at the Lake Placid Games, the single most memorable moment being when we missed the shot of Team USA goalie Jim Craig, an American flag draped over his shoulders after his team beat Finland 4–2 to cinch the gold medal, searching desperately in the stands for his father. One of our ace cameramen, Al Mountford, saved the day by capturing the unforgettable sequence, enabling us to show it on tape mere seconds after it happened.

You weren't supposed to insert taped material into a live broadcast in those days, but there was no way in hell I was going to pass up the chance to broadcast this extraordinary moment that remains etched on the minds of all of those who saw it.

"Great shot, Ralph!" Roone Arledge bellowed into my headset, "That's the shot of the Lake Placid Games!"

And it was an Emmy-Award-winning shot.

The hockey team was indeed *the* story of the Lake Placid Games; a bunch of overmatched, no-name college Davids pulling the carpet out from under a slick team of Russian Goliaths. At the time, the Americans didn't have a chance at a medal, at least in my opinion. Play-by-play announcer Al Michaels and colour commentator Ken Dryden agreed with me, and so, apparently, did ABC, which elected not to cover Team USA's games live.

I will forever admire the team's accomplishment, but I do not look back as fondly on their leader and coach.

As far as my television work was concerned, I found Herb Brooks extremely difficult to deal with. Team Canada, which by now was back on the Olympic hockey scene, was much more accommodating. Those in charge of the Canadian program seemed to understand what we, as television people, were up against and trying to accomplish.

I completely understand Herb's predicament, with a team that faced a monumental task, and it was important to protect them, to a degree, to keep them focused on their mission. And you certainly can't argue with the results.

That said, in speaking with others who have had dealings with Herb, his behaviour in Lake Placid was very typical. He was, simply, a difficult man. A great coach, to be sure, but from a TV point of view, a major pain in the butt.

If you watch the splendid movie *Miracle*, you see veteran actor Kurt Russell doing a bang-on job of portraying the single-minded Brooks, who put everything in his life, including his family, on hold in pursuit of his dream. Oh well, I guess if his family had to deal with his relentless drive, I shouldn't really complain.

That said, I wasn't coaching or playing hockey. I was trying my best to provide quality television.

Seldom does everything work out perfectly at such a huge undertaking as an Olympic Games. Lake Placid was no exception.

As far as I was concerned, Lake Placid had no business hosting the 1980 Winter Olympic Games. The small town (population 2,600) in upstate New York got them by default. There had been only one other bidder, Vancouver and Garibaldi in British Columbia, but they withdrew before the vote could be held. The town had staged them in 1932, when only eight sports were contested, but the Winter Olympics had grown immensely in the intervening forty-eight years.

When I arrived ten days before the Games in an effort to get the lay of the land, I had a feeling this wasn't going to be a smooth-running operation, particularly for fans attending the Games. In fact, it turned out to be a disaster for fans.

There weren't nearly enough hotel rooms, and transportation was unimaginably disorganized. If you missed the bus destined for your hotel after attending an event, you had no way to get back to your room—assuming you were lucky enough to have a room.

The restaurants were packed, so it was extremely difficult to get a meal. I was lucky in that ABC had rented the restaurant in our hotel. Also, Calgary House opened its doors to me. The folks from Calgary had a contingent there because they were bidding for the 1988 Games, and the delegates went out of their way to make me feel comfortable. But ordinary people had very few options.

To give you an idea of what we were up against at the venues, the guy who ran the Olympic arena was also the local barber. This was the guy I had to deal with—and I didn't need a haircut. I couldn't seem to get him to co-operate, and to get the best coverage of an event like hockey, you really need the arena staff in your corner. It was as though he was going out of his way to be difficult. With all the pressure I was under, I certainly didn't need some small-town arena operator standing in my way.

Finally, I met with the guy and asked him exactly what the hell his problem was.

"I don't have one pin from ABC," he angrily informed me.

You must understand, collecting pins at the Olympics is an event itself. You have no idea the lengths some people will go to to collect as many pins as they can. This guy was going to disrupt my broadcasts simply because he didn't have one of our pins.

I called over to the broadcast centre and got a hold of Marvin Bader, Arledge's assistant, and asked him to send me over as many pins as he could. Once this gentleman got pins for himself and his crew and his Zamboni driver, he was putty in my hands.

There were still some fun and games to be had. The night before the final game between the U.S. and Finland, Al Mountford, our Canadian cameraman, knocked at my door at 1 a.m. There were always beautiful girls stranded in the lobby of our hotel, and he had two of the most gorgeous women I have ever seen on his arms.

"Ralph," he said, "these girls have nowhere to sleep tonight, so I'm taking one and you take the other."

I told Al we had the big game tomorrow. Forget it! As I drifted off to sleep, I thought to myself, now *that's* dedication to your job.

The flip side of being in a small village is that you get to bump into just about everybody at one time or another. I enjoyed that aspect of it.

Team USA stole the spotlight at the Lake Placid Games, but American speed skater Eric Heiden was a close second when he became the first individual to win five gold medals at one Games. He won the 500-, 1,000-, 1,500-, 5,000- and 10,000-metre races, not to mention the hearts of Americans, setting four Olympic records and one world record in the process.

From where we were staying, we could see the speed-skating oval because it was outside at the local high school. We had a bird's-eye view of the proceedings.

I went back years later, in 2005, for a visit. The arena looked just the same, as did everything else. It was still a little village. I was in the Olympic museum, looking at the exhibits, and a guy walked up to me and told me he was the curator. I told him who I was and his eyes opened wide.

"I've been waiting years and years to meet you," he informed me. "Why?"

"Do you remember the night a guy cleaned your compound outside the arena and cut three camera cables?"

"Sure I do."

"That was me. I was a kid in college and my job was to clean up around the arena. I didn't mean to cut your cables. It was an accident."

We managed to get new cables, but it sure gave us a scare. He gave me a souvenir T-shirt and hat from the museum.

* * *

Sarajevo, host city of the 1984 Winter Games, was such a beautiful place. I have always regretted that it was the one time I didn't make a pre-Games scouting trip. I imagine if I had, I would have learned so much more about this historic and spectacular place. Talk about a missed opportunity.

ABC hired me once again to produce hockey, and I was well ensconced with the network at that time—that summer, they used me to direct basketball at the Olympics in Los Angeles.

Before I arrived in Sarajevo, I did a little homework about Yugoslavia just so I wouldn't land unprepared. It is one of the most multi-ethnic places I've ever been to, with Muslims, Turks, Serbs, Christians, Croats, and more. Ironically, I sent my wife a card from Sarajevo, and on it I wrote: "This is the one place in the world where there won't be trouble. Everybody lives in harmony here regardless of his or her religious beliefs."

The first couple of days there, I wandered around to get my bearings. I was astonished. They have a market, and on one street you could buy gold trinkets and on the next it would be silver jewellery and another street it might be bronze baubles. They were called the streets of gold, silver, and bronze. What better place to hold the Olympics?

I went down to a part of town where they had replicas of two footprints in cement and a plaque where Archduke Franz Ferninand had been shot, the event that triggered World War I. They say a guy got drunk in a bar, wandered out into the streets and stumbled upon the Archduke, whose convoy was lost. The drunk shot Franz Ferdinand—and started a world war.

The whole place had such an air of mystery to it. If you walked into a pub, you'd be greeted with a haze of smoke, and through it you would see three tables and a bar in a mostly darkened setting. You would almost expect Humphrey Bogart to appear from out of nowhere as you sat there and sipped your beer.

The first thing I noticed when I went to the broadcast centre was this huge pile of snow across the street. I asked a local what it was, and I was informed it was where all the locals were told to park their cars. They were only allowed to travel by taxi while the Olympics were on. All those with private cars were told to stay off the roads, and when it snowed, the cars were buried. Talk about sacrifice.

It was a great Olympics because of the ambience of the city. Each morning, you were awakened by the sounds of the church bells as well as chanting from the mosques. Our crew stayed outside the city, which made it even more romantic for me. The Austrians had built a park on the outskirts of Sarajevo that had deer and rabbits running through it. There were three Austrian hotels there, and I stayed in the main building. I ran into Roone Arledge and he said, "Guess which suite I got?"

Turns out he got the Archduke's room—the one he stayed in before he was assassinated. I went up to the room to take a peek at it because it had such historical significance, especially for me, since my grandfather and uncle fought in the First World War. It's impossible to put into words how it feels to be inside such a room.

One of the big thrills of staying in that park was the fact I was able to get up and run every morning with Peggy Fleming, the famous figure skater. Peggy was a five-time U.S. champion, three-time world champion, and the 1968 Olympic gold medallist who was working as a commentator for ABC. I saw her coming back from a run one morning and she mentioned to me that she ran every day—then asked if I'd like to join her. Of course I would. I never missed a morning jog. She was so beautiful. Being a typical Canadian male, I always ran behind her. What a great view to start the morning!

That year we added Mike Eruzione, who had captained the Miracle on Ice team four years earlier, to our broadcast crew. "Miracle Mike" was a happy-go-lucky guy who added another dimension to our broadcast. People love to hear intelligent analysis from somebody who has been there. On top of that, I could go out for dinner with him and not feel totally confused by the conversation, the way I did when I went out with Ken Dryden. Ken was in the booth again. He and I used to go downtown together a lot, where all they seemed to serve was pizza. If I remember correctly, I always paid for the pizza. You owe me one, Kenny. Al Michaels did the play-by-play, but he was a big star by now so he didn't want to go out to dinner with me anymore.

We broadcast from two arenas: the Skenderija Sports Hall, which opened in the late 1960s, and the Zetra Arena, built specifically for the games. In a sad footnote, the Zetra Arena was all but destroyed eight years later by shelling during the Bosnian War. The wooden seats were used to make coffins for war casualties, and the surviving parts of the structure were pressed into service as a morgue. The nearby Koševo Stadium, where the opening and closing ceremonies were held in the winter of 1984, was used as a graveyard. Although it took many years, the stadium and arena were rebuilt. The latter reopened in 2004.

The hockey at the 1984 Games was rather uneventful, as the Russians, featuring the likes of goalie Vladislav Tretiak and skaters Alexei Kasatonov, Igor Larionov, Sergei Makarov, and Vladimir Krutov, won the gold medal easily. They won all five of their games in the preliminary round, then swept the medal round. In seven matches, they outscored their opposition 48–5.

The Americans, coming off their miraculous win four years earlier, placed seventh. Is it merely a coincidence that both of their gold medals (Squaw Valley in 1960 and Lake Placid in 1980) have been won on U.S. soil? The Czechs claimed the silver while Sweden took the bronze medal.

The Canadian team, coached by Dave King, featured a number of players who would go on to varying levels of success in the NHL: J.J. Daigneault, Bruce Driver, Doug Lidster, James Patrick, Russ Courtnall, Kevin Dineen, Patrick Flatley, Dave Gagner, Kirk Muller, Dave Tippett, and Carey Wilson. They defeated the Americans, Finns, Austrians, and Norwegians, but were shut out 4–0 by Czechoslovakia in the final game of the opening round. In the medal round, they were also shut out by the Russians (4–0) and Swedes (2–0). They ended up ranking fourth.

The 1984 Winter Olympics were notable in that they were the first Games to be held under the presidency of Juan Antonio Samaranch. Also, Jure Franko won Yugoslavia's first-ever Winter Olympics medal, capturing silver in the giant slalom. Ice dancers Jayne Torvill and Christopher Dean of the United Kingdom made a huge impact, earning perfect marks of 6.0 for artistic impression in the free dance, something no skaters before or since have accomplished.

This would turn out to be the one Olympics for which I didn't win an Emmy, yet at the same time I have a great fondness for the 1984 Games because Sarajevo was simply so beautiful. I felt a little sad when it was time to leave, and swore I'd return one day. I have yet to do so. That's life, I guess.

Still, I have so many fond memories. I nicknamed my driver Niki Lauda because of his mad, high-speed driving. The cook who worked at our hotel—her name was Pearl—was a doctor. All kinds of professionals helped out in whatever capacity they could during the Games, just to be a part of history. Pearl was a beautiful woman who one day asked me to join her for a little shopping excursion. She had $500 that she wanted to spend in the international store, but locals weren't allowed to shop there. I took her into the store, showed the people my passport and bought all the things she wanted. She was delighted.

Half of my crew was Yugoslavian. They were great people. Today, I can't help but wonder how many of them survived the war. Just another sad aspect of what happened after those Games.

Although I met many sporting legends through my work at various Winter Olympics, it was my friendship with a most unlikely musician that I cherish most fondly.

When I arrived in Sarajevo, I was fit to be tied. I was tired and a little grumpy, having worked the NHL All-Star Game in New Jersey immediately before boarding a plane for Sarajevo. It was a terrible flight. And when we arrived, they put everybody's luggage on the runway, and we had to find our own bags. There were hundreds of ABC bags, with nametags that all looked alike. There were upwards of two hundred people wandering around looking for their luggage, when finally our boss, Roone Arledge, told us just to grab a couple of bags each and we'd sort things out at the hotel.

We were further held up because broadcaster Keith Jackson didn't have the proper credentials. All in all, it was a miserable experience and I couldn't wait to get to my room to relax.

It was ten o'clock at night when I got into my room, and the first thing I heard was music blaring from the room beside me. I'm thinking, what the hell is this? At the Olympics, everyone works on different schedules, at all hours, so you're expected to be mindful of your neighbours. In other words, keep the bloody noise down.

I walked into the room, grabbed my bag and whipped it against the wall. It made a heck of a racket. Next thing I knew, there was a quiet tapping at my door, and when I open it, there was a little fellow standing there, kind of squinting at me with a big smile on his face. He said, "Hi, neighbour. I'm in the room next door."

"Are you the son of a bitch who's playing the loud music?" I asked.

He looked at me with a big smile and said, "Yeah, I need to play my music."

I said, "Have you ever been to the Olympics before? Because here are the rules: no music before 9 a.m. and no music after 9 p.m. That is the rule between you and me. And if you don't follow that rule, I'll kick the shit out of you!"

I paused and added, very pompously, "I'm Ralph Mellanby, the hockey producer for ABC."

He looked up at me, stuck out his hand and said, "Hi, neighbour, I'm John Denver."

Turns out ABC had hired Denver to do some work on the Olympics. I was a huge John Denver fan, but because it was so late and he wasn't wearing his signature round glasses, I hadn't recognized him.

He said, "You seem to have had a tough day; how would you like a nice Tuborg beer?"

He grabbed a couple of beers, sat down on my bench, and that night marked the beginning of a lifelong friendship.

When all the NHL general managers arrived, I invited the likes of Cliff Fletcher, Bill Torrey, and Glen Sather over to our hotel one night and asked John to come down to just meet them. He brought his guitar and entertained us for ninety minutes. It was amazing!

The following year, CBC covered the World Skiing Championship in Aspen, Colorado, where Denver lived. The TV people saw him sitting in a bar in Aspen and walked up to him with a proposal. They mentioned they were all friends of mine and then asked if he'd tape an opening welcoming the TV crew to Aspen.

He said, "It'll cost you."

They knew right away they probably couldn't afford his asking price, but were pleasantly surprised when John said, "That'll be one Tuborg, please."

I have so many great memories of Sarajevo. Someday I'll go back—I promise!

* * *

The 1998 Winter Olympics in Calgary represented another great highlight in my career. It was the most ambitious project I undertook during my career in television.

I was put in charge of producing the world feed—or as they call it, the host broadcast—for all the events. I was named executive producer and, after twenty years with *Hockey Night in Canada*, left the show for good.

The host broadcaster has to do nearly everything for the visiting broadcasters. In other words, if you are watching a hockey game in Moscow or Beijing, you would see the same video, but with announcers from the home country. This time, it wouldn't be a matter of showing up to the Games a few weeks in advance to get my bearings, then relying on my experience and instincts to carry me through.

On the contrary, I was in for five intensive years of preparing for this monstrous, yet very flattering assignment. It was a total commitment that required me to move to Calgary in 1985. There are only two or three guys in the world who are qualified to do this job, and as a result of this experience, I happen to be one of them. I did the same thing afterwards in Barcelona and Atlanta. It was the Calgary Games that put me on the Olympic trail full time and gained me a worldwide reputation.

When the offer came, I was quite content working at *Hockey Night* and doing the Olympics as a hired gun for the American networks, as a producer or director. It never occurred to me the Olympics would become the focus of my working life.

Well, the phone rang one day and it was my pal Peter Sisam, the vice-president of sales and marketing for CTV. We had a rather strange and mysterious conversation, and at the end of it I felt as though I had just spoken with a spy. Right off the bat, Peter told me our conversation was confidential, then informed me that his network had won the competition to be the host broadcaster for the Calgary Games, which was a huge coup, considering the sports infrastructure the CBC had at its disposal.

I didn't know this at the time, but I found out later that ABC had told CTV, "You'd better get Mellanby, because we've invested a lot of money in our coverage and we don't believe you have the people capable of doing the job."

So of course I was flattered to be chosen, but had I known about that call, I probably would have asked for a lot more money!

Shortly afterward, I got a call from Pip Wedge, another CTV veteran who had been my executive producer when I was doing variety television at CFCF, and he delivered the same message: the network was very interested in having me join them as executive producer for the world feed.

To be honest, I wasn't convinced I was qualified. I had done Olympic basketball and hockey, but that was all. I had a basic understanding of the infrastructure, but I also knew there was plenty I still had to learn. After all, this was a massive undertaking. Besides, I had just signed a long-term contract with *Hockey Night*—and I had never broken a contract.

At the same time, I knew it was a dream job that would put me on the world stage. It was a huge step up for me and I knew it could lead to me doing more Olympics in the same capacity.

The funny thing was, I kept saying no to CTV because of the deal I had just signed with *Hockey Night*. Then Murray Chercover, the president of the network, called me and invited me to come see him. I told him I didn't think it was a good idea—again, because I was already under contract.

"Besides," I said, using an old negotiating ploy to drive up my price, "I don't think you can afford me."

I was already scheduled to work on the Games on a freelance basis for ABC, so it wasn't as though I would miss out on Calgary if I turned them down—I would just keep doing what I had in the past.

Eventually, I told Chercover the only way he'd ever get me would be to go to my boss, Ted Hough, and convince him to release me from my contract. Little did I know it was already in the works. Chercover and Hough got together and made it happen. The deal they made, between the two of them, was that I would do both jobs for one year. I'd have an office in Calgary, where I would begin preparations for the Calgary Games, and at the same time I would continue to do *Hockey Night*, all the while grooming my successor, Don Wallace, who wound up lasting just two years on the job. (Guess I was a tough act to follow.)

I came home and told my wife, Janet, and her initial response was, "You mean you're going to get two salaries? Wow!"

It turns out the budget had already been set, and strictly speaking, CTV *couldn't* meet my price. I ended up being paid by two separate entities—by CTV directly and out of the host broadcaster budget—to make sure I got what I contracted for. Plus, I was still getting paid by *Hockey Night* that first year.

I settled into my new job quite nicely. I had an office at CTV in Toronto on Charles Street in addition to the one in Calgary, and quite frankly, I was used to juggling two or three things at once—I'd produced baseball and hockey simultaneously—so that didn't bother me. It was the way I was brought up in television. I could handle the heavy lifting.

Making the task easier was the fact that I had friends in Calgary—Cliff Fletcher, the general manager of the Flames, was a great friend, and my pal Glen Sather had his place in Banff and allowed me to rent his coach house for five years.

I love working on projects where you start with a clean page. As usual, I stumbled and bumbled around, making mistakes along the way, but I was determined to get the best coverage, the best mobile units, the best technicians—this was going to be an all-star Canadian Olympics. I was going to make it the best Winter Olympics ever.

And as it turned out, I got what I wanted across the board. CTV wasn't loaded with talent, so I was able to recruit people from other networks to work freelance for me. I got Jim Thompson, for instance, was had been vice-president of TSN, to come out of retirement and produce alpine skiing for me. I got John Shannon for hockey—at that point he was working at TSN, though he would later take my former job as executive producer of *Hockey Night*. As my senior producer, I hired Doug Beeforth, who had been at *Hockey Night in Canada*, but only after he resigned. It was a principle of mine that I wouldn't raid my old show.

CTV knew this was a golden opportunity for the network and was prepared to do whatever it took to make the Games a huge success. I walked into Douglas Bassett's office at CFTO—he was the power behind the throne at CTV—and had one of the shortest meetings I have ever been involved in.

He said, "You can have whatever you want from CFTO."

So I got Gerry Rochon, their executive producer and an old pal of mine, to handle the opening ceremonies. It was also my daughter Laura's first big TV assignment. Just out of college, Laura worked as a production assistant on figure skating, and my brother Jim was one of the hockey producers.

It was a masterpiece of Canadiana, the way all of Canadian broadcasting—private, public, over-the-air, and cable—pulled together to help me. One of the strengths I brought to the table was the fact that I had worked with the majority of the people we brought in to do the Games—I wasn't just a CTV guy. People around the world, after the Calgary Games, said we had set the bar higher than ever before.

As I travelled around the world in the years to come, all the broadcasters I met said the Calgary Games were the best ever.

Everything worked; there wasn't a glitch. And you have to understand the broadcasters and reporters are the only guys who go from
Games to Games, so they know what they are talking about.

The late Bill Pratt was the president of the Calgary Olympic
Organizing Committee, and talk about a character. This guy
marched to his own drummer, and believe me when I tell you, everybody fell right into place behind him.

I had met him years before when he used to run the Calgary
Stampede. He was such a presence. Bill always wore cowboy boots
and a cowboy hat, which the International Olympic Committee
hated him for—it didn't fit their image.

I was in Calgary working a Flames game for *Hockey Night* one
night, and Doug Mitchell, my friend who would later run the
Canadian Football League, told me, "You've got to meet this guy."
Doug told me Bill was building the Saddledome, and at this stage it
was just a hole in the ground.

"You'll be doing *HNIC* out of there, so it's an opportunity for you
to have a say in where the camera positions will be and other things
that will affect your broadcast," Mitchell said.

I went up to Bill's office, and there was a model of the Saddledome
sitting in the middle of the room. He wasn't the president of the
Olympic committee yet; he was just building the Saddledome.

Doug introduced me, and Bill just said, "Yeah, yeah, yeah." He
couldn't have been less interested in Ralph Mellanby. Doug went
into a spiel about how I wanted to have *HNIC* in the Saddledome and
Bill said, "Let's stop the bullshit. I don't need some hotshot from the
east coming out here telling me how to build my stadium."

Doug was mortified.

I said, "Never mind, Doug. Mr. Pratt, I'll tell you something.
There are *two* reasons why I should have some input here. For
starters, I know more about televising sports and camera locations
than anybody in this country."

"Okay," he said. "What's the second thing?"

"I'm doing this for nothing."

He smiled and said, "I like the second reason."

So I ended up being a consultant on the construction of the Saddledome and, true to my word, I did it for free. I got the cameras where I wanted them for all events, and since I knew it would be built as a multipurpose facility, I put cameras all over the building. By the time I got the job on the Olympics, Bill was the new president of the organizing committee. He and I ended up having a great relationship, and I felt good about that because Bill did not impress easily— at least, he never gave me a single compliment throughout the project. Later, I found out I was part of a big club in that regard.

Juan Antonio Samaranch, who was the president of the International Olympic Committee from 1980 to 2001, sent a note that he was coming to Calgary and he was to be referred to as "Your Excellency." Talk about being full of yourself. Pratt shook his head and said, "This guy is the head of a sports agency—that's all. There's no damn way I'm calling him 'Your Excellency.' He's not royalty. Who the hell does he think he is? Anybody who calls him 'Your Excellency' is fired!"

And he meant it. Bill Pratt wasn't about to kiss anybody's ass.

I remember him sitting there, with his cowboy boots up on his big mahogany desk, and he said to me, "Ralph, I want you to remember one thing. You're doing this and I'm doing this for several reasons. Number one is we're doing it for Canada. Number two is we're doing it for Alberta. Number three, we're doing it for Calgary. So fuck the IOC. These bastards will never come back here after the Games are over."

And he was right. They never came back, and they absolutely detested Bill Pratt because he wouldn't stand for their crap. It's one of the things I admired most about him.

I had an idea for the opening ceremonies that would make them stand out. I said to Bill, "When we light the Olympic torch, why don't we light up the Calgary Tower at the same time?"

In the back of my mind, I figured the idea would get shot down immediately because there's only supposed to be one Olympic flame, but it was worth a shot.

Pratt said, "Yeah, let's do it."

Then, acting cautious, I said, "Wait a minute, Bill. The IOC says there is to be only one Olympic flame."

"Fuck the rules!" he barked.

So we had two flames. When the stadium flame was lit—*bang!*— the tower flame followed. Both stayed on until the end of the Games. To me, Bill was the hero of the Calgary Games. I loved him!

I prefer the Winter Olympics. The Summer Games are spread out all over the place, and you don't get the same sense of community. And they're too commercial for my liking. At the Winter Games you see so many familiar faces—you're always bumping into your pals. It's still a smaller, more intimate Games—like family.

Besides, let's be honest, Canada is a country that excels at many of the winter sports.

As far as the competition was concerned, it was a strange Olympic Games. There were great performances: Finland's Matti Nykänen winning three gold medals in ski jumping; Dutch speed skater Yvonne van Gennip winning three gold medals and setting two world records; and the great Alberto Tomba of Italy winning two golds in alpine skiing. The Battle of the Brians pitted Canadian Brian Orser against American Brian Boitano in the men's figure skating competition. And while the host country didn't win a single gold medal, they were pleasantly surprised by the performance of Elizabeth Manley. All eyes had been on Katerina Witt of East Germany and Debi Thomas of the U.S., who were expected to finish first and second—it was just a question of who would claim the gold medal. Witt prevailed, but Thomas had to settle for the bronze when Manley outshone her to win the silver.

But it was also an Olympics where an inexperienced ski jumper, Eddie "the Eagle" Edwards of Great Britain, garnered more headlines than some of the truly talented athletes. ABC played up Eddie the Eagle as one of the great all-time lovable losers. And there was also the Jamaican national bobsled team, the inspiration for the movie *Cool Runnings*, which starred the late John Candy.

As for the hockey, the Soviet Union won yet another gold medal, with Finland taking the silver, and Sweden the bronze. Canada, made up mostly of amateurs with a handful of fringe pros as well as bona fide star goaltenders Sean Burke and Andy Moog, finished fourth.

As amazing as the opening ceremonies were, the closing ceremonies were memorable for all the wrong reasons. I nearly destroyed the stage. We had Canadian singer k. d. lang on stage singing, and I had the bright idea of sending all the athletes on the stage to join her. It was a secret that we would do it. Well, the stage wasn't built to handle that kind of weight and it nearly collapsed. Luckily, it held the masses and a catastrophe was avoided.

Veteran Canadian newscaster Lloyd Robertson was a friend of mine before the Games, but we grew closer because of the time we spent together in Calgary. I ran into him at the broadcast centre one day, and he seemed to be quite distraught. He told me CTV was experiencing technical problems while he was on the air and it was driving him to distraction. He would call for a certain event to be shown and it wouldn't come up. It didn't matter that Lloyd wasn't the one at fault, he was the host and it was his face on the tube. He felt horrible. The CTV network got better as the Games went on, but in the end they were panned in the press for their shoddy work. Meanwhile, the CTV crew assembled under my direction to be the world broadcaster was showered with praise.

I was able to take advantage of the contacts I'd developed working with ABC over the years. For instance, I wanted a camera to go down the ski jump on a rail beside the skier, but I couldn't afford it on my budget. I went to Roone Arledge and told him of my idea and he said, "Sounds great. Let's go fifty-fifty on the cost." ABC had the big bucks and wasn't afraid to spend them. I wanted to use three helicopters instead of two, so ABC chipped in. I wanted to put a camera in the valley so we could show the entire ski run, and once again, it was ABC to the rescue. You just never know when helping somebody will pay dividends.

As another example, with the Games just a few weeks from getting under way, I got a call from Peter Sisam, who told me we had a real problem. We were twenty days away from the opening cere-monies, and I was told Key Porter Books, which had the rights to publish the official booklet of the torch relay, had no accreditation and no good camera positions.

I knew I had to find a way to make things happen. As host broad-caster, I had a special finish-line compound where I could take cam-eras for post-event interviews. So I put them on my towers and gave them host-broadcaster credentials and saved their book. Who would have dreamed that, twenty years later, Fenn Publishing (which now owns Key Porter) would publish my first book, *Walking with Legends*, as well as this book? I don't think I would be able to help them under today's conditions, with the heightened security and without charac-ters like Bill Pratt to make things happen.

One thing I always tried to do when I worked in television was to hire the siblings of my friends when they were looking for work. Quite often, these were the grunt jobs, the stuff that goes on behind the scenes, but it gave them the opportunity to get a foot through the door of the world of television. And it put a few dollars in their pockets.

I received a call from Bobby Ackles, whom I knew from my days broadcasting Canadian Football League games. He asked if I might be able to hire his son Scott to work at the Calgary Games. When I interviewed Scott, he immediately impressed me as a bright young lad, so I hired him to work as an intern on the opening and closing ceremonies—his first job. Scott did a fabulous job for us, and he is now the president of the Calgary Stampeders. I ran into him years later and he told me he has had a lifelong groin injury from lugging cables to the top of McMahon Stadium during the Games. He also told me he met his wife while working at the Winter Olympics.

* * *

I had a hand in the coverage of the 1992 Winter Olympics in Albertville, France, this time as a consultant. In that capacity, I made several trips to France along with Bill Pratt and the Calgary organizing committee. We tried to help them out.

It turned out to be a very tough Olympics for the French. The venues were spread out all over the region, several of them fifty miles or more from Albertville. That made it very unusual. I speak French, which helps, and I enjoyed the trips and the people. I helped them with the bobsled and luge, and of course with the hockey, too. These were sports the television people in France were not used to shooting. I advised them on technical matters, where to put their compounds, where to establish their cameras—and how to deal with the tough international sports federations.

Calgary had set the standard in terms of how to do things. I went over to share my experiences with them, but they weren't very receptive to my suggestions. Every time I would suggest something creative, they would balk at the idea. They had their own way of doing things and they didn't want to break the mould. They weren't very innovative in terms of their television techniques, which was a little frustrating for me.

I didn't do anything during the actual Games. In fact, I left the day after the opening ceremonies. At that point, I had done as much as I could, and they were either going to pull it off or they weren't. There wasn't anything more I could do for them.

At the end of the day, the French host broadcasters did an okay job, but it wasn't what I would call a ground-breaking Olympics. In my opinion, they really succeeded because of tremendous support from the European Broadcasting Union.

Even though I wasn't there for the Games, I do have one long-lasting memory of being in Albertville during the preparatory stage. I had the good fortune of having dinner with Jean-Claude Killy, the French skier who won the triple crown at the 1968 Winter Olympics in Grenoble, France, taking gold in the giant slalom, slalom, and downhill events. He served as co-president of the Albertville Olympics. He seemed to me a real Olympian—a first-class guy—and in our conversations I realized how much he loved his country.

* * *

The 1994 Winter Olympics in Lillehammer, Norway, marked the first time that the Winter and Summer Games did not take place in the same year. In retrospect, if I had to pick an Olympics that I had the most fun at, it would be these.

I was part of CTV's negotiating team, along with Johnny Esaw, to get the rights to televise the Games. Part of the deal we made was we'd help co-host the broadcast—we would do figure skating and hockey. Even though I had left CTV at that point to take a job as the head of venue production in Atlanta, I still felt obligated to Doug Beeforth and John Cassaday and the others at the network, so to fulfill that obligation, I agreed to do hockey.

During my two pre-Games scouting trips to Norway, I fell in love with the country and its people. They reminded me of Canadians in many ways. What I found particularly striking was that they were not the least bit pretentious. That was true of the host city itself: it was a ski resort town, and they didn't change a thing to make it seem as if it was anything other than that. The streets were icy in the winter, and they left them icy. If it snowed, they just left it—didn't clear it. They basically said, "This is who we are and this is what we are going to do." I thought that was very Canadian. And the women? They had the most beautiful women I have ever seen. They also reminded me of Canadian women.

There were two arenas out of which we would be working. One, the Fjellhallen, was built in an underground cavern carved out of a mountain in Gjøvik, about twenty-five miles south of Lillehammer. The other, Håkons Hall, was a larger building that was closer to the action. I knew right away this would be an easy assignment for me. At every other Winter Olympics I did, I had to take on local people and integrate them. This time, my whole crew was made up of Canadians who were used to covering hockey, so there was no training involved. It was a lot like working an NHL game in Toronto, Vancouver or Montreal.

I had my own car and driver to go back and forth between our lodgings and arenas, which added to the ease of covering these Games. Also, I had no dealings with on-air talent—I was solely responsible for the world video feed. I did, however, always brief the Canadian and American networks on what I was up to.

I have always been impressed by the way people in television help one another. Henry Irizawa, our director, hadn't told anybody that his wife was coming over for the Games, and he wondered if we'd be able to provide her with accommodations. He was staying with me, my brother Jim—who was the isolation director—and a technical producer in a small cabin with four little one-person bedrooms.

Ostentatiously, I said, "Don't worry. I'll go to the organizing committee and I'll make sure we get an extra bed for your wife in your room."

Well, when I went to them, they said, "No way! She's not allowed. It wasn't pre-arranged."

On the night she arrived, there were about eight of us out for dinner, and we knew there were some empty rooms in the village. So away we went, and stole a bed from one of our pals. We carried it back to our cabin and put it beside Henry's bed. Voilà! She had a place to sleep.

We were just like a bunch of schoolkids out on the prowl. In fact, we dubbed ourselves "Mellanby's Marauders" and had quite a laugh over the whole caper. It was soon the talk of the media village. My daughter Laura, who was producing figure skating, even phoned me about the Marauders.

At night, we'd go out to a bar and meet up with NHL general managers. It was one big party. The three girls who worked the bar we went to were like a trio of Anita Ekberg clones. I tell you, *Charlie's Angels* had nothing on these three beauties. The single guys in our crew were constantly hitting on them, and finally the rumour started to circulate that one of the guys had hit paydirt with the most beautiful of the trio. The next day, we had to broadcast a big game and he was half-asleep. I understood why, but that didn't stop me from giving him the business.

"Wake up!" I said to him. "You've got a job to do. You might be a hero to the rest of the crew, but you're not my hero. You were out playing all night; just make sure you get your graphics right!"

When the Olympics ended, we had our closing party and of course I bumped into the guy. He told me he was proud of what he'd accomplished. I assumed he meant the job he'd done at the hockey games, but he laughed that off. "No. It was because I was the only guy on the crew to get shit from you, but the way I see it, I got shit for the right reason. Thanks."

I said, "Congrats also on Anita," and we both laughed.

Most Olympic Games are memorable for the events that take place during the competition. This year, though, it was a soap opera leading up to the Games that grabbed headlines. American figure skater Tonya Harding's husband, Jeff Gillooly, hired a thug, Shane Stant, to club fellow American skater Nancy Kerrigan in the knee. Gillooly and Stant were arrested and Kerrigan, who was terrorized by the attack, went on to win a silver medal. Harding placed eighth.

Sweden won the gold medal in hockey, defeating Canada 3–2 in a shootout in the final game. Teenage sensation Peter Forsberg scored the deciding goal when he moved in on Canadian goalie Corey Hirsch, deked to his left and let the puck lag behind and slide into the empty cage as Hirsch followed his move. The goal was later immortalized on a stamp in Sweden. Žigmund Pálffy of Slovakia led all scorers with 10 points, while teammate Miroslav Šatan led all goal-scorers with 9.

Local hero Johann Olav Koss was the darling of the Games, capturing three speed skating gold medals and setting three world records in the process.

One thing happened in Lillehammer that I found quite interesting. The Japanese NHK Network had something I'd never seen before: a high-definition truck. They were doing hockey and asked if I'd like to come into their truck to direct a period with them. To me, it sounded like a great opportunity—a chance to look into the future of TV broadcasting.

So I got my brother to fill in for me as producer, and away I went.

They had three cameras, and I was directing it like a normal hockey game, doing the things I had done routinely for years. The Japanese director was going nuts because in hi-def you don't cut from camera to camera to camera while the play is on because it's too distracting for the viewer. And because the screen is wider and the images more detailed, static shots are favoured over camera movement.

"Oh no, don't do that—don't do that," came this voice from over my shoulder.

It didn't take long for me to realize how unhappy they were to have invited me into their truck. Here I was, this great guru of hockey television, and I was screwing up their feed. I did about five minutes and got the hell out of there. They looked relieved.

It was the last time I worked in a truck. At the end, my young brother Jim said, "Ralph, you've still got it!" That made me happy because I was sixty at the time.

* * *

Not all of my Olympic memories are fond ones. In fact, my final experience with the Olympic Games was really a story about the one that got away and perhaps the main reason I got out of televising the Olympics.

I wanted to head the host broadcasting team for the 2002 Winter Olympics in Salt Lake City. I was working in Atlanta at the time and decided that this was the Games where I wanted to be *the* guy again. I didn't want to be working for a general manager or for anybody else. I wanted to run the show, just like in Calgary.

Don Baer, who had worked with me at the Goodwill Games and was working with me in Atlanta, was the former vice-president at NBC Sports. We had become very good friends. So I figured what the heck and asked him, "Why don't you and I put in a bid to be the host broadcaster?"

There was no hesitation. He jumped at the idea.

I felt we needed somebody on our team with ties to Utah, and we both knew the famous Osmond family—Don knew them from his days at NBC, and I knew them from my days working in variety television. So we got hold of Alan Osmond and asked if he would be interested in joining the bid with us. We told him he and his family could be involved in the opening and closing ceremonies. The Osmonds are loved in Utah and still live there. Alan loved the idea and was very excited about it, as was the rest of the family.

It was one of the biggest disappointments in my life when we didn't win with our bid. I was heartbroken, so much so that that's when I decided to give up on the Olympics.

I took numerous trips to Salt Lake City to meet with the Olympic executives—Frank Joklik, president of the Salt Lake Organizing Committee, and vice-president Dave Johnson. We were very suspicious of the SLOC executive. They struck us as amateurs. Joklik and Johnson both ultimately resigned amid allegations of bribery, and Mitt Romney took over as president of the SLOC. He was brought in to save the day after the event was judged to be running nearly $400 million short of its revenue benchmarks in 1999. It was a mess.

Romney came in and made positive changes that resulted in the Games actually turning a profit of more than $100 million. Romney contributed $1 million to the Olympics, and donated the $825,000 salary he earned as president and CEO to charity. I wish I'd been dealing with Romney when I submitted the bid—I think I might have stood a much better chance of winning. At least we would have been a level playing field.

There were five bids for the TV rights, and I am convinced ours was the best—certainly the bid that was going to cost the least amount of money. I spent $25,000 of my own money to help put the bid together, and Don did the same thing.

We aimed high. They way we saw it, our group included an American and a Canadian with illustrious TV backgrounds, as well as a member of one of the first families of Utah. As we made our pitch, however, I felt the judges were barely paying attention. I sat there thinking, we don't have the inside track. We had wasted our time and our money. The organizing committee didn't seem to like us at all.

When we left the room, I turned to the others on our committee and said, "There's no chance we're going to get this."

To be clear, Romero was tremendously qualified and experienced and was a great choice. It was the process and the organizing committee that got to me.

Alan said, "What are you talking about, Ralph? We gave a great presentation. And you told me our bid was going to cost the least amount of money to do it because we are the only real North American bid."

I said, "We don't have a hope."

The whole process sickened me and turned me right off the IOC. Looking back, I couldn't help but remark on the contrast from my first experiences with the people who ran the Olympics—people like Lord Killanin, Princess Anne and Prince Albert of Monaco, I realized it had all changed; it was now very insular, and if you weren't part of the inner circle, you had to have the right international political connections.

When Juan Antonio Samaranch stepped down as president of the IOC in 2001, the committee created the Olympic Broadcasting Services (OBS) to serve as host broadcaster of future Games and give it rights to do the Olympics forever under the banner of IOC Television.

As a result, unlike Calgary in 1988, the Winter Games in Vancouver in 2010 will not be televised for viewers around the world by Canadians, but by the consortium of broadcasters chosen by the IOC. That is sad.

It is a political mess. Some people think I'm an ingrate for feeling this way because of all the good the Olympics did for my career. But an IOC member once told me I'm not off track in terms of the way I feel. I once asked him, given the choice, if he'd rather be an IOC member or run a major worldwide corporation. He said he'd rather be an IOC member because he could make more money.

Most members of the IOC demand to be treated like royalty.

They want the best suites at the best hotels, to have cars and drivers, and many other favours. In the old days, they used to pay their own way, for heaven's sake. Those were the real Olympics.

Doug Mitchell, a member of the Calgary '88 bid team, loves to tell the story of the IOC member from Pakistan who told him, "I didn't vote for Calgary because you didn't deliver the girls to me."

I have served on many IOC commissions, but at that level you're not party to, or on the receiving end of, all the infighting, the pay-offs—even scholarships given to children of IOC members. Of course, they deny it. But let's be honest about something: my friends—former IOC members Paul Henderson (not the hockey player) and Dick Pound—are the exceptions that prove the rule. They serve on principle. Of course, they are Canadian.

Alan and the rest of the Osmond family were terribly disappointed about losing in their own city. I told Alan later they should have sung at the presentation.

When we found out about the bribery scandal, we thought they were all going to be charged and sent to prison. In 2000, a US federal grand jury indicted the former president and the former vice-president of the Salt Lake Olympic Bid Committee and the organizing committee for their roles in the city's bid to host the 2002 Games. In 2003, a federal court judge acquitted them.

To me, Salt Lake was an absolute disaster, and a major disappointment after I'd had the good fortune to deal with so many good people around the Olympics in the past. I hope the people running the 2010 Winter Olympics in Vancouver are very careful in terms of their money and integrity. You often need to have a Bill Pratt on your side to tell the IOC and sports federations to go screw themselves, to put them in their place. It's not necessary to bend over backwards to give these freeloaders everything they want. The decent IOC members, however few they may be, are always willing to help and give the host city what it wants and deserves.

Salt Lake City notwithstanding, I do have many fond memories of my participation in covering the Winter Games. I know I made my mark, and all things considered, I am proud I was never invited to be an IOC member.

I recall bumping into Roone Arledge and Keith Jackson of ABC at a broadcast convention. Keith was introducing me to people and saying, "This is Ralph Mellanby, Canada's Roone Arledge."

Roone heard this and immediately turned around and chimed in, "No, no. I am America's Ralph Mellanby!"

I loved him for that. I was so flattered to be compared to such a great American television executive—even if it was meant as a joke.

In my opinion, ABC built the Olympic movement through its exceptional television images and the dollars they paid for American television rights from 1964 through 1988. Their reward? CBS and later NBC came in with more money and stole the Games away.

As Roone said to me, "Ralph, don't fall in love, like I did, with the Olympic movement. When it comes down to the USA and Canada, it's all about money to those guys, not loyalty."

I couldn't have said it better myself!

11

THE SUMMER GAMES

My experience working for ABC on the 1976 Winter Olympics in Innsbruck had been a fantastic one, so I was absolutely delighted when I got a call from Guy Desormeaux, who had directed *Hockey Night in Canada* in Montreal for years. CBC was to be the host broadcaster for the Summer Games in Montreal, and Guy was responsible for the production.

Guy wondered if I would be interested in directing basketball, and right away I said I was. It was funny, though—I had been *his* boss for years, and now our roles would be reversed. I was okay with that because we had a great relationship. As it turned out, I was the only freelancer on the production team. All the rest were CBC staffers. I had a sense that ABC had recommended me for the job.

I was interested in the position—who wouldn't be?—but I certainly wasn't going to do it for scale. "What's the deal?" I asked.

Truth is, I *would* have done it for scale because of my long association with Guy, but I wasn't about to tell him that. He gave me the standard fee —$5,000 for two and a half weeks' work. That was pretty low, especially when you factor in the time that goes into preparing and attending the many seminars. I had been paid $25,000 to do the Winter Olympics, but that was ABC and this was the notoriously low-paying CBC.

I said, "Sorry, I can't do it for that."

"Well, Ralph, that's what we're paying everybody else."

I was rolling the dice a little bit, but I knew he didn't really have anybody that could do the job. So I passed—for now.

A little while later, he called me back and said, "I'll tell you what I can do. We have a suite at McGill University...it's the Dean's Suite. I was going to use it for a VIP, but I guess you are the VIP."

It had three bedrooms, so it meant I'd be able to bring my wife, Janet, my kids, Laura and Scott—who were twelve and ten, respectively—and also my in-laws, Fred and Anne Cochrane from Saskatchewan. I had gone to the Winter Games on my own, so I looked at this as a great opportunity for my family to experience a trip of a lifetime. Some things in life are more important than money. Certainly, family is one.

I told my wife and she said, "What's the use of us going there for three weeks if we don't have tickets to the events?"

Good point. I never had an agent, but on this one I probably could have used one.

I went back to Guy and said, "Send me a list of the tickets that are available."

I then sent him a rather extensive list of ticket requests, figuring I would shoot for the moon, since this was a one-time deal. He accepted—I got all my tickets—and we had a deal.

The next time I was in Montreal, I went over to see the accommodations, and it was a beautiful suite, conveniently located right on a subway line. My family also had the use of the cafeteria at McGill, a swimming pool—pretty much everything you could ask for. It made it really special to have my kids there. It was my only time, out of the thirteen Olympics I covered, that I had my entire family with me. That made the assignment extra-special.

I was thrilled that the Games were being held in my old stomping grounds. I cherished my years spent in Montreal, and some memories stay with me, even today.

One in particular was working on a TV show called *The Mayor Speaks* with Jean Drapeau, which ran every Sunday. I was a great admirer of the man who held the office of mayor from 1954 to 1957 and again from 1960 to 1986. Among his many achievements was securing the Olympics for his city, along with the world's fair, Expo 67, attracting major-league baseball and building the subway system. Sadly, Drapeau is now remembered by many for the huge cost over-runs for the Olympic Games facilities, which took the city three decades to pay off.

Regardless, he was my friend and I recall fondly the days when he would arrive at the studio well before show time. I'd arrive about an hour before the show and he would already be sitting in the lobby, having driven himself to the studio. He would do a report on the city each week, and then he would chat with an invited guest. It was really an easy show for me to produce and direct.

I also knew the mayor via hockey. Every time the Canadiens won the Cup, he'd throw a party up on Mount Royal at the Pavilion. It was a lavish, invitation-only affair that included players, members of the press, and people from the broadcast crew. One year, after the Habs had won a number of Cups in a row, they didn't win it. I recall my wife complaining that there was no party. I had to explain that there's no reason for a party if the Canadiens don't win the Stanley Cup and, while Montreal won most of the time in those days, they didn't win it all the time.

I always felt the 1976 Games in Montreal were underrated. Maybe the taxpayers resented them after being stuck with the tab, but the broadcasters and press thought it was a great Games. Montreal is one of the most cosmopolitan cities in the world, and it's very easy to get around. And in 1976, there wasn't nearly the sort of security presence that there is today, following the 9/11 attacks.

Basketball was to be one of the marquee sports at the Montreal Games, and Canada had a pretty good squad. The majority of games were to be played at the Étienne Desmarteau Centre, with the men's and women's finals to be played at the Montreal Forum.

I'd played basketball in high school, even won an Ontario championship, and I still played recreationally, so I was totally familiar with the sport. I also had the good fortune to have a close association with the coach of the Canadian men's team, Jack Donohue—one of the nicest men I have ever met in all my years of televising sports.

I was allowed to hand-pick my crew, so I leaned heavily on the people I'd worked with at CFCF in Montreal. I was ten years removed from working there, but I still knew who the best techs were. As usual, many of them were the guys who had worked with me on hockey. Unfortunately, none of them had played basketball, so they didn't really have a feel for the sport. I wasn't too worried about the audio guy or technical director in this regard—but the cameramen would need to be taught the finer points.

So I went to Donohue and asked him if, after one of the national team's practices, he'd be willing to give the crew a little seminar. "I'll get them to bring their running shoes and gym gear and they can have a little game amongst themselves," I added.

He said, "Sure, I'd be happy to help."

He brought his assistant coach with him and, over the course of about forty minutes, ran through the basics of the game. Then he bellowed, "Okay, let's have a game now."

He decided to ref a game between the technicians and the production staff. You should know that the technicians always hate the production staff—it's just one of those things in the TV business.

What unfolded was one for the books. My biggest regret is I didn't have the cameras rolling. There was no YouTube in those days, but if there were I am certain this scrimmage game would have gotten millions of hits on the Internet. I have never seen basketball played like that. There was blood all over the court from guys smashing into one another. It was absolutely fierce—full-contact basketball. These guys thought that basketball was hockey on hardwood!

Jack looked at me and said, "Ralph, this is hopeless. You'd better stop the game before somebody gets killed!"

When the Games finally arrived, I was pumped. I had gone to the opening ceremonies of the Winter Games with Curt Gowdy, the ABC announcer, and I will never forget a warning he gave me: "Ralph, be ready emotionally. When your country, Canada, walks in, you're going to cry."

"No I won't," I scoffed. I'm a hardened professional, I told myself. I won't get all caught up in that.

Well, I attended the opening ceremonies with my wife and kids and my pal Ron Harrison, the director for *Hockey Night in Canada* who later became the show's executive producer. As the host nation, Canada was the last to enter the stadium, and when they did, the tears started rolling down my cheeks. It was unbelievably emotional. You think about your mom, your dad, your career...you're just so proud to be a Canadian.

We also went to the closing ceremonies, which weren't as sentimental as they were funny. Midway through the proceedings, a streaker made his way onto the field. At first, the crowd was shocked to see the young man running buck-naked around Olympic Stadium, but eventually shock turned to laughter and then applause.

It was a first in Olympic history and it has not been repeated.

As I hoped, my family thoroughly enjoyed the Games. They went to most sports at least once, and even saw Princess Anne ride in the equestrian event.

One of our biggest thrills was attending the boxing finals at the Forum. I was very fortunate to be given Molson's private box, and my family and I had it to ourselves. The United States had an amazing team, with Sugar Ray Leonard winning the gold medal in the light welterweight division and the Spinks brothers, Michael and Leon, winning gold in the middleweight and light-heavyweight divisions respectively.

As for my TV involvement, things did not run smoothly. When my event, basketball, moved to the Forum, I had to leave my hand-picked crew—my security blanket—behind and work with CBC people. CBC–Radio Canada was having labour problems at the time, and the crew insisted I direct in French, even though my video switcher and audio people spoke English.

I was lucky enough to have a buddy of mine, François Carignan, working with us, so I sat him beside me in the truck. I had to direct English so the guy in the truck, from English CBC, could understand me, and then I had to give the cameramen directions in French—not only in French, but in perfect French.

My French wasn't bad, but it wasn't perfect. When the cameramen wouldn't respond to my direction, I'd poke François in the ribs and he would come in on my intercom and give the instructions in perfect French. In response to the poking, he'd say, "Can't you just touch me, Ralph?"

Some of the cameramen knew what I meant, but they wouldn't respond. They were being jerks—and these are guys who had worked on hockey for me, but because of the labour dispute, they were very militant. In a crew meeting I told them, in French, "This is for Canada and for the world." One of the guys looked at me and said, "I don't give a shit about Canada!"

I had more cameras (twelve) than I was used to working with. In an effort to run things as smoothly as possible, I gave the cameramen strict written instructions before each game on what I expected from them so I didn't need to do a lot of directing. I made out shot lists in French so they could put them on their cameras. For instance, if there is a free throw, do this. If there's an outside shot down low, do that. If there is a time out, do this. That reduced the amount of verbal instruction I needed to give them during the game. It wasn't perfect, but it was effective.

I never forgot what they put me through, and I never forgave. It was a terrible thing to do. It was a shame their politics and labour problems were affecting our broadcast.

The day before the men's gold-medal game, the head of the union (also a cameraman) came up to me and asked—in English—if I could get him tickets for the game. I just looked him in the eye, shook my head and walked away. He had worked for me in hockey, but after all he had put me through, I couldn't believe he was standing before me asking for a favour. The nerve!

In the end, we got the job done. When I told the ABC guys what grief I had been through, they couldn't believe it. Since the U.S. won the gold medal, they were happy and also liked the coverage so much that they later hired me—a Canadian—to direct basketball at the Los Angeles Games in 1984.

My assistant, François, is now the head of Radio-Canada's Olympic broadcasting. More than thirty years later, I think his ribs are still probably sore.

* * *

My experience at the 1980 Summer Olympic Games was short and not so sweet. I had been hired by NBC, and this time my fee was substantially more than I earned in Montreal—US$40,000.

At least, that's how much I was supposed to earn.

NBC, which was stuck in third place among the big three U.S. networks in the late 1970s, had bid huge money to win the Olympic television rights away from ABC, and in 1977 they hired Don Ohlmeyer, who had produced and directed Olympic telecasts for ABC, as executive producer of NBC Sports. He was the one who hired me to direct basketball—both men's and women's games. I would work with producer Bob Goodrich, whom I knew from the 1976 Winter Olympics in Innsbruck. And you certainly didn't have to train an American crew on how to cover basketball.

When I went to the seminar with all the announcers, producers, and directors, held at the famous Copacabana nightclub in New York, I found that a lot of the guys were former ABC employees who had been lured away by NBC. Mike Weisman and Terry Ewert were the head producers, and I respected both of them. When they introduced me at the seminar, they made a point of telling the people what a great job I had done in the previous Games in Montreal, which made me feel very good. I got a smattering of applause.

Ohlmeyer, who was kind of a hero of mine, explained to me what they wanted and needed. Don said, "I am going to depend on you a lot because you have experience with these guys. I'll be calling you a lot." By "these guys," he meant the Russians.

I couldn't wait for the Games. For one thing, it was a treat to be working for an American network, where I knew no expense would be spared. And this assignment was going to be a breeze—there would be no directing in French this time. English only.

Well, it would have been a breeze had the Americans actually gone to the Olympic Games. On December 27, 1979, the Soviet Union invaded Afghanistan in order to prop up the pro-Soviet government. President Jimmy Carter gave the Soviets a deadline of February 20, 1980, to withdraw their troops. The deadline passed unheeded, and the United States Olympic Committee decided to boycott the event.

As a result of the U.S. boycott, NBC cancelled its plans to broadcast the Moscow Games—150 hours of coverage. With that decision, my paycheque vanished. I was euchred. I never received a dime.

Years later, when I lived in Atlanta, I met President Carter at a lunch at the Druid Hills Club and I told him, "You cost me forty grand!"

"Ralph," he said, "if I were you, I would also be upset." He was a great president and a great guy. Very charming.

It was very disappointing to have to sit at home and watch the Canadian coverage of the Games. They took the host feed and I thought they did a pretty good job. I enjoyed the Games, but I really missed the experience of being there.

It turned out to be the only Olympics I worked that I didn't make any money from. I asked Ohlmeyer for a small fee for the pre-Games work I had done for the network—I'm still waiting for the cheque.

* * *

Shocked at having lost the 1980 Olympic Games to NBC, ABC made a monster bid, won the rights to televise the 1984 Games and vowed never to lose them again. (They did lose them, but that was the sentiment of the day.)

I wasn't surprised to get the call from ABC to ask if I'd be interested in doing basketball for them. That's one of the great things about being a freelancer—you aren't officially aligned to one network and you are appreciated for your expertise. It seemed I was now known as the hockey guy in winter and the basketball guy in summer, and that was just fine with me. I also felt like part of the ABC family.

My brother-in-law, Fred Cochrane Jr., was a big builder in L.A. and he always kept a place in any development he built. He had built an apartment complex in Santa Monica, right on the ocean, for Lawrence Welk, the famous musician and band leader whose TV show aired from 1951 through 1982. Welk called his style of music "champagne music," so not surprisingly the white building was called Champagne Towers. Fred had a penthouse in this complex, and he'd offered me the use of it anytime I'd like.

Of course, ABC provided me with accommodation as well, in a hotel at the airport, but it was comforting to know that, if I had a little bit of downtime, I could enjoy a change of scenery. Hey, if you're working on the west coast, you might as well take advantage of some of the best beaches in the world. In any case, Santa Monica was not far from my venue, the Los Angeles Forum.

Also, because I had worked a lot of National Hockey League games in Los Angeles, I knew lots of people there, so unlike my experiences in most other Olympic cities, I knew I would have plenty of company.

Another bonus was the fact that Jack Donohue was once again coach of the Canadian men's basketball team. I had a few lunches with Jack to get caught up on what was shaking with the Canadian program and what I might expect in Los Angeles. I trusted Jack to educate me about who and what I should be looking out for in the Olympic tournament.

The American men's team, by the way, was being coached by the legendary (and controversial) Bobby Knight and featured such future NBA stars as Patrick Ewing, Michael Jordan, Chris Mullin, Sam Perkins, and Alvin Robertson.

As in the past, my primary responsibility would be to cover the American men's and women's teams, although I would also direct many games involving other countries for the world feed. Our play-by-play man was Keith Jackson and the colour analyst was Digger Phelps, coach of the Notre Dame Fighting Irish. Digger was a wonderful guy and a very informed and polished analyst. Keith, Digger, and I grew quite comfortable hanging out with one another, and the guys loved to get away once in a while, so I'd often take them to the Beach Club in Santa Monica, where my brother-in-law was a member. The club was located on the ocean, on the estate that once belonged to silent-film star Marion Davies, the lover of newspaper magnate William Randolph Hearst.

It was a lasting thrill to work with a real pro like Jackson, who was *the* college football announcer. He was also known for his work on *Wide World of Sports* and in the early days of *Monday Night Football.* He was so versatile, it might be easier to list the things he *didn't* do. He also did play-by-play for *Monday Night Baseball,* NASCAR stock car racing, and worked ten Summer and Winter Olympics. To use the phrase some say he made famous, "Whoa Nellie!" He called speed skating in 1980 when Eric Heiden was the darling of the Games. Strangely, he was offered the opportunity to do play-by-play for the Olympic hockey in 1980, but turned it down. That was the year the American pulled off the upset of the century, winning the gold medal—the Miracle on Ice!

As a director, it was my job to get to know the talent's personalities and make their lives as simple as I could. They are, after all, our link to the viewing audience. Even though I was a freelancer, I felt my relationship with Keith improved with each passing day. Keith was a fun guy, but when it came to work he was total business. He seemed to have a critical eye about everything, and he certainly didn't like to waste time.

Anytime he had to tape something he'd say, in his booming voice, "I hope this is one take—it'll be one take for me!"

Yes, he was a real pro.

Being Canadian, I had an affinity for the our teams, and the Canadian men's basketball team had a decent showing in Los

Angeles, finishing fourth behind the United States, which won gold; Spain, which captured silver; and Yugoslavia, bronze. The Russians boycotted the Games, so once again the much-anticipated matchup between the U.S. and the Soviets was not to be. The Canadian women also placed fourth. The United States won gold, South Korea took silver, and China went home with bronze.

For me, being at an Olympics wasn't always about sports—it was more about the people I worked with and the people I met. I only regret that the venues were so spread out, so I didn't get to see any of the other events, and also missed seeing many of my old friends.

That said, there's always the chance to forge valuable, lasting relationships with the folks you work with. We had a really likeable kid working with us as a go-fer, and one day he said to me, "I want to be in television."

I'd heard that before, but this kid seemed quite genuine—a real keener. When I was directing games that didn't involve the American teams, I would bring him into the truck with me, where he would sit behind me so I could teach him. He was a great kid, really eager to learn.

I got to really like him, but I never learned his name—well, to be honest, I guess I knew it at the time, but I quickly forgot it. But he was very thankful to me when the Games concluded.

Years later, when my partner, Brian Robertson, and I founded the *Governor General's Performing Arts Awards in Canada*, I needed the co-operation of the Kennedy Center. George Stevens Jr., the son of one of the greatest movie producers of all time, ran *The Kennedy Center Honors*, an annual TV special that celebrates figures from the world of performing arts who have achieved a great deal in their careers—filmmakers, singers, dancers, musicians, actors. Our *Governor General's Awards* were based on these shows, and neither Brian nor I hid that fact.

I went to Washington to see Stevens, and being unfamiliar with the area, I got lost in the Kennedy Center and was late in arriving for our appointment. When I finally arrived, I walked into his office. It had to be a hundred feet long, and the walls were lined with photos of Hollywood legends—mostly from his father's films such as *A Place in the Sun, Giant, Shane, The Diary of Anne Frank* and *The Greatest Story Ever Told*. A younger fellow sat at the near desk, while Stevens was way at the back.

Stevens, who was on the phone, took the receiver away from his ear and said, "Mellanby from Canada?"

I said, "Yes."

"Just a minute—I'm speaking with Katharine Hepburn."

Don't think that didn't intimidate me!

Meanwhile, the young guy at the other desk walked over to me and gave me a big hug.

I wondered what the heck was going on, but it turned out he was the kid I'd helped during the Olympics in L.A. He was George Stevens Jr.'s son.

He looked at me and said, "I told my dad, anything you need, you get!"

I was so pleased and thrilled to hear that, though I still couldn't remember his name. Turns out it is Michael Stevens, and he's the co-producer of *The Kennedy Center Honors* as well as a series of specials for the American Film Institute.

My meeting with George was great. He gave me so much information that would benefit me with my show—how they handled their honourees, transportation and other details—and he did it all for free! We thought for sure we'd have to pay for his valuable help.

For that, I have to thank Michael Stevens. It's just another example of how, when you do something to help people, you are often rewarded for your kindness.

Without question, the most memorable night I had at the 1984 Games was at a special dinner engagement.

One day, while I was relaxing beside the hotel pool, Digger Phelps dropped by and wondered, "How would you like to have dinner with Bobby Knight?"

Did he have to ask? "I'd love it!" I said.

Bobby had led the Indiana Hoosiers to three NCAA championships and won the National Invitational Tournament crown one year. Six times, he had been named coach of the year in the Big Ten conference, and four times he was the college basketball coach of the year for the entire country. You'd think a guy with that kind of track record would be noted primarily for his accomplishments, but not Bobby Knight. As many of you will recall, his volatile temper—manifested in countless courtside outbursts and the tossing of chairs across the basketball court—gained him even more notoriety than his ability to win titles.

I knew I was in for quite an experience.

Digger and I were already at our table in the restaurant when Knight arrived. Digger introduced me as the Canadian who had directed basketball at the Montreal Olympic Games.

Knight looked at me, and the first thing he said was, "What the hell is a Canadian doing basketball on American TV for ABC?"

I was speechless. After composing myself, I told him I'd played high school basketball on an Ontario championship team and had been offered several scholarships to play college basketball in the United States. I also shared with him my experiences televising the Games in Montreal, and all the hassles I faced, and when I was done, he looked at me and said, "Okay, that's legitimate."

Phew!

I'll tell you, I learned a lot about basketball that night, sitting at dinner with two legends, but I made one big mistake. I asked Knight why he wasn't playing Ewing more, because Patrick was one of the biggest college basketball stars in the country.

He glared at me with a look that screamed, "How dare you ask me that!"

"Are you the goddamn press?" he said.

"No. I'm just interested and it's going to become a pretty big story."

"It already *is* a story. The son of a bitch isn't playing and I'll play whoever the hell I want to play."

I guess, at the end of the day, Ewing didn't fit Knight's system, which was run-and-gun.

* * *

The groundwork for television coverage of an Olympic Games is laid well in advance, often as many as four or five years before the Olympics are actually to be held. So even though I had no idea whether or not I would actually work at the 1988 Summer Games in Seoul, South Korea, I was still asked to join the Calgary delegation that travelled there to meet with the Koreans for an exchange of ideas. I had never been to Korea and was really looking forward to the excursion.

What I found out, however, was that the exchange of information was a one-way street—we told them everything we were doing at the Winter Games and got nothing in return from them about the Summer Games. That, I soon found out, was typical of the Koreans. Their attitude absolutely shocked me. They were perfectly willing to listen to what we had to say, scribbling down our ideas, but when it came time to reciprocate, all we got back was many blank stares. It was very frustrating.

We had a meeting with Dr. Kim Un Yong, who was a vice-president of the International Olympic Committee and was in charge of the Seoul Games. He wasn't much help, either. Dr. Kim was rumoured to be next in line for the presidency of the IOC, but he ultimately left the organization in disgrace after being accused of various wrong-doings, including bribery and embezzlement. He eventually went to jail. This became a regular event for many IOC members.

The trip wasn't a total waste of time. At least I saw Seoul, visited most of the venues, and was privy to some of their preparation work.

I hadn't really planned to be part of the Seoul Olympics, but was pleasantly surprised to be asked to produce volleyball for NBC. During the Winter Games in Calgary, some of the high-ranking NBC people came to visit us. I showed Mike Weisman, an executive producer at the network, around as much as I could while still attending to my duties as the head of world TV coverage.

It was Weisman who asked me to join the TV team heading to Seoul. I had never done volleyball and, truth be told, knew little about the game. Like a lot of kids, I had played a bit in high school, but that hardly made me an expert.

Weisman said he always thought volleyball coverage was very stagnant, and I agreed with him. He said he wanted to put a team together that included Teddy Nathanson and myself. Teddy was a superstar at NBC who had directed twenty-one Wimbledon tennis championships and thirteen Super Bowls during an illustrious thirty-seven-year career with the network. It was said that he was like a great athlete in that he made the others around him better at their jobs, but he also had a quirky side. He was absent-minded and forgetful and, believe it or not, always wore elbow pads and a neck brace while directing. He often forgot these—as a matter of fact, he also often forgot his eyeglasses.

Here's a story he loved to tell. Once, he was driving across the country to Los Angeles, and he stopped in the desert to get gas for his car. His wife, Edith, went into the washroom, and when she came out, Teddy was gone—he'd taken off without her! I'm not sure how far down the road he got before he realized his mistake. But that was Teddy.

Teddy and I reinvented the way volleyball is covered, with low angles and a camera on top of the net for isolations. We planned to shoot from well behind the server. We mounted robotic cameras on the posts that held the net up, and these were able to pivot to give us some amazing shots.

NBC wanted to see what our coverage would look like, so we arranged to do a test run, shooting a match involving the Olympic team at Temple University in Philadelphia. I was to travel there to meet up with the NBC crew, which included announcers Bob Trumpy and Chris Marlowe. Trumpy was the network's football guy—imagine for a moment, Weisman had put together his volleyball team with a

Canadian hockey producer, his main football director and his head
football announcer. He really did want new coverage for the
Games—it was a stroke of genius!

What should have been a simple trip to Philadelphia nearly blew
up in my face when I got stopped at the airport. I had a briefcase with
me, stupidly, that contained all the plans and scripts. The customs
and immigration agents wouldn't let me into the United States
because I didn't have a work permit.

I called the people at NBC and told them of my predicament,
and they weren't sympathetic. This was my show and there was no
way I could be absent. The network managed to get me booked on a
later flight, and this time I left the briefcase behind and told the
agents I was on my way to see my son play hockey—Scott was with the
Philadelphia Flyers at the time.

The meeting that had originally been scheduled for the afternoon was now postponed till evening, which pissed off everybody—
the production crew, as well as the talent, whom I had never met. I
arrived embarrassed for having held everybody up. The meeting
finally got under way, and there I was, laying out the plans, when two
well-dressed men walked in and said, "Is there a Ralph Mellanby
here?"

I put up my hand and said, "Yeah, that's me."

"Step outside," they said. "We're from U.S. Customs and
Immigration."

"I'm just listening in on the meeting," I bluffed, but they weren't
buying it.

"Yeah, right. You're running the meeting. You are here working
and you don't have a work permit."

There was dead silence in the room. I was escorted into the
hall—and I was scared shitless because I was thinking I'd not only
lose my contract, I might go to jail.

We got out in the hall and suddenly I saw their faces break out
into little grins.

"You can stop worrying," one of the "agents" said. "We're just two guys Teddy Nathanson met at the bar. Actually, we're in the insurance business. You were set up."

Well, was I relieved. They really looked like feds to me.

I was mad, but at the same time I realized it was good for the meeting and good for the morale of our group. Everybody got a big laugh out of it—they were all in on the gag!

Afterward, we met for a few beers and Marlowe and Trumpy really got into the whole idea of being part of this team. They liked the new way of doing volleyball. The test run went well, except that Teddy forgot his glasses and a neckband. I had to lend him my glasses. He was sure a different guy.

I'd brought in Peter Greene, who had been a world-class volleyball player in his day, to be our spotter. Peter, who was a golfing and tennis buddy of mine, was a teacher at the Banff School of Fine Arts. I figured I'd better bring along somebody who knew a lot about volleyball. He got under Nathanson's skin. It used to be that when a team was serving and lost the point, it was called a "side out." Peter would call "side out" and Teddy would freak.

"Don't say 'side out'!"

I said, "Teddy, that's the terminology."

"I don't care. I don't want to hear 'side out' anymore. Call it anything you want, but don't call it side out!"

So we called it "change of serve." Teddy was brilliant, but he was also weird.

I went to Korea a bit early, and Teddy came too, with his wife, Edith. My brother Jim and daughter Laura were also working for NBC. Jim was doing sports news and Laura the daily summaries. Having family there always make the event so much more special for me.

The coverage during the Games was great. Trumpy did an excellent job of calling the action and Marlowe, who had been a great player for the United States, provided first-rate analysis and insight. Our biggest obstacle was trying to stickhandle around the Korean officials who were supposed to be helping us.

When it comes to international events, you are at the mercy of those in charge of the world feed. I had a mixed crew that included some Koreans. My venue manager, who was also Korean, was terrific. In fact, she and my translator, another woman, turned out to be gems—they were easy to deal with. But I found the men could be real jerks. Not only were they not helpful, but they seemed to take delight in seeing you struggle. The senior venue manager for the Seoul organizing committee was someone from whom we had trouble getting any co-operation. Asking him for anything was like talking to a wall. He could never give us a decision on anything—it seemed that nobody there wanted to be held accountable, so you always had to go up a step on the food chain to find someone willing to make a decision. At the end of the Games, we even offered him a gift, and he refused to take it. He hated us. The feeling, as Teddy said, was mutual.

But not all the Korean men I met caused me grief. In fact, when the Games were over, my venue manager took me to meet her father, who was a doctor. Teddy and I went to their house for dinner and had a delightful time. She was a beautiful lady and her father was very well mannered. Both he and his wife were gracious.

The American men's and women's teams both won gold medals, so it was a very festive time. After the men won their gold medal, I invited the entire team to our compound for a beer. Well, wouldn't you know it, they drank us dry! They went through all our beer. That pissed me off—before our crew even had a chance to finish mopping up, the players had finished the stock.

Beer turned out to be the least of my brother's worries. One night, Jim and I headed over to the Itaewon, a district filled with restaurants and shops where tourists hang out. We went to a bar and enjoyed some beers and great conversation before heading back to the hotel.

The next thing I knew, my phone was ringing and it was Jim. I could hear the panic in his voice.

"My passport is gone!" he said. "I think I may have left it in the bar."

"Then you'd better get your butt back to the bar to see if it's there," I said. If you lose your passport at the Olympics, you might as well pack up and head home—if, that is, they'll let you out of the country.

By the time Jim got back to the bar, it had closed, but fortunately someone answered when he banged on the door, and sure enough the staff had his papers. What a relief!

One of the great guys I met in Seoul was Ferdie Pacheco, the famous cornerman for many boxing champions, including Muhammad Ali. He was a personal physician, too, and worked for NBC as a boxing analyst—he was always called "The Fight Doctor." Ferdie used to hold court in the hotel lobby, and I used to like hanging around him because I was a huge fan of professional boxing. I would talk boxing with Ferdie all the time.

I told him I'd directed Ali's fight against George Chuvalo at Maple Leaf Gardens, and he was impressed. I also attended Ali's first bout with Joe Frazier at Madison Square Garden, courtesy of the NHL. For me, there's something magical about a big-time boxing match. I was very fortunate to attend a fight between "Marvellous" Marvin Hagler and Thomas "The Hit Man" Hearns in Las Vegas as a guest of CBS. The seats were at ringside; I looked around and there was Frank Sinatra some twenty feet away from me, clicking away with a camera—he was taking pictures for *Life* magazine. Wow!

When you're on the road, it's customary for TV people to take shots at one another—all in fun, I must add. Well, the 1988 Seoul Summer Games were the Ben Johnson Olympics, so there I was, the proud Canadian, rubbing Trumpy and Marlowe's noses in the fact that my guy had beaten their guy, Carl Lewis, in the premier event of the Games, the 100-metre race. Johnson crossed the finish line in world-record time with his right arm raised and his index finger extended to illustrate to the world his standing as the fastest man on the planet.

The next morning, I got on the bus to our arena, and boy, did I get it back. Johnson had been caught with a banned substance, stanozolol, in his system, and was stripped of his gold medal, which was then awarded to Lewis. The guys on the bus were ready for me.

"You Canadians," Trumpy and Marlowe said. "Nothing but a bunch of cheaters!"

I had to put up with that for the rest of the Games.

As the years go by, time has proven that Johnson was not unique to track in taking performance-enhancing drugs. Johnson won the gold, but even if he hadn't, someone who won it eventually would have been caught using drugs. That was the culture of the sport back then. It may still be that way today, for all I know—they just have more sophisticated ways of hiding it.

The officials were looking for a sacrificial lamb, and Ben Johnson was their man. I think he has been mistreated as a Canadian since then, too—especially by the media. In my books, he is still a great champion.

You never know who you'll bump into at an Olympics. Prior to the start of the Seoul games, there was a big meeting of all the producers, directors, and talent. It was held at a hotel a considerable distance from where we were staying, and when it was over, I managed to miss the bus taking us to our seminar. I had misread my schedule and had the wrong time.

So I was standing outside the hotel when this big, black limousine pulled up and I saw a guy walking toward it.

I said, "Are you with NBC?"

He said he was.

"I'm Ralph Mellanby and I'm producing the volleyball at the Games."

He said, "I'm Tom Brokaw. Hop in."

Brokaw, it turns out, was a great mountain climber who had been to Banff and climbed the Canadian Rockies. I never saw him again, but I'll never forget our chance meeting and a great conversation about Canada and the mountains.

When the Games finished, I couldn't get home fast enough. Of all the Olympic cities I have worked in, Seoul is the one place I have no desire to return to.

* * *

My participation in the 1992 Summer Olympics in Barcelona was minimal compared to my duties in previous Games. I was the head of venue production, which is a pretty fancy title for a job with precious little responsibility. In a nutshell, I was responsible for making sure there were no problems that would hamper television at the venues and giving daily reports to Manolo Romero, who was in charge of running the world TV feed. I was to be his eyes and ears. It meant I also had to put up with a lot of bitching and moaning.

Oh well, I also managed to squeeze three trips to Barcelona out of the deal, so it wasn't all bad. I was there with the IOC television commission, as part of CTV's bid for the broadcast rights (they didn't win) and on a preparatory survey trip. So by time the Games rolled around, I knew my way around a bit.

Despite the fact that I should have been able to relax and enjoy the Barcelona Games, it was not one of the most pleasurable experiences of my working life. My big problem was a bit of culture shock. I didn't realize it during my exploratory visits, because in that situation you're travelling with a group and there isn't really any pressure to get your job done. But once I landed in Barcelona and began working, it became apparent that the Spanish way of doing business was very different from what I was accustomed to. I am a typical North American who likes to eat his dinner between 5 and 6 p.m. They don't eat until 11 p.m. They arrive for work at 7 a.m., and I'm not much of a morning person. They have a three-hour lunch—usually with booze—then they have a siesta. When they finally go back to work, they stay until 10 p.m., and then they go to dinner. After a few days of this routine, my head was spinning.

Fortunately, I found a restaurant near my hotel that served fast food, because I certainly couldn't wait until 11 p.m. to eat my dinner. The owner eventually expanded the menu to include full meals after I told him the Americans and Canadians coming to the Games would want to eat much earlier. He made a killing during the Olympics—he actually built a second restaurant. He gave me a free meal at the end and said, "Thanks. That was the best tip I have ever received." Well, if only I'd invested more than an idea!

One of my major concerns heading to the Games was whether I would have to learn to speak Spanish. I needn't have worried. It turned out the fact I spoke English and French was enough to get by—I was told that in Barcelona the official language is Catalan, and most of the people there hated the Spanish as they had been conquered by Franco. I could relate, having lived in Quebec. So, no Spanish lessons.

What saved me was my driver, Eduardo. He spoke perfect English and told me he eventually hoped to move to the United States. He was the same age as my son and became my pal. Eduardo really knew the town and the culture. It wasn't until the Games were nearly over that I found out his father was the president of the Bank of Spain—not a bad contact.

I am certain Eduardo liked my company, too. He arranged it so that he became my permanent driver, saving me from having to go to the motor pool every day.

"Do you need a driver every day?" he asked.

I said yes.

He said, "I'm your guy."

"I thought I have to go to the motor pool."

"Never mind," he said. "I can beat that system."

And he did. Smart kid!

The theme of the 1992 Summer Games was "Friends for Life," and he became a great friend.

Barcelona is a fantastic city, the second largest in Spain, with a population of more than 1.6 million people. It has a Mediterranean climate, which means mild, humid winters and very dry summers. There are seven beaches totalling 2.8 miles of coastline. And, I am happy to report, they have some wonderful golf courses. I was able to get a few games in before the Olympics began at a seaside town outside of the city.

During the Olympics, I was to report directly to Romero. If there were problems, I would let him know. He would need to know the problems, even though it was his venue managers who were responsible for solving them. Given my experience at previous Games, this was not exactly an onerous task. Still, in my heart I felt I could have contributed more had I been put in charge of producing at one of the venues—say, basketball or volleyball. But those tasks went to Europeans and I had to be satisfied with the fact that I was at least at the Games. Also, I was able to help with the production of the opening and closing ceremonies because I had done them both in Calgary.

I was able to set my own schedule, which was nice. It was the first time the Games were broadcast in high-definition, so that was a learning experience. And prior to the start of the Games, there were seminars for some of the major sports, and I was able to participate in them. I was the main speaker at the volleyball seminar.

I didn't run into too many problems with my duties. The Germans were going to go home because they thought the contract had been broken. Apparently, their major complaints centred on the food and the Spanish support staff, who did not speak German.

All in all, it was a great Olympics. This was the first time professional athletes were allowed to compete in basketball and the United States, not surprisingly, cleaned up. The Dream Team, led by Magic Johnson, Larry Bird, Michael Jordan, Charles Barkley, Scottie Pippen, and David Robinson, steamrolled its way through the preliminary round, winning five straight, then winning three playoff games to win the gold medal. The American women also won gold.

Other highlights included Vitaly Scherbo winning six gold medals in men's gymnastics, including four in one day. American Evelyn Ashford won her fourth gold medal in the women's 4 × 100 relay, making her just the fourth woman in history to achieve this. After being a demonstration sport, baseball was elevated to an Olympic event, and the gold medal was won by Cuba. Thirty-two-year-old Linford Christie won the gold medal in the men's 100-metre sprint, becoming the oldest Olympic champion in that event.

I try to be on my best behaviour when I am at high-profile events such as the Olympics, but every now and then I let my guard down. One day, I was out for dinner with a bunch of my pals on La Rambla, a street where everybody goes to shop and eat and which is the main tourist area. On this day, well, I got a little drunk. In my celebratory state I went to a fortune teller who didn't speak a lick of English— she spoke only Catalan. I'm not certain what the heck she said to me, so I have no idea if my fortune came true. John Cassaday, the president of CTV, and Peter Sisam, a network vice-president, were there for meetings on future Olympics, and they never let me forget about that one.

Barcelona was a memorable experience. It is a beautiful and unusual city filled with history and remarkable art and architecture. But if you visit, be prepared to eat late.

* * *

My participation in the 1996 Summer Olympics in Atlanta began with my being a part of the team that tried to get the Games for Toronto. I was on the bid team led by Paul Henderson. That's not the famous hockey player who scored the winning goal for Team Canada at the 1972 Summit Series; *this* Paul Henderson was the coach of the Canadian Olympic yachting team and was later president of the International Yacht Racing Union. Today, he is a valued IOC member.

I was *the* Canadian television guy at the Olympics by 1990, and a lot of my pals suggested that I get involved with the Toronto bid because of my experience at previous Games. We had a Toronto group that we called the "Twelve Disciples," and we later added people like former Canadian prime minister Joe Clark to the bid team.

The vote was to take place in Tokyo, and Toronto was the front-runner all the way. That is, until we arrived in Tokyo. Everything that could go wrong for us did. Remember the protest group Bread Not Circuses? They were a bunch of anti-poverty activists who, in an unprecedented move, were allowed to meet with the committee evaluating the sites. They argued that the money spent on the Olympics should be spent on housing. Also, when Bob Rae's New Democratic Party won the Ontario provincial election in 1990, it was a deadly blow for the bid. Henderson invited him to join us in Tokyo, but he refused, and that sank our ship. When the premier won't show up, it's perceived as a bit of slight. The new government's political stripe couldn't have helped; I think the IOC started to wonder whether the Toronto bid could actually deliver the money it had promised. If we had the Conservatives or Liberals in power in Ontario, I believe Toronto would have hosted the Olympics.

I travelled all over the world with the Toronto group. At the same time, I would always be running into the Atlanta delegation. I was always very cordial to them. They didn't really care for Henderson, but they got along with me because they knew who I was. I wouldn't say they welcomed me with open arms, because at that point we were in competition, but they didn't treat me with animosity, either.

One American in particular that I grew friendly with was the late Chuck Fruit, the marketing guru at Coca-Cola who had gained his reputation earlier with Budweiser. I met him through other Games, particularly in Calgary in 1988. In Atlanta, there was Turner Broadcasting and there was Coke—so Chuck later opened a lot of doors for me.

Throughout the process, Toronto was ranked number one, and we believed in our hearts that we would be chosen to host the 1996 Olympic Games. Our insider sources kept telling us the IOC wanted to come to North America, and with only Toronto and Atlanta bidding from North America, I liked our chances.

John Cassaday had taken over as president of CTV from Murray Chercover, and while we were in Tokyo he offered me the job as vice-president of sports for the network. He told me Johnny Esaw was retiring and he wanted me to replace him.

I was extremely flattered, but I said, "No." I explained that we felt we were going to win the bid for the Olympics, and I was committed to Paul Henderson to head up the worldwide television operation.

"Well, what if you lose?" Cassaday asked.

"We're not going to lose."

That's how absolutely sure I was. I didn't think there was any way on earth we would lose the bid.

In the end, I regretted my decision. Truth be told, even if we didn't win the bid, I thought I'd be the number one TV guy if Atlanta won. They liked me.

When the Games were awarded to Atlanta, we were just devastated. It was a surprise to everyone—the conventional wisdom was that Athens was our biggest competition. They certainly were a sentimental favourite to host the Olympics in the centennial year of the modern Games. But Athens lost, too, as did Belgrade, Manchester, and Melbourne.

All the Olympic bidders have a closing party lined up, because they all think they are going to win. When we lost, I went to our party and who did I see at the bar but Canadian businessman and sportsman John Bitove as well as Trevor Eyton, the industrialist. Both were members of our bid committee. They were sipping rather large drinks, and I walked over and said, "Can I join you?"

Trevor looked at me and said, "I know you are an IOC guy." In fact, I wasn't. "We should have bought the bastards."

I harked back to Bill Pratt of Calgary, who'd told me the IOC could be bought. I didn't believe him at the time. Now, I'm not so sure, given that history has shown that corruption has had its place at the IOC.

Bitove looked at me and said, "What are you worried for? You're going to work in Atlanta anyways. We're the guys who won't be there."

They were decimated. I didn't feel that way. The fact is, my brother Jim was having quadruple bypass surgery the next day, so he was my top priority, even though I had worked so hard on the bid. Family always comes first. I took a red-eye flight back to North America to be with Jim. Thank the Lord, the operation was a great success.

Atlanta had been perceived as a long shot, if for no other reason than because Los Angeles had been the host city in 1984. Our feeling was that their bid was very weak, but we forgot how powerful Coca-Cola was, and they were involved. Nothing like having a monster corporate sponsor on your side.

Later, the Atlanta folks called me and asked if I would be interested in being the host broadcaster. I said of course I would. Don Baer, a former executive at NBC Sports, and I decided to put in a bid, but didn't go very far.

The next thing I knew, I was informed that Manolo Romero had been chosen to do the world broadcast and there would be no formal bidding for the position. I was dumbfounded.

I asked why, and I was told it had to do with politics.

Typical, I thought. We're North Americans and the Games are being held on North American soil, yet we still get aced out by a European. Why bring in an outsider who is already busy in Barcelona to be the guy? But Romero went back a long way with the IOC.

Romero did a smart thing, though. He hired three guys off our Atlanta bid team, including me, to be part of his crew. That certainly placated Don and me. And I helped the organizers in the choice of a site for the broadcast centre, which was the World Congress Center.

My job in Atlanta, as director of venue production, was the same one I'd done in Barcelona, but on a much larger scale. I had a lot of other things going on—other international events, and Brian Robertson and I were starting up the *Air Farce* TV series for CBC and the Governor General's Awards. But I felt I needed to be in Atlanta to devote as much attention as possible to the Games, so, in 1991, I decided to move there.

I knew I would be doing a lot of commuting, and Atlanta was a great city to live in. It made sense to have a base there.

The Games, from a television standpoint, were immaculate. It was also a TV dictatorship. I had learned that from having worked for and with Romero over the years, and I knew that in order to do the job I had to accept that. I knew I wouldn't have a lot of say in terms of how things were run. Just production—forget our expertise in other areas.

I loved being involved in the Atlanta Games even though, at the end of the day, the organizing committee was rather mediocre. They were very insular and parochial. There wasn't a lot of sharing of information. Television people around the world have a saying that the only real amateurs at the Olympics are the members of the organizing committee, and it holds true most of the time. They do it once and they never do it again. They are mostly rookies who lack the necessary experience to mount a truly great Games.

One thing I learned over the years is that the organizing committee should not be made up exclusively of people who were on the bid committee. Any Olympic veteran will tell you this. Winning the bid doesn't mean you know how to run the Games. You need the input of people who have run them before.

Right away, I could see that the people who had helped win the bid had been given the most important jobs with the organizing committee. We wouldn't necessarily have gone down that road if Toronto's bid had succeeded. We weren't even sure that Henderson, who headed up the bid, would be president of the organizing committee.

I made up my mind that I would try to give the Atlanta organizing committee the benefit of my expertise. For instance, they had about three different heads of transportation, and one day the newest came into my office and told me that everybody had told him he should talk to me. We had never met.

I said, "Sure. I'm a team player. What would you like to know?"

He said, "What is the best transportation system you have ever seen at an Olympics?"

I replied, "I have never seen a good one. They were all very poor."

He thought I was being a smart ass and started telling me how, now that he was running transportation, I'd never be able to say that again. Clearly, I had rubbed him the wrong way, even though that was not my intention. I told him I would be happy to help him in any way I could, but transportation always has been a problem and likely always will be. You have to turn the city upside down to host the Olympics, and transportation is one of the first casualties. Needless to say, soon thereafter there was a new head of transportation—and I avoided him.

Another day, about a year and a half before the Games were to begin, a woman came into my office and said, "I'm Shirley Franklin," which didn't mean a whole lot to me at the time. Of course, she became the mayor of Atlanta in 2002—the first woman to be mayor of that city. *Time* magazine named her one of the top five big-city mayors in 2005. She was one of my favourite ladies.

She said, "I'm new, and I'm here to work with Billy Payne [the president of ACOG, the Atlanta Committee for the Olympic Games]. I don't know the Olympics and I have never worked the Games."

She then asked me if she could take me into her confidence and I said yes.

She said, "I need someone who can help me understand the nuances of this, and everybody tells me you are somebody I can trust."

I told her the best thing she could do was accompany me on field trips to other events, such as the Pan-American Games, the Asian Games and the Commonwealth Games in Victoria, British Columbia, and I'd try to show her how things work. Shirley was so smart she really didn't need to join me, but years later, after she became the mayor of Atlanta, I ran into friends who told me she credited me with being a big help to her. I was very flattered and appreciated her kind words.

The Games themselves were average. There was a heavy reliance on corporate sponsorship, and many considered the Games to be too commercialized.

The venues were great and the people were terrific. But everything that surrounded the Games made them tawdry. The mayor, Bill Campbell, closed down many of the downtown parking lots and leased them out to souvenir vendors and people who set up tents and operated temporary nightclubs. It was ridiculous—embarrassing. The city had committed to do a lot to make itself a showcase, but failed to deliver on its promise. As far as I could see, all it did was put in new streetlights downtown. Big deal. In fairness, Billy Payne—a hero of mine—did build great venues, as well as the Centennial Olympic Park, which left Atlanta with a great legacy.

Transportation, as I predicted, was a disaster. It always is. It didn't affect the broadcast operation, because we made our own transportation and security arrangements.

I loved Billy Payne, but I think he needed more experienced people on his organizing committee. Billy went on to replace Hootie Johnson as chairman of Augusta National Golf Club, home of the Masters Tournament, and I'm sure his Olympic experience will help him to be a great success in that venture.

One highlight of the Games occurred during the opening ceremonies, when boxing legend Muhammad Ali lit the torch to officially begin the Games. If you didn't have tears in your eyes watching Ali, shaking from the effects of Parkinson's disease as he lit the torch, then you might have wanted to check your pulse to see if you were still alive.

In terms of the athletic events, I was thrilled when Canada's Donovan Bailey won the gold medal in the marquee event, the men's 100-metre sprint. There would be no steroid scandle this time, and Bailey was unofficially dubbed the world's fastest man. However, Michael Johnson of the United States won the 200- and 400-metre races and soon proclaimed that it he, not Bailey, should be considered the fastest man on the planet.

This later led to a match race between Bailey and Johnson in Toronto's SkyDome. They had agreed on a distance of 150 metres, and Bailey blew Johnson (who pulled up short) out of the water, taking home the $1.5 million prize for doing so.

Carl Lewis won his fourth Olympic gold medal in the long jump event, while the American women's soccer team also won gold.

Unfortunately, the Atlanta Games will also be forever remembered for the bombing at the Centennial Olympic Park just after midnight on July 27. Eric Robert Rudolph planted a knapsack containing three pipe bombs in the busy area, then left. Two people died and 111 were injured.

A happier memory has to do with helping an old friend get involved in the event. The organizing committee was looking for someone to train their venue announcers, who had to speak both English and French and get the sporting terminology just right. I told them I knew just the person: Don Goodwin, the former head of CBC Sports. He was semi-retired—although he still does events such as the Canadian Open tennis tournament to this day. I called Don and warned him to expect a call from the Atlanta committee. He said he'd love to do it, and that he'd love to join me in Atlanta.

"How much dough does it pay?" he asked.

Funny how money is usually at the root of most decisions people make.

"I don't know," I said.

They interviewed two or three other guys, but they picked Don. He was happy with the generous fee, by the way.

When it came time to choose an announcer for the opening and closing ceremonies, the organizers decided that, rather than hire a famous name, they wanted someone that no one would recognize—that way, the voice wouldn't be associated with anything but the Atlanta Olympic Games. The announcer would have to have a great voice, of course, but would also have to be able to handle more than one language.

I told them, "You already have that person on board as a freelancer."

"Who?"

"Don Goodwin. He's here training all the venue announcers and doing a wonderful job."

I called Don and told him about the opportunity, and was surprised when he replied that he really wasn't interested in the job. He said he was too busy.

I said, "I think the fee is around $30,000," and he immediately said, "Count me in!"

They interviewed Don, and he got the job. As I predicted he was terrific and I was very proud of him. I was ecstatic to have another Canadian involved.

It truly was an anonymous job—in the years since 1996, I have even asked some of Don's friends if they knew who the voice of the opening and closing ceremonies was. They had no idea. Don gets a big chuckle out of that. He tells me even some of his former employees didn't know he was the guy.

When I look back at Atlanta, I feel sorry that the staging of the 1996 Games have been underrated. The venues were immaculate and the sports well administered. The Olympic Park, in spite of the bombing, was a great success, and the television coverage was monumental.

But the damn transportation!

* * *

When Sydney, Australia, got the 2000 Summer Games, I got a call from David Hill, the president of Fox Sports, who told me the organizing committee didn't want Manolo Romero to handle the broadcasting. Guess I'm not the only one who wasn't a charter member of Romero's fan club. Apparently, he'd had a falling out with the executive of the Sydney organizing committee.

So the Aussies called an Australian TV executive, Jim Fitzmaurice, who had worked with Hill, to ask about whom they might hire as executive producer to run the world television feed. Both mentioned my name.

"Mate, you've been well recommended," David Hill told me.

The committee invited Janet and me to come for a week to discuss the job. I took a week's vacation and didn't tell a soul where I was headed.

As a side note, a pickpocket stole my wallet in the Atlanta airport. It was an omen. Fortunately, we were able to arrange with my brother-in-law to meet up with us in Los Angeles and slip me some money while we waited for our connecting flight.

We travelled first class and could not have been treated better. I met Michael Knight, the president of the Sydney committee, who told me he was very impressed with my resumé and that everybody on the committee wanted me to be in charge of the world feed. I'm sure it didn't hurt that I was Canadian, and therefore came from another Commonwealth nation. Naturally, I was thrilled. I began looking forward to living Down Under for four or five years, and was up to the challenge.

I toured all the venues and met with the telephone company people, and then Jim Fitzmaurice took us to his palatial estate on his lake for a barbeque. What a great trip! I had made a lot of friends in Australian television over the years, and thanks to this trip, I was able to expand my network even more. I was so confident I had the gig lined up that I offered many of them jobs with the host broadcaster.

Then Knight called me in to his office to meet with him and the chairman. "Samaranch has called me, Dick Ebersol from NBC has called me and several members of the IOC have called me, and they are insisting Romero be in charge of the world feed. You can't do it."

It was like a kick in the stomach! Once again, Manolo Romero had aced me out of the job.

I looked both of them in the eye. "Either I run the world television feed or I'm out. I will not work for that man again."

They simply said, "Sorry mate, but we can't afford the political fallout. But we still want you on the team."

I said, "Not with Romero!"

* * *

The next kick in the pants came a little later, near the start of the Atlanta Games. I had been acting as a consultant for Fox when they acquired the rights to NHL hockey. The network had never covered the sport, so they needed someone to advise them on which producers, directors and talent they should use. I spent a year helping them; it was fun, financially rewarding, and I loved working with David and the people at Fox.

One day, Hill called me and said he had something confidential he'd like to discuss with me. He informed me that Fox was planning to put together a group to become the first network to get the world-wide rights for five Olympic Games. This was huge—unprecedented. It was a stroke of pure genius!

Hill said that he and Rupert Murdoch, who owned Fox, wanted me to fly to Los Angeles for a secret meeting. Needless to say, I was in.

David swore me to secrecy—they didn't want NBC to find out about their plans. I assured him I could be trusted. They were so secretive about the meeting that they didn't even want to hold it at their TV studios. We were to meet at the corporate headquarters of the 20th Century Fox movie studio, around the corner from my hotel.

Being a movie buff, I was quite interested in seeing the lot. They sent a limo to my hotel, ready to drive me around the corner to the meeting, but I said no, I'd prefer to walk.

I walked up to the front gate with my briefcase, and I was greeted by an old security guard who told me had had worked there for decades and decades.

I said, "Can you direct me to the administration building?"

"I can tell you how to drive there," he said.

"What do you mean?"

"Nobody has ever walked up to the gate before and asked how to walk to a meeting," he said. "You're a first."

He directed me where to go, and I walked through the back lot. Being somewhat directionally challenged, I didn't find it right away. But then I spied an old friend, Geoff Mason (who had been the executive producer of ABC Sports when I worked there). He was waving at me, and I picked up the pace because I was going to be late. I was happy to see that Geoff was also part of the group. Hill, Mason, and I were the only three Olympics experts attending the meeting. The rest were Fox brass, about twenty people in all. Rupert Murdoch was even there to say hello before departing and letting us get down to business.

David laid out the plans. He said he and Rupert were going to Lausanne, Switzerland, to bid on five straight Olympics. Juan

Antonio Samaranch of the IOC knew they were coming, but not the purpose of their visit.

The plan sounded a little bit like pie in the sky to me. I kept saying, "David, you'll never get it. The IOC hates Fox."

Actually, they hated Rupert because he was such a huge media mogul. And it wasn't hatred so much as jealousy.

After the meeting was over we went to David Hill's home and enjoyed a wonderful California evening, not to mention a barbeque. I continued to tell Hill, "You'll never get it."

He said, "You son of a bitch, Mellanby. Just make sure you don't tell anybody."

"Why would I tell anybody? I want to be a big part of this. I'll be the executive producer for five straight Winter and Summer Olympics."

He said, "You can bet you will be. You're going to be a Fox guy."

With that, I sure as hell wasn't going to blab. I flew back to Atlanta and didn't tell a soul.

As fate would have it, I was scheduled to attend a meeting with NBC while Hill and Murdoch were to be in Switzerland. Who should be there but Alec Gilady, an Israeli member of the IOC who also worked for NBC; indeed, he was known as "the delegate from NBC."

After the meeting, we moved on to lunch at the Fox Theater Restaurant. We were all eating and enjoying ourselves, when suddenly I noticed that the NBC bigwigs had gone upstairs to an empty part of the restaurant. There was a big kafuffle, and the next thing I knew they were leaving the building, led by Gilady and Dick Ebersol.

The rest of us wondered what the hell was going on. Coincidentally, Romero was there, and he wouldn't say a word.

I found out later that a phone call had been placed to Gilady at the restaurant. I don't know for sure, but I heard it was Samaranch. My guess is it went something like this: "You'd better tell our friends at NBC that Fox just bid for five Olympic Games. NBC had better be prepared." Again, that's just my well-educated guess. David Hill later confirmed he heard a similar story from an IOC insider.

Shortly thereafter, it was announced that NBC had secured the rights to every Olympics, Winter and Summer, through 2008. It sickened me to hear it. I remembered Gilady and company storming out of the restaurant and realized once again that politics had won out. This was a period when U.S. networks were bidding aggressively for the rights to carry sports. Fox snatched NFL rights away from CBS in 1993, which cost CBS in terms of prestige and affiliations with local stations. Fox also got the rights to Major League Baseball from ABC and NBC in 1995. In 1998, CBS would succeed in outbidding NBC for *its* NFL package. But rather than opening the Olympic rights to competitive bids, the IOC elected to maintain its relationship with NBC.

I later asked Gilady if he got a call from the IOC during that lunch, but he wouldn't tell me.

In the newspapers, it came out that it was NBC's idea to bid on five Olympics all along, but I don't believe it. Having been in on the meeting at Fox, I know it was their idea first.

The Australian network that covered the Sydney Games offered me a job, but I declined. After thirteen Olympic Games, I was done—I didn't want to work on them anymore. I'd had my fill of the IOC's nonsense, and later, when I got the chance, I said so right to the faces of Canadian IOC members Dick Pound and Paul Henderson.

No one was more of a fan of the Olympic ideals or the Games than I, but to this day I don't even watch a minute of any Olympic Games. I hate the fact that professional athletes are allowed to compete, and regret the commercialism. I find myself longing for the days, back when I started, when the Olympics were not just a business, but a dream come true for the amateur athletes of the world, and a place where new stars are born and the world could celebrate.

12

ONCE IN A LIFETIME

One of the most amazing things about working in television is the opportunity you get to cross paths with some of the most famous people in the world. Not just athletes, but movie stars, politicians, singers—you name it. My wife, Gillian, says I should have called this chapter "The People You Met Once in Your Life." Well, "Once in a Lifetime" is close enough.

After more than fifty years in the business, I feel very fortunate to have found an occupation that suited me perfectly and, quite frankly, a business I had no intention of entering. Fact is, the television business as we'd come to know it was less than ten years old when I joined it, and who knew back then what a powerful medium it would become?

My dad was quite adamant that I follow his footsteps into the newspaper business, and I even got to work as a copy boy one summer. There was no doubt that, if I didn't become a professional baseball player, that was the business I would choose. All my relatives felt the same—that I was destined to be a newspaperman just like Dad.

My Grandma Mellanby was a well-known psychic in Hamilton. She used to attend the Church of Spiritualism, and she was amazing. Once, my dad lost his Christmas present—a hat. She said to Dad, "I never see you wearing your hat," and he said, "I don't know where it is."

Grandma Mellanby said, "It's at the very bottom of your front hall closet at the back."

Truth be told, she hadn't peeked inside that closet—she just sensed things. She amazed everyone.

Grandma Mellanby used to tell me all the time, "You're going to be great. You're going to be wonderful."

I'd say to her, "Yeah, Grandma, I'm going to be a professional athlete."

"No you're not; you're going to be in the entertainment world."

In those days, there wasn't any television—just radio and movies. It's amazing. She died in the early 1940s, and even back then, she knew what path my life would take.

I think the greatest joy of my career wasn't doing the shows and covering all the events I was fortunate to be a part of, it was the famous people I met along the way. I would have never met these celebrities had I not been in television.

I was very lucky when I started in television to be at a local station like CKLW in Windsor. It was a great learning experience because in those days, in the 1950s, local television wasn't like it is today. Today, it's just news and information—they bring in the big network shows during prime time. In my day, local stations produced a lot of their own programming—and 75 per cent of the shows went out live because videotape was still unheard of and film was expensive. We did kids' shows, women's shows, housekeeping shows—you name it. In sports, we did "studio boxing" and "studio wrestling." There would be 100, maybe 150 spectators in attendance, usually by invitation, and these bouts were staged to promote the big events that would take placed in larger venues across the river in Detroit.

Not only was there a lot of activity, but I got to do every job because we weren't unionized. You can't do that today. People are more specialized. My dad always encouraged me to try to do every job on the way up to familiarize myself with the industry.

One of the shows I worked on was *The Bill Kennedy Show*. It started in 1956 and was the number one afternoon show in Detroit and Windsor. Bill had been an actor in Hollywood, appearing in movies— and it was his voice you heard as narrator during the opening of the television series *The Adventures of Superman*. Bill would interview stars on his show. I have many, many pictures of myself and the rest of the crew with Bill's guests—the likes of Liberace, Charlton Heston, John Wayne, and Robert Mitchum. Detroit was a huge media market—the third-largest in the country behind New York and Chicago—so they would make the trip to promote their movies and other efforts.

I was part of the stage crew back then, as an assistant. It seemed like I was always an assistant to somebody in those days, and every job I had I thought was going to be my job for life. I truly loved everything I did! To me it was play. Being around all these stars was a bonus. I'd go home and tell my mom, "Jeanette MacDonald was in today." MacDonald, of course, was the lovely singer and actress who starred in four movies nominated for the Best Picture Oscar. My mom, Marie, was thrilled.

MacDonald was appearing in a Broadway-style show in Detroit and when she came to our studio, she brought a makeup person and her own lighting man with her. Television was still in its infancy, and celebrities didn't trust us to make them look their best.

Another star I'll never forget dropping by for the day was Kirk Douglas. He was my hero in the movies. Not only was he the biggest star of the day, but he was my kind of guy—a man's man. The crew was really excited about him being there. I worked with a stagehand named Luke Adam, who was a bodybuilder. Kirk, who was a weightlifter too and had a great body, looked at him and said, "What's your name?"

"Luke."

"You're a weightlifter, huh?"

"Yes."

"Won't do you any good. Look what it did for me!"

We all laughed. What a guy!

Doing that show I learned that the biggest stars were all the best people. They had the confidence, the swagger. They didn't feel they had to mistreat the little people just to make themselves feel better. It was the same way in sports.

I also worked on *Dance Party*, and we had some of the best young musical stars as guests, including Buddy Holly, Ricky Nelson, and Paul Anka. I was a floor manager on that show. They'd bring in the artists with the top hit songs of the day and they would lip-synch to their records while the kids danced—the same idea as *American Bandstand*, which wasn't yet being broadcast nationally.

I'll never forget the day Paul Anka appeared. He was seventeen years old and had a huge hit record with "Diana." The same day we also had actor Sal Mineo on the show. He was best known as an actor—particularly for his roles in the James Dean pictures *Rebel without a Cause* and *Giant*—but he'd also made a venture into pop music. We had to have the police at our studio to control the large gathering of teenagers that had come to see them.

I remember speaking with Mineo, and he was so nervous about being on the show. Anka and his people, on the other hand, were pissed off because they were second banana.

I also worked one season as a cameraman on *The Soupy Sales Show* in Detroit. I always said Soupy hired me because I was a good ballplayer and he wanted me with his company softball team. All the stations played in a summer softball league every Sunday morning at Palmer Park in Detroit.

Soupy's producer, Pete Strand, had been one of my lecturers at college. Soupy later went to New York around the same time I moved to Chicago. He actually had two shows in Detroit—a kids' show at noon, which got about 90 per cent of the viewing audience in its time slot, and a variety show at 11 p.m. at night. I worked on the kids' show.

What I liked about Soupy was that he was such a big sports fan. He played first base on the softball team and he'd do what we called the "Soupy Shuffle" to entertain the few fans that would come out to watch our games.

* * *

One of my great experiences was having the opportunity to meet all three Kennedy brothers—Jack, Bobby, and Ted.

In those days, organizations would buy time on television and broadcast their own shows. One of these, *Meet the UAW–CIO*, was funded by organized labour and the host was Guy Nunn. I was a cameraman on that show, and one day Senator John F. Kennedy was a guest. I remember looking at him through the camera and thinking he was the most handsome man I had ever seen.

When he walked into the studio and sat down in his chair to be interviewed, the charisma just radiated from him. It was still too early for me—and most anyone—to guess that he would go on to be president.

I met Bobby after JFK was assassinated. It was at the Grey Cup in Toronto the year before he, too, was assassinated. I was executive producer of the Grey Cup telecast and had been invited to a pre-game party that Bobby Kennedy also attended. The Kennedy and Bassett families were good friends, and John Bassett of CFTO and the *Toronto Telegram* had invited Bobby to perform the ceremonial kickoff.

I spoke with Bobby and told him I had met his brother. I told him I had to get back to the mobile where I was working, and as I started walking away, I said, "Good luck with the kickoff."

He said, "I just hope I don't screw it up!"

He didn't. The Kennedys were great lovers of football, so I wasn't surprised when he booted the ball about forty yards down the field.

I met Ted Kennedy when the Boston Bruins held "Bobby Orr Night" at the old Boston Garden. That night, they played an exhibition game against the Russians, and Don Cherry never forgave Bruins GM Harry Sinden for what he perceived as an egregious slight. Cherry, who was coaching the Bruins, was absolutely livid that the Bruins would honour the greatest player in the history of the NHL during an exhibition game—against the Russians, of all people! In protest, he didn't dress many of his best players for the game. Of course, the Russians won.

Ted Kennedy was at the game, which I worked on for *Hockey Night in Canada*. When I was asked if we wanted the senator as a guest on one of the intermissions I said of course. I went down to the studio, which was actually a converted dressing room, and met with him. The mayor of Boston walked in with the entourage and Senator Kennedy. I was standing at the back of the studio, near the washrooms and showers, and I pulled him aside to let him know who I was and to talk about his appearance on the show.

"What will we talk about?" he asked.

"No politics," I said, "just sports and perhaps a little bit about your family."

That relaxed him a little bit. It was just before he was about to go on when I noticed his hair was a little messy.

"Maybe you'd like to use the washroom to fix your hair," I said.

"No, to tell you the truth I have to take a piss," he replied.

And off he went. Obviously, a regular guy.

Scotty Morrison, who was in charge of the NHL's on-ice officials, was a guest on the show before Senator Kennedy, and when Ted came back from the bathroom, we were just about to go to a commercial. Scotty was on for three minutes, and we reserved seven minutes for Ted.

As our host, Dave Hodge, threw to the commercial, our floor manager barked out, "You, Morrison...get out! You, Kennedy...get in!"

The entire room fell silent. All the PR work I'd done with Ted Kennedy was ruined. Still, he was a great guest.

After the game there was a party for Bobby at some great big mansion. I was invited. Senator Kennedy was also a guest at the party and we had a wonderful talk about his brothers. I told him about meeting Jack and Bobby, and he seemed quite pleased about that. He, of course, regaled our small group with stories about the old days at the Kennedy compound. By the way, just like me, he loved his drinks.

* * *

I met President Bill Clinton when he spoke at a reception in Atlanta, where we had assembled our Olympic staff. I introduced myself to him as a Canadian and he told me how much he liked Canada. I always get a big thrill talking about my country.

I also got to meet many of Canada's top politicians over the years, including Tommy Douglas, who was named the greatest Canadian ever in a CBC poll in 2004. The former premier of Saskatchewan is known for his dedication to social causes and is considered the father of Canada's public health-insurance system.

I met him at a football rally for the Saskatchewan Roughriders. It was a thrill, not only because of all he had done for Canada, but also because of our mutual connection to Saskatchewan—my first wife, Janet, of course, was also from Saskatchewan. I walked up to him and thanked him for what he had done for the country and then told him I'd married a girl from Regina.

He looked at me and said, "That just shows you have the ultimate good taste."

I met another son of Saskatchewan, John Diefenbaker, Canada's thirteenth prime minister, when I took him for a tour of Maple Leaf Gardens.

He said, "I want to tell you something: you have the second most important job in Canada behind mine—running *Hockey Night in Canada.*"

He said our show was so important to Canadians because it united the country—especially on Saturday nights.

I met his successor, Lester B. Pearson, several times. During the 1972 Summit Series he told me, with that lispy voice he had, that he was a much better hockey coach than he was a prime minister. He was a real jock—he had played hockey at Oxford University and coached the University of Toronto men's team. He was also a star baseball and lacrosse player in his youth.

Peter Lougheed was never the prime minister of Canada, but he could have been. He dedicated his political life to the province of Alberta, serving as premier from 1971 to 1985. He was the face of the province and built a great legacy.

I met him at the NHL All-Star Game in Calgary in 1985. I used to take Janet to all the All-Star Games. Unlike the playoffs, where you had a series of games, the All-Star events were just one game, one night, and the league always threw a big party for its sponsors so it was a real social engagement—especially for the wives.

Peter was the special guest on this occasion, and he spent quite a bit of time trying to convince Janet—who, like him, was a graduate of the University of Alberta—that she and I should move back to Alberta. I was standing there laughing, because I had no intention of living in Alberta. Little did I know...

In 1985, after I accepted the job of running the Calgary Winter Olympics, there I was, living in Alberta! Lougheed had a place in Banff, just down the street from the coach house I'd rented from Glen Sather, and we'd have breakfast together occasionally at Melissa's Mistake, a great restaurant. He told me quite frankly he never wanted to be prime minister of Canada. He was a Conservative, as was I, and was truly passionate about Alberta. He really helped teach me a lot about the province during our breakfasts.

Another of my favourites was René Lévesque, the founder of the Parti Québécois and the twenty-third premier of Quebec. René was an announcer in French television when I first met him at the Montreal Press Club. He was a good friend of one of my top cameramen, Jimmy Grattan, who produced our intermission features. It was Jimmy who introduced me to René.

Once, I was in New York with Jimmy to shoot a feature on Rod Gilbert of the Rangers. We went to a restaurant, and who was sitting in the corner with two beautiful women, but René. He was in New York to do a famous talk show and said, "These two ladies who worked in TV invited me for a drink." Some story! We just smiled. Neither Jimmy nor I ever told a soul we saw René out on the town in Manhattan with a couple of women.

I am a great admirer of Lévesque's, even though I acknowledge that a lot of Canadians don't respect his political beliefs or his desire to have Quebec separate from the rest of the country. I understood what he was trying to do. Sometimes it takes dramatic measures in our country to gain attention and get results. Peter Lougheed once told me he thought Alberta might separate first, before Quebec, so you never know.

I met Brian Mulroney before he was the prime minister. I was staying at a hotel in Montreal and went down to the restaurant to have lunch, and he was sitting with Ronald Corey, the president of the Montreal Canadiens. Corey was Mulroney's campaign manager and invited me over to meet him. We had a wonderful chat and shared the fact we were both staunch conservatives.

Ralph Klein, the twelfth premier of Alberta, used to call me "the other Ralph in Calgary." He was the mayor of Calgary when we first met. Today I am on the board of advisers for the Calgary Stampeders of the Canadian Football League, and former CFL commissioner Doug Mitchell always has me to the game when they play the Argonauts in Toronto. The last time I went to the game, Ralph was there—I hadn't seen him since the Olympics.

He sat beside me for the entire first half of the game so we could catch up. He was another guy who got his start in the media. He was a reporter for a local television station and he used to meet at a pub with other reporters and would complain about all that was wrong with the city. His pals convinced him to run for mayor, and that's exactly what he did. He was the mayor of Calgary from 1980 to 1989 and was a big help to me during the Olympics.

The guy I was closest to in terms of political personalities was Otto Jelinek. Born in Prague in 1940, Otto was a world-class figure skater before becoming a Canadian politician—a right-wing conservative and staunch anti-Communist.

I served on two government commissions for Otto when he was Canada's minister of sport. He put together the Fair Play Commission, a group that included myself as well as former CFL star quarterback Russ Jackson and NHL superstar Jean Béliveau, among others. I really enjoyed our meetings, not so much because we were trying to get fighting out of hockey—one of our top priorities—but because the people on the committee were all interesting Canadians and became lifelong friends.

Once in a while, Otto and I would play golf in Durham Region, just east of Toronto. He was the only guy I ever met that had a full complement of clubs—all the irons and all the woods—but he only used his 5-iron, wedge, and putter. And he always beat me! He insisted that was how he'd learned to play—with just three clubs. And he'd shoot in the low- to mid-80s. Amazing!

When freedom came to the Czech Republic, he moved back to Prague, where he lives with his sister, running the family business. Otto was really passionate about sport in Canada and did an amazing job of raising funds for all our athletes. I was proud to have him as a friend.

* * *

Back to the entertainment business.

I got a call from a guy I played tennis with who, after he retired, became a limousine driver, squiring around celebrities. Not bad work if you can get it. The guy that owned the limo company liked him so much, because he had such a great personality, that he was always assigned to chauffeur the biggest stars when they were in Toronto. As fate would have it, he was assigned to drive Orson Welles.

Now, I was a big fan of Orson Welles while I was growing up. Who wouldn't be? He was a genius—an Academy Award–winning director, actor, and writer whose 1941 film *Citizen Kane* is considered by many experts to be the greatest movie of all time.

Orson was in Toronto to appear on a television show, and the driver and I were both members of the Toronto Boulevard Club. The driver called me and said, "Ralph, Orson says he wants to meet somebody in the business, and you're the only guy I know. I told him you're a sports producer and he's really excited about meeting you. Why don't we take him to dinner at the club?"

I was flabbergasted.

"Sure," I said.

"Don't bring your wife; just come by yourself. It's just us guys, Ralph. Oh, and by the way, we have to buy dinner."

I was excited beyond belief. I had read his book, *The Making of Citizen Kane*, and was pretty well versed on Orson Welles. When I walked into the club and saw him, I knew I was in the presence of greatness. He was a huge man, and what set him apart was that he wore a cape.

The dinner lasted about five hours, and he did most of the talking. I just sat there, peppering him with questions. I was in love with Rita Hayworth growing up and Orson had been married to her from 1943 to 1948, so I asked him about her. There was no question that he wasn't happy to answer. Of course, we talked a lot about *Citizen Kane*.

He told me something I'll never forget. "Collaboration is the nature of our business, Ralph," he said. "To be honest, when we made *Citizen Kane*, I had no idea what I was doing. I had worked in radio and theatre and wasn't familiar with the film industry. I got the best cinematographer, the best set designer, the best this, the best that. I put them all together and it worked for us. I knew about acting, but as for the rest, I learned as we went along.

"I asked them all, 'What haven't you been able to do in the past?' In all cases, we did it in the movie."

Orson was the first director to put ceilings on the sets so he could shoot from low angles. Another thing he did was dig a big hole in the middle of the concrete floor of the studio to get one shot. It was a six-foot hole.

Norman Jewison told me the same thing. His meetings were famous. He used to lie on his back on the floor while conducting the staff. He was a different cat. He also told me the same thing Orson told me about trusting the people you work with.

Jewison loved to move the camera from side to side, because he was a television director. He was famous at the CBC for directing variety and entertainment shows. He told me that, when he made his first feature film, he was operating the same way he had on television, moving the camera constantly. On about the fifth day he asked the cinematographer, "How am I doing?"

"You're doing a great job with the actors, but nobody will ever cut this fucking picture."

"Why?"

"Because you never stop moving the camera."

Norman was shocked, but he said, "Then teach me."

For me to have the privilege of meeting two of the greatest movie directors in history was amazing. Again, two more famous personalities I never would never have met if not for my chosen career.

In Montreal, I used to do a show called *Nightcap*, where we interviewed celebrities. The announcer, who came from England, was David Bassett. He was very good and an amazing character. When we had Jackie Robinson on the show, I was shocked to see how old he looked for a man in his forties. He looked like he was a hundred.

Zubin Mehta was the conductor of the Montreal Symphony, and he would later become assistant conductor of the Los Angeles Philharmonic and other great things. He was David's guest one night, and when Mehta arrived at the studio, he had a friend with him.

I walked into the waiting room, called the green room—I can never figure out why, because they're never green! Anyway, he was in the green room accomanied by a lovely lady. Back then, the guests didn't have their managers or an entourage hanging around with them. I had met Zubin once at a rehearsal for the Montreal Symphony because a friend, Mev Berman, was the assistant conductor and chief oboist. Mev was also a sports nut. He invited me to the rehearsal.

I was probably the only guy in the building who knew about Zubin's guest, Maria Callas. She was the American-born Greek soprano and has been called one of the most distinctive and recognizable voices of the twentieth century.

Zubin introduced her, and I just about fainted, I was such a big fan. I looked at her and said, "Is there anything I can do for you?"

all the while thinking to myself that *she* was the one we should be interviewing.

"Yes, I'd love a cup of tea."

Now, you must understand, we were in a facility with a lousy little cafeteria, and I had no idea what the tea was like. Regardless, I raced over to the cafeteria and told the women who worked there, "Grace, give me the best tea you have."

"We only have one—Lipton's."

She handed it to me in a paper cup and I said, "No. This is for somebody really special—Maria Callas."

Grace wasn't happy. She had no idea who I was talking about, but she found me a proper cup and saucer and I took it to Maria.

When David and Zubin left to tape the show, I asked her if she'd like to join me in the control room because I had to leave to direct. I didn't want her to be left alone in the green room.

"I'd love to," she said. "I've never been in a television control room."

I introduced her to the guys in the control room, but they weren't impressed. They had no idea who Maria Callas was, either. She sat there throughout the show, and when it came time for her to leave, I asked her if she'd enjoyed herself.

She said, "I think what you do is marvellous, but the tea was lousy."

We both laughed. Today my wife, Gillian, and I have the complete DVD collection of the work of the late Maria Callas.

Two of my favourite guests on *Nightcap* were Pearl S. Buck, the Pulitzer and Nobel Prize–winning author, and Canadian writer Farley Mowat.

When I met Mrs. Buck, she was a lovely older lady and she looked at me and said, "You look just like my son."

Mowat came in to do his segment wearing a kilt. My script assistant Gayle, a beautiful, peppy girl, said, "I always wondered: what does a Scotchman wear under his kilt?"

Without hesitation, Mowat lifted his kilt and revealed to her the answer.

Well, let me tell you, Gayle's face turned a hundred shades of red and she just about fainted. She ran out of the studio in horror!

Guess what he had under the kilt—nothing! Don Cherry loves that story.

* * *

One of my great pals through the years has been Alan Thicke. An actor, writer, and producer, he was a northern Ontario guy from Kirkland Lake who was always around the hockey world. He both loved and played the game.

I knew him when he produced *The Alan Hamel Show* in Vancouver. Thicke was married to Gloria Loring, the singer and star of *Days of Our Lives*, at the time, and he always loved hanging around with the NHL hockey players and *Hockey Night in Canada*. We became close and still are. He flew in from California and served as MC when I was honoured in Windsor. I even put him on our *HNIC* team to play in the NHL slo-pitch softball tournament, and he was a pretty good left fielder. He is a decent hockey player, too.

I'd put Alan in the top ten Canadian TV stars, but he has always been a very down-to-earth guy. My son Scott went to play a charity hockey tournament in Las Vegas that was put on by the famous film and television producer Jerry Bruckheimer. Scott was sitting by the pool at his hotel with a couple of his NHL friends when Thicke walked over.

He said, "Are you Scott Mellanby?"

"Yes, I am."

"I just want to tell you I am a good friend of your uncle."

"My uncle?"

"Yeah, your uncle Ralph."

"That's my dad."

Alan looked at him and said, "Jesus Christ, are you ever lucky!"

* * *

Ted Zeigler was a kids' entertainer in Chicago when I worked there, and he later moved to Montreal to become "Johnny Jellybean," the third and final performer to play the role.

I was a backup director to my friend Gerry Rochon, and once in a while I'd direct Zeigler's show. We got to know each other well, and even though he was a network star, he was another of those down-to-earth guys. When I got my dogs, Ted came out to my house with his kids and helped me build a fence to house them.

He later moved to Los Angeles and became a talent agent, one of the biggest in Hollywood.

I was in Los Angeles doing a Kings series during the NHL play-offs and decided to look him up. We hadn't seen each other in years, but I figured I'd take a chance.

Ted said, "I have something to do today, but I'd like you to come along. I want to give you a big surprise."

He picked me up at my hotel by the airport, and off we went. We travelled for what seemed like an eternity, all the while talking about the good old days at CTV. Finally, we came upon a little house and parked the car. A tiny woman with an English accent greeted us at the door and invited us into her very humble one-bedroom cottage.

We were standing there when who should walk into the room but Stan Laurel, the famous actor, writer, and comedian and one half of the world-famous comedy team Laurel and Hardy. This was Ted's surprise for me.

Ted was actually helping take care of Stan, who had to be in his late eighties at the time. Ted was a great-hearted guy. We were there for about an hour and a half and they served us coffee and donuts while we chatted.

What amazed me was how sharp Laurel's mind was. He talked and talked about Oliver Hardy and the films they made. As a kid, I loved to watch the Laurel and Hardy movies, so meeting him was beyond a thrill for me.

I told him, "I still see you on TV all the time."

He nodded and then said he never got a dime from those films when they were rebroadcast. There were no residuals for the stars of his era.

"When you signed a contract back in the '20s and '30s and '40s, it was a one-time payment," he said. "We have no money."

It was a joyous day to be with Ted and to meet Laurel, but I was also very saddened to see such a famous star in need of money. I wondered how an industry could let such talented people just fade away.

Ted is gone now, and I hear his son runs the agency. Thanks, Ted, for one of the greatest thrills of my career.

* * *

Once, while I was on a flight home to Toronto, I saw a friend of ours from the Boulevard Club, Laura McCormick, sitting in first class. Laura worked in fashion and also played tennis. She was sitting with a lovely lady at the front of the plane, so I joined them for a while.

Laura's travelling companion, it turned out, was Edith Head, the greatest costume designer in Hollywood history. She was going to Toronto, to our club, to put on a charity fashion show of her ten greatest costumes. We got to speaking, and she told me she also loved playing tennis and had a tennis court at her home in Hollywood.

As we left the plane, she invited me to the fashion show that evening and asked me to bring my wife. The Boulevard Club was absolutely packed with people that night, yet when she saw me, she lit up.

Janet was a little nervous to meet her, but Edith made us both feel so welcome. Edith gave me a standing invitation to play tennis at her court, but I never got the chance. She died shortly after.

You never know who you'll bump into on a flight. Once, I was on a flight from Los Angeles to Toronto when Jim Nabors sat down in the seat across the aisle from me. Jim was a major star at the time, playing dim-witted Gomer Pyle, first on *The Andy Griffith Show* and later on the spin-off *Gomer Pyle U.S.M.C.* He was a very warm-hearted man and we chatted quite a bit during the trip.

When we arrived in Toronto, I asked if Jim wouldn't mind meeting my kids, Scott and Laura. He was going on to Ottawa, but said he'd love to. They were big Gomer Pyle fans and always said he looked like a friend of ours named Bill Burrows, a fine producer at CTV whom my kids called Uncle Bill.

Jim came out with me, but the kids didn't seem impressed. I think they were eight and ten years old at the time. He was very gracious, and Janet was quite impressed. After a while, I thanked him and we went our separate ways. I've never seen him since.

On the way home in the car, I said to the kids, "You guys didn't seem too thrilled."

"We thought it was uncle Bill," they explained.

* * *

I met Bud Greenspan, an eight-time Emmy Award winner, when we lived in New York. He was financially strapped when I met him and had nothing on the go, so I lined him up with the CTV brass and he went on produce and direct many great Olympic films with their help. In Calgary and at several other Olympics, I helped get prime camera positions for his crews, and he was very grateful. Today, he is still my friend and still "Mr. Olympics."

When I stayed at Glen Sather's coach house in Banff, CTV used to send a lot of TV and movie personalities to stay with me. Among the big names I entertained was Sir Peter Ustinov, the famous British actor and writer. He was one of the most interesting people I ever met. And just like Orson Welles, he did most of the talking, which was fine by me. He also had a great sense of humour, or as he called it, a sense of the ridiculous. Peter was the greatest storyteller I have ever known.

Steve Allen, the comedian and American television personality, also stayed with us at one point. The best, though, was Canadian actor Lorne Greene, star of the TV western *Bonanza*. Lorne was coming in for the Banff Film Festival, and his son arrived before him.

His son said, "Boy, this is a great thrill. My dad has always wanted to meet you."

Of course, the feeling was mutual!

*   *   *

Gary Blye was producing an Andy Williams Christmas special for my company in Toronto in 1990. Glen Campbell was the headline guest, and we also had Canadian-born impressionist Rich Little on board. We had no room in the show for anybody else, but Gary said to me, "There's somebody you *must* get on the show. She has never been on English television before."

I said I didn't think we had room, but he was insistent. "Even if it's only for one song, you have to get her on. You won't regret making Canadian television history."

I reluctantly agreed and asked, "How much is this going to cost me?"

"I think I can get her for $10,000 plus expenses."

The singer's name was Céline Dion. I remembered her name, because at the Calgary Olympics the guy organizing the opening ceremonies had mentioned her, but I couldn't include her at that time because we were only using Alberta stars.

When she came in to do the Andy Williams show, along with her manager and future husband, René Angélil, we went to meet with her. Because she was a late addition to the show, we didn't have a proper dressing room for her. The room we gave her was like a closet, and I apologized to her.

She would have nothing of it. She was all smiles and just glad to be a part of the show. Talk about being gracious. What wonderful young lady—what a pro!

Céline sang two songs, one in French and one in English, and just as Gary Blye predicted, she was the hit of the show. She brought down the house.

Think you could get her for $10,000 today? Gary was right—we were part of showbiz history.

* * *

I have, in both my books, had a chance to tell you about the great athletes and entertainers who helped make my career. I was lucky—so lucky!—to have worked as a freelance producer and director for all the top networks in the world.

This career has led to many interesting stories and I wish to thank you for letting me share them with you.

INDEX

INDEX

INDEX